A Driftwood Altar

ALSO BY MARK FORD

A Driftwood Altar

essays and reviews

Mark Ford

with an introduction by Nick Everett

WAYWISER

First published in 2005 by

THE WAYWISER PRESS

9 Woodstock Road, London N4 3ET, UK
P.O. Box 6205, Baltimore, MD 21206, USA
www.waywiser-press.com

Editor
Philip Hoy

Editorial Advisors
Joseph Harrison   Clive Watkins   Greg Williamson

A CIP catalogue record for this book is available from the British Library

ISBN-10: 1-904130-16-X
ISBN-13: 978-1-904130-16-1

Printed and bound by
Cromwell Press Ltd., Trowbridge, Wiltshire

For Mercy

Contents

Acknowledgements

Acknowledgements are due to the various publications in which these essays and reviews originally appeared, sometimes in slightly different forms and with different titles:

Essays in Criticism: "Elizabeth Bishop at the Water's Edge", Vol. LIII, no. 3, July 2003, pp. 235-261. (Reprinted by permission of Oxford University Press).

Journal of American Studies: "Inventions of Solitude: Thoreau and Auster", Vol. 32, no. 3, 1998, pp. 201-219. (© Cambridge University Press, reprinted with permission).

P.N. Review: "*Mont d'Espoir* or *Mount Despair:* Early Bishop, Early Ashbery, and the French", 114, Vol. 23, no. 4, March - April 1997; "A Wide and Wingless Path to the Impossible: the Poetry of F.T. Prince", 147, vol. 29, no. 1, September - October 2002.

Poetry Review: "James Schuyler and Englishness", Vol. 92, no. 3, Autumn 2002; "The Prince of Morticians: Thomas Lovell Beddoes", Vol. 93, no. 4, Winter 2003/04.

London Review of Books: "That Goddam Ginsberg", April 23, 1987; "Georges Perec", February 2, 1989; "The Well-Wrought Ern", September 9, 1993; "Genius in Its Pure State: The Literary Manuscripts of Raymond Roussel", May 22, 1997; "Harry Mathews and the Oulipo", March 20, 2003; "The Madness of Marinetti", May 20, 2004; "Love and Theft", December 2, 2004.

Introduction

This selection of Mark Ford's literary essays and reviews takes its title, *A Driftwood Altar*, from that of a poem by John Ashbery (from his 1992 volume *Hotel Lautréamont*), in tribute to the poet whose work first and most profoundly showed Ford a way forward for his own. Wave after wave of new American poetries arrived on British shores in the wake of *The New American Poetry* of 1960, from the confessionalism of Lowell and Berryman to the deep imagism of Bly and Merwin and the austere late Modernism of Olson and the Black Mountain poets. For Ford and myself, however, as British students in the early 1980s (when we met and became friends), aware and appreciative though we were of the original examples of these others, it was Ashbery who seemed absolutely where it was at. He somehow managed to be irreverent, witty, funny, bizarre as well as genuinely urban, and yet at the same time serious and moving and absolutely central to poetic tradition. There was nothing wrong with the senior British and Irish poets of the time – Hill, Heaney, Hughes etc. – but all were using their powers to define cultural problems. What distinguished Ashbery particularly was that he offered, as they did not and did not want to, a genuine and contemporary continuation of the Romantic tradition suggested in Keats's famous definition of "negative capability": "when a man is capable of being in uncertainties, Mysteries, doubts, without any irritable reaching after fact and reason" (which Ford quotes here in his piece on James Tate). Ashbery's poetry did not seek to articulate ideas about experience but to present ideas instead as one ingredient of experience among many; it sustained uncertainty, refused to reduce experience to some crystallized image or symbol or pat generalization, and instead tried to evoke the random, irreducible nature of existence. To William Carlos Williams's famous Modernist adage, "no ideas but in things", came Ashbery's characteristically witty Postmodernist correction: "no ideas, not even in things".

In the twenty or so years since then, as well as developing his own very different versions of negatively capable poems, collected in *Landlocked* (1992) and *Soft Sift* (2001), Ford has continued to find different strains and varieties of this "Other Tradition" (to use another Ashbery title, from *Houseboat Days* (1977)) of Mysteries and uncertainties in the work of other authors, many of whom feature in the essays and reviews collected here. The title *A Driftwood Altar* thus also suggests the quality that more than any other unites these diverse pieces. Our predisposition towards reductive meaning, as Ford abundantly shows, is very strong; a lot of ingenuity is required to overcome it – all the more to overcome it without completely alienating or boring the reader. But how? Ford's authors avoid "depth" and "significance" in a variety of ways. The constant surprises of James Tate's bizarre narratives help them remain below the threshold of reasonable interpretation. Georges Perec's pre-programmed arbitrary constraints on form (and sometimes content) cut across the natural tendency to write "significantly". Unlikely though it initially sounds, James Schuyler, as Ford interestingly shows, found models in the English rural journals of Kilvert and Woodforde and Gilbert White of how to describe things "for their own sakes" and to "accommodate the random trivialities of experience without either loading them with significance, or making them seem mere illustrations of chaos and contingency". Harry Mathews's fictions use multiple conflicting narratives, resisting overall coherence with each plot development. Like Ashbery's long poem *Flow Chart* (1991), their scale is the opposite of emphatic; such points as they make are not reinforced but moved beyond and left behind. The varieties of negative capability

14

are striking. But in all cases one is left with the sense not that life has been simplified and ordered, but that its disorder and randomness have been acknowledged and evoked.

Like Ashbery, the examples I've given here – Tate, Perec, Schuyler and Mathews – are all, loosely speaking, Postmodernist authors: the forms of negative capability Ford cherishes and explains so well are essentially Postmodernist. There are writers of the Modernist period here, but far from being representatives like Eliot and Pound of High Modernism, all display attitudes and approaches which anticipate (and indeed in some cases influence) the pluralism and indeterminacy of a later generation. Thus, for Ford, Mina Loy's "Songs to Joannes" anticipates the "decentering fluidities characteristic of Postmodern poetics"; Roussel's stories "fit together like so many Chinese boxes, but lead nowhere beyond their own implausible recoveries and conjunctions"; and Marinetti's Futurists "first developed the tactics that were later deployed by practically every revolutionary avant-garde of the century, from the Dadaists to the L=A=N=G=U=A=G=E poets". And in even the earliest, and only nineteenth-century, writers treated here, Beddoes and Thoreau, Ford finds models in their different ways of Postmodernist pluralism and fluid uncertainty. Beddoes's *Death's Jest-Book* is described as a "startlingly prescient work" that anticipates the "black humorous worlds of such as Samuel Beckett and Ionesco" and that in its "conflicted, doomed, self-defeating form, at once fragmentary and endlessly expansive", looks forward to Postmodernist epic structures. And Thoreau's "dispersal of the self" in the course of *Walden*, so different from his friend Emerson's concrete "self-recoveries", as Ford cleverly demonstrates, provides Paul Auster with one model and example for his examinations of the complexities of identity in his *The New York Trilogy*. The exception that proves this rule is Auden, whose long poem "The Sea and the Mirror" is given detailed exposition here as a rejection of his earlier view of the magical, religious properties of poetry not unlike Prospero's rejection of his magical power in *The Tempest*. Turning away from the extreme gestures of

The Orators (1932), which remains a favourite for Postmodernists,
and genuflecting once again before a literal Episcopalian altar, Auden
now sees poetry as no altar at all, not even a driftwood one.

The turmoil in Auden's life that informed this change of direction
in his work is vividly conjured by Ford. It may seem surprising in a
book largely about experimental work to find biography invoked so
frequently. However, the characters behind literary innovation and
experiment loom large here, and in the company of Roussel and
Marinetti and Breton and Beddoes, Auden, shuffling out into the
East Village in his slippers and shades, amazingly seems the least eccentric. Such larger-than-life characters are reason enough to ignore
the programmatically anti-biographical approach of much contemporary academic criticism; but Ford has sound critical reasons too.
For him the author's life can no more be dismissed as irrelevant than
it can be invoked as the solution to a work's conundrums. One gets
a sense of his subtle awareness of how works and selves create each
other from the fact that his most thoroughly and satisfyingly biographical piece here is about a poet, Ern Malley, who didn't actually
exist, but who was invented in the early 1940s by two young Austral-
ians, as a hoax to mock the pretensions of Modernism. At the same
time, Ford avoids crude and reductive biographical criticism. Both
here and in the brilliant book-length study, *Raymond Roussel and the
Republic of Dreams* (2000), the treatment of Roussel, whose eccentricities, literary and personal, and sexuality (especially at this distance in time) would have tempted many others into more aggressive
speculations and interpretations, is a model of tactful, sensitive and
unintrusive criticism. Malley and Roussel emerge as strange twins
here; both, in their very different ways, are Fordian ideals in being
wholly naïve rather than knowing experimentalists. The cynicism in
Malley's work is all his creators', while he, as invented poet, remains
untarnished, utterly and earnestly absorbed in the Modernist angst
they invented for him. This, as Ford delightedly shows, contributes
substantially to his enduring appeal. Roussel meanwhile, though real

flesh and blood, is if anything even more miraculous in being a thoroughly unselfconscious dandy who considered his bizarre and outrageous literary experiments destined to achieve widespread popularity. The intriguingly elusive, scarcely credible personality behind such rarefied and aesthetic work helps to preserve its intensity too, and indeed must, I think, along with the undue neglect of his work in the Anglophone world, have played a significant part in Ford's decision to write a book about him.

A Driftwood Altar more generally conveys an almost continuous sense of incredulous awe in the presence of the strange innovators it describes, the essays like so many paeans from prudence to extravagance, sobriety to intoxication, caution to adventurousness, sanity to craziness. Not that I am biographicalizing here; perhaps I just mean from responsible criticism to good art.

Ford's intelligent and tactful approach to biography exemplifies the balance of two vital qualities – literariness and humanity – that distinguishes all his critical writing. He is certainly indebted to the literary journals, the *London Review of Books*, the *New York Review of Books*, the *Times Literary Supplement* and the *New Republic*, which commissioned many of these pieces and which encourage essayistic prose that is both intellectually rigorous and accessible. But his writing's simultaneous total literariness – no one is more literary than Ford – and total humanity are his own and stand behind the creativity, readability, humour, and so much else that is good in his work. Together they account for his ability to make narrative and description do so much of argument's job that explicit argument has barely to dot the i's and cross the t's. Separately they act as correctives to each other too, and thus help Ford steer clear, on both the academic and the journalistic sides, of contemporary critical writing's most common pitfalls: his literariness prevents his writing ever becoming overfamiliar, matey, imprecise or laddish; and his humanity prevents it ever becoming pedantic, abstract, pompous or donnish. (Not a single sentence in the book, you'll be glad to hear, begins "I would suggest

17

...") Consistently perceptive, engaging, informative, elegant writing about difficult, experimental modern and contemporary poetry (and prose): what Ford offers here you simply won't find anywhere else.

– Nick Everett

The Madness of Marinetti

F.T. (Filippo Tomaso) Marinetti liked to describe himself as the "caffeine of Europe". He was undoubtedly the most daring and inventive artistic propagandist of the twentieth century, and Futurism, the movement he launched with a manifesto published on the front page of *Le Figaro* on February 20th, 1909, reconfigured the popular notion of modern art and the modern artist more widely and decisively than any of the other 'isms (Fauvism, Cubism, Expressionism, Imagism, Vorticism) now gathered under the umbrella heading of Modernism. His movement is also, of course, inevitably associated with another 'ism, that which took its name from the *Fasci di Combattimento* (organizations of First World War veterans) marshalled by Mussolini in 1919 into the *Partito Nazionale Fascista*.

Marinetti was born in 1876 in Egypt to wealthy Italian parents. He was educated in French at a Jesuit lycée in Alexandria, and sent to Paris in 1894 to take his *baccalauréat* at the Sorbonne. There he immersed himself in the lush, swooning raptures of late Symbolism, and composed, in French, a series of somewhat mind-numbing long poems; in their way these endless free-verse hymns to the immortal powers of the sea ("Ah! Ah! / Laugh beautiful Waves! Laugh / a vast adamantine laugh up to the stars!") make as good a case as his electrifying manifestos of the need for change. "Les vieux marins" (which won a prestigious poetry prize and was publicly recited by Sarah Bernhardt), "La Conquête des Étoiles" (an epic in nineteen cantos about a battle between the sea and the stars), "Destruction" (a set of lyrics equally vague and cosmic), all illustrate precisely the style and subject

19

matter Marinetti would soon be condemning as "passéist": as point number three of the Manifesto of Futurism puts it: "Up to now literature has exalted a pensive immobility, ecstasy, and sleep. We intend to exalt aggressive action, a feverish insomnia, the racer's stride, the mortal leap, the punch and the slap."

It was Alfred Jarry, prince of iconoclasts, who first suggested to Marinetti how much a well-aimed punch or slap could accomplish. His *Ubu Roi* of 1896, with its famous opening neologism – "Merdre" – had caused the kind of public scandal long poems about the sea and the stars, however anarchistic in intention, could never ignite. Accordingly, Marinetti had his own Jarryesque *Le Roi Bombance* staged by the same producer, Lugné-Poë, at the same theatre where *Ubu Roi* had opened, and was gratified when the thunderous sound effects with which it represented a priest's digestive system provoked the desired uproar. "No work", he flatly declared, "without an aggressive character can be a masterpiece" – though in later tracts Marinetti denounced the very notion of a "masterpiece". Of all the early twentieth–century movements that have attracted the label "avant-garde" (first used in this sense in 1910), Futurism was the one that most fully deserved the militarist implications of the term. Art, like battle, "can be nothing but violence, cruelty and injustice". "We will glorify war", point nine of the manifesto notoriously proclaimed, " – the world's only hygiene – militarism, patriotism, the destructive gesture of freedom-bringers, beautiful ideas worth dying for, and scorn for woman."

Marinetti's manifestos are such a shrewdly calculated mix of outrageousness and buffoonery, of bullying, histrionics and self-parody, that – like a triple espresso – they almost invariably succeed in setting the reader aquiver, normally, at this safe distance in time, with laughter, but at other moments with an uneasy dismay at the urge to destroy they serio-comically encourage and release. D.H. Lawrence, for instance, was deeply stirred by Marinetti's "purging of the old forms and sentimentalities", as he wrote in a letter of June 2nd, 1914, by his "revolt against beastly sentiment and slavish adherence to tradition and the dead mind ... I love them [i.e. the Futurists] when they say to the child 'all right, if you want to drag nests and torment kittens, do it, lustily!' But I reserve the right to answer 'all right, try it on. But if I catch you at it you get a hiding.'" The Marxist critic Antonio Gramsci was also initially exhilarated by the "impetuosity of their youthful energies", their conviction that an alliance of artistic and technological innovation would sweep away bourgeois culture once and for all:

> They have destroyed, destroyed, destroyed, without worry-ing if the new creations produced by their activity were on the whole superior to those destroyed ... *They have grasped sharply and clearly that our age, the age of big industry, of the large proletarian city and of intense and tumultuous life, was in need of new forms of art, philosophy, behaviour and language.* This sharply revolutionary and absolutely *Marx-ist* idea came to them when the Socialists were not even vaguely interested in such a question.

He had hopes their experiments would help inspire the creation of an organically revolutionary proletarian art, but later dismissed the whole Futurist movement as a mere spasm of naughtiness easily tamed by the threat of a "hiding", comparing them, in 1930, to "a group of schoolboys who escaped from a Jesuit boarding school, whooped it up in a nearby wood, and were led back under the policeman's stick."

Violence – introducing "the fist", as Marinetti put it, "into the ar-tistic battle" – played a crucial role in both the aesthetics of Futurism, and in the way the movement presented itself to the public. Mari-netti's genius was to find ways of translating aspects of the thought of such as Nietzsche, Bergson, and Georges Sorel, whose *Reflections On Violence* advocated the need for continual and violent class struggle, into a series of manifestos, publicity stunts, and theatrical events that generated excitement, fury, riots, and enormous amounts of media

21

coverage. Marinetti was gifted with an unerring sense of the workings of publicity, which he exploited shamelessly; he was more than happy to write up each scandalous, triumphant Futurist happening himself, and dispatch his reports over the wires to Europe's leading newspapers. He understood from the outset the importance of timing: the founding Futurist manifesto was scheduled to appear on December 24, 1908, but was pulled by Marinetti at the last minute when an earthquake hit Sicily, killing 20,000 people, and engrossing the public's attention. He had no qualms about using the vast fortune he inherited from his father in 1907 to subsidise his publishing house, his magazine *Poesia*, and his general campaign to position Futurism as the brand leader in avant-garde art movements. It was a friend of his father's and a major shareholder in *Le Figaro*, Mohammed El Rachi, who negotiated the prominent positioning of his initial call to arms.

The manifesto opens with a group of decadents staying up late, trampling their "atavistic ennui into rich oriental rugs, arguing up to the last confines of logic and blackening many reams of paper with our frenzied scribbling." But while thus plumbing the depths of their souls, they find themselves suddenly stirred by the mighty rumbling of a huge double-decker tram, "ablaze with coloured lights", and decide to abandon the dreary pursuit of "Mythology and the Mystic Ideal". Fast cars are what they need, and, fortunately, have:

> We went up to the three snorting beasts, to lay amorous hands on their torrid breasts. I stretched out on my car like a corpse on its bier, but revived at once under the steering wheel, a guillotine blade that threatened my stomach.

They tear through the streets, until Marinetti has to swerve to avoid two wretched cyclists blocking his way, and crashes into a ditch; there he experiences the primary Futurist initiation rite:

> Oh! Maternal ditch, almost full of muddy water! Fair fac-

tory drain! I gulped down your nourishing sludge; and I remembered the blessed black breast of my Sudanese nurse ... When I came up – torn, filthy, and stinking – from under the capsized car, I felt the white-hot iron of joy deliciously pass through my heart!

It is only once "smeared with good factory muck – plastered with metallic waste, with senseless sweat, with celestial soot", that he and his confrères can proclaim their manifesto, and hymn the beauty of speed: "A racing car whose hood is adorned with great pipes, like serpents of explosive breath – a roaring car that seems to ride on grapeshot – is more beautiful than the *Victory of Samothrace*."

Speed is at the heart of Futurist morality: "One must persecute, lash, torture all those who sin against speed." Speed is "*pure*", the new good, slowness "*unclean*", the new evil:

Speed = synthesis of every courage in action. Aggressive and warlike.
Slowness = analysis of every stagnant prudence. Passive and pacifistic.
Speed = scorn of obstacles, desire for the new and unexplored. Modernity, hygiene.
Slowness = arrest, ecstasy, immobile adoration of obstacles, nostalgia for the already seen, idealization of exhaust and rest, pessimism about the unexplored. Rancid romanticism of the wild, wandering poet and long-haired, bespectacled dirty philosopher.

Particularly criminal are tardy Sunday crowds, the hopelessly slow gondolas plying the Venetian lagoons, and those "cemeteries of empty exertion", museums, libraries, and academies:

Come on! set fire to the library shelves! Turn aside the ca-

23

nals to flood the museums! ... Oh the joy of seeing the glorious old canvases bobbing adrift on those waters, discoloured and shredded ... Take up your pickaxes, your axes and hammers, and wreck, wreck the venerable cities, pitilessly!

There was a personal context to Marinetti's hatred of all antiquity. One day, he liked to tell journalists, he was driving extremely fast towards the Arch of Constantine in Rome when a bit of stone from Nero's aqueduct fell and damaged the paintwork of his car. Italy's crumbling ruins were not only virulently passéist, infecting the nation with the "smelly gangrene of professors, archaeologists, ciceroni and antiquarians", but posed an unacceptable threat to the modern motorist.

The founding manifesto suggested the movement was already in full swing. "The oldest of us is thirty," Marinetti revealed (he was in fact thirty-two), "so we have at least a decade for finishing our work." That "we" was also misleading, for the group did not as yet exist, and there was only one paid-up Futurist, Marinetti himself. The manifesto was actually an advertisement for members rather than a justification of an already existing body of art. That it struck a chord, however, is not in doubt; he later claimed to have received a mailbag of some 40,000 letters in response, and within a matter of months the group had been conjured into being, and included the painters Umberto Boccioni, Carlo Carrà, Gino Severini and Giacomo Balla (whose love of new technology extended to naming one of his daughters Elice (propeller)), the architect Antonio Sant'Elia, and Luigi Russolo who was both a painter and a musician, and inventor of the *Intonarumori* or Noise Intoners that shook European concert halls in the pre-War years, with their simulations of explosions, crackles, gurgles, buzzes, scrapings, splashes and booms.

One of Marinetti's most cunning and effective strategies was to elide the gap between genres, and between artistic and political matters. While Symbolism fastidiously distanced itself from the business of everyday existence, Futurism took the opposite approach, claiming it would revolutionise every aspect of life, even offering, in a manifesto by Balla and Fortunato Depero, a "Futurist Reconstruction of the Universe". Marinetti organised his campaign like a political leader determined at all costs to make the headlines, and with the advantage that all publicity, however negative, spread the Futurist word. On July 8th, 1910, for instance, he and his followers scattered 800,000 copies of the manifesto "Against Passéist Venice" from the campanile of St. Mark's, and then harangued and baited the crowd. A "terrible battle" ensued, and hosts of passéists, as Marinetti tells it, got "knocked around". The manifesto proposed filling in all the canals, pulling down the "leprous, crumbling palaces", burning all the gondolas ("rocking chairs for cretins"), and converting the city into an industrial and military port that would soon dominate the Adriatic. The Futurist aesthetic, he assured his enraged listeners, would transform Venice from the "greatest bordello in history, the saddest hospital in the world", into a thriving modern metropolis that would attract a "shrewd, wealthy crowd of industrialists and businessmen!"

Futurism took a stance on everything, from typography to clothing to cooking, and its aggressive calls for change should be seen in the context of the burgeoning Italian nationalism that would culminate in the reign of Mussolini. Futurist theatrical events, known as *serate*, often involved burning or shredding the Austrian flag. These *serate* were a cross between a political rally and a variety theatre revue, and many, like the denunciation of Venice, led to brawls between the Futurists and their opponents. The incendiary nature of their pronouncements normally guaranteed a ruckus, but Marinetti also suggested the use of a range of provocative tactics: a powerful glue could be spread on some of the seats, and itching or sneezing powder on others; the same seat could be sold to ten different people who would then squabble in the aisles, while complimentary tickets should be handed out to anyone "unbalanced, irritable, or eccentric and likely to create uproars with obscene gestures, pinching women, or other freakishness."

Futurist *serate* were particularly good news for fruit and vegetable vendors: the events drew audiences of three or four thousand, many of whom came armed with tomatoes, potatoes, oranges, and eggs with which to pelt the merry pranksters. Marinetti evolved a Futurist style of declamation which seems to have been highly effective: the Futurist speaker, he counselled, should "metallize, liquefy, vegetalize, petrify, and electrify his voice", and gesticulate both geometrically, "giving his arms the sharp rigidity of semaphore signals and lighthouse rays", and topographically, "creating in midair cubes, cones, spirals, ellipses, etc." He also made use of sound effects, such as automobile horns, saws, electric bells, and hammers, and a number of blackboards scattered about the auditorium on which he'd inscribe theorems, equations, and "synoptic tables of lyric values". At a performance in London in May of 1914 of *Zang Toumb Toumb*, he also had a telephone installed on stage, into which he barked orders to his only English disciple, the painter C. W. Nevinson, who would then bang two enormous drums in an adjoining room.

Zang Toumb Toumb, translated into English here for the first time, is Marinetti's most impressive embodiment of his theories of "words-in-freedom" and the "wireless imagination". It describes the Bulgarian-Serbian siege of Adrianople in 1912-13, which Marinetti covered as a war correspondent for the French newspaper *Gil Blas*. In his "Technical Manifesto" of 1912 he argued the Futurist writer should destroy syntax, abolish the adjective, adverb and punctuation, use verbs only in the infinitive, and double up nouns into compounds such as man-torpedo or woman-harbour (a rather revealing choice of examples). Instead of conjunctions one should use mathematical signs ($- \times + : - = > < -$) and musical symbols. The goal of these innovations was to "**destroy the I in literature**" (this in large bold text), "that is all psychology. Man, utterly ruined by libraries and museums, ruled by a fearful logic and wisdom, is of absolutely no more interest. So abolish him in literature. Replace him with matter." In *Zang Toumb Toumb* (the sound of a shell exploding) Marinetti set about deploying these techniques and all kinds of typographical innovation to recreate verbally, and pictorially, the smells, sounds, sights, textures and terrors of the siege.

> **patatraaaak boom zoomb-toomb** Turkish shell on the bridge whirlwind dust-mire-wood-hate-terror-blood-hail-of-meat-guts-corridas-minced-meat-fat shattering of machine guns masks of bloodymud

While there is no room for pity or sentimentality in Marinetti's depiction of chaos and slaughter, certain passages still conflict oddly with the heroic concept of war as hygiene propounded in the manifestos. The section representing the experiences of a trainload of sick soldiers is especially visceral and immediate, cataloguing with gruesome thoroughness "the smells of all the sicknesses stuffed in the train": "fecal smell of dysentery honeyed stench of plague sweat ammoniacal smell of the cholera patients sweet stink of gangrene consumptives acidulous smell of the fever patients ..."

The text ends, however, with a recovery of Marinetti's vision of nationalist military might and male potency. He was an ardent supporter of Italian entry into the First World War, and much Futurist activity of late 1914 and early 1915 had an anti-neutralist focus: Balla designed anti-neutralist clothes in the colours of the Italian flag, and anti-neutralist shoes dynamically shaped to deliver "merry kicks to all neutralists". Sporting these outfits, they burst in on the lectures of pacifist and Germanophile professors in the University of Rome, disrupted the opening night of a Puccini opera, burnt Austrian flags in public, and organized street demonstrations. "Italy power Italian-pride brothers", Marinetti intones in the final paragraph of *Zang Toumb Toumb*, "glory domination cafés war-stories Towers guns-virility-chases erection range finder ecstasy **toomb-toomb.**"

In the event the First World War, characterised by Marinetti as "the most beautiful Futurist poem that has ever seen the light of day", brought to an end the first and brightest phase of the movement. It took the lives of Boccioni and Sant'Elia, and led to the defection from Futurist principles of Carrà and Severini. Its horrors failed to dent Marinetti's enthusiasm for battle, however, but then, though he did receive a minor wound, he experienced the war pretty much on his own terms: he worked mainly as a propagandist, roaming around the front at will, infusing the troops with "Italian pride" in the *arte-azioni* (art-in-action) in which they were participating, organising patriotic Futurist entertainments that now included dances of the shrapnel, the machine-gun, and the aviatrix, and composing increasingly fragmented words-in-freedom poem-collages that attempt a "dynamic verbalisation" of trench combat.

Marinetti probably met Mussolini in 1915; certainly that year he claimed him as a Futurist, adducing both his "lightning-swift conversion to the necessity and virtue of war", and his use of Futurist propaganda tactics in his political campaign for intervention. It would be a mistake, however, to think of Futurism as inherently right-wing; its revolutionary ideals appealed to Ultra-leftists as well, and Marinetti greatly prided himself on the movement's impact on avant-garde Russian artists such as Mayakovsky and Malevich: "I am delighted to learn that the Russian Futurists are all Bolsheviks", he crowed in an essay of 1920, "Beyond Communism", in which he pointed out that Lenin's trains were all decorated with designs derived from Boccioni, Balla, and Russolo. The Futurist Party Political manifesto of 1918 advocated an eclectic range of radical measures that included easy divorce, Free Love, obligatory gymnastics in the open air, a minimum wage, the right to strike, equal pay for women, the abolition of the secret police and universities, the modernisation of all cities that live off tourism, and massive redistribution of the land. It argued for replacing the Senate with an assembly of twenty "technicians" all under the age of 30, and for the total overthrow of the "suffocating, medieval theocracy" of the Church: "The Italy of Tomorrow is to be the sole religion."

Many of these ideas were discussed at the First Fascist Conference in Florence in October of 1919, and in the following month's General Elections were put to the nation by a Futurist-Fascist alliance. They gathered little support, and Mussolini quickly distanced himself from Marinetti and his new band of followers, few of whom, alas, rivalled the first wave of Futurists in talent or originality of expression. Marinetti resigned from the Fascist party in 1920, but four years later rejoined in the hope of persuading Mussolini to make Futurism his regime's official art form. But *Il Duce* had other ideas: the Fascist art he promoted, far from embracing modernity, sought to ground his autocracy in the mythology of Ancient Rome. For all Marinetti's finagling and intriguing, Futurism played only a minor role in the *civitas fascista*, which celebrated order and discipline rather than dynamism and intoxication. The most renowned and amusing of the manifestos of his later years was his attack on pasta, which he condemned as "heavy, brutalizing and gross", as "anti-virile", and as inducing "scepticism, sloth and pessimism". Pasta is "no food for fighters", whom it weighs down as they charge into battle, nor lovers, for it is "not favourable to physical enthusiasm towards women". In its place he suggests dishes that would stimulate the palate, rather in the manner of his compound words, by fusing the unusual: salami bathed in hot coffee and flavoured with eau-de-Cologne, mortadella and nougat, roast lamb in lion sauce, sardines and pineapple – all to be eaten while inhaling a carefully chosen perfume, and stroking some distinctive and appropriate substance, such as velvet or emery paper.

"Thanks to us," Marinetti wrote towards the end of "Beyond Communism", "the time will come when life will no longer be a simple matter of bread and labour, nor a life of idleness either, but *a work of art*." In the light of the totalitarianism about to engulf Europe, such a claim seems more than a little sinister, though – if you ignore the bluster – the Utopianism it expresses is not so very far removed from the ideals of, say, Ruskin or William Morris. Futurism, as Gramsci noted, was the first avant-garde art movement both responsive to modern technology and aimed at the masses. It faced squarely, indeed deliberately embraced, the dilemma outlined in Walter Benjamin's 1936 essay, "The Work of Art in the Age of Mechanical Reproduction". Marinetti is the evil genius of Benjamin's conclusion, the artist who most fully proves his thesis that "all efforts to render politics aesthetic culminate in one thing: war." Futurism, like Fascism, reveals a new stage in mankind's "self-alienation", which has now reached "such a degree that it can experience its own destruction as an aesthetic pleasure." For Futurists and Fascists only war, Benjamin argues, can "supply the artistic gratification of a sense perception that has been changed by technology. This is evidently the consummation of '*l'art pour l'art*'".

Marinetti never, of course, saw himself as a late decadent, as the final exponent of art for art's sake. Futurism was to be a means of obliterating the past, not of being obliterated by it. At its purest it advocated a commitment to the concept of change as the only way for each new generation to fulfil its potential. The founding manifesto imagines the movement's successors, "younger and stronger men", bearing down on the band of now ageing, vagabond Futurists, eager to "throw us in the wastebasket like useless manuscripts". What's more, Marinetti promises, they will welcome their supplanters – "we want it to happen!"

> They will come against us, will come from far away, from every quarter, dancing to the winged cadence of their first songs, flexing the hooked claws of predators, sniffing dog-like at the academy doors the strong odour of our decaying minds, which already will have been promised to the literary catacombs.

> But we won't be there ... At last they'll find us – one winter's night – in open country, beneath a sad roof drummed by monotonous rain. They'll see us crouched beside our

trembling airplanes in the act of warming our hands at the
poor little blaze that our books of today will give out when
they take fire from the flight of our images.

It was not, in the event, their books and images so much as their con-
ceptual techniques, nearly all of which derived from Marinetti, which
ended up having the most powerful influence on later art movements:
Dadaism and Surrealism and Absurdist Theatre all borrowed heavily
from Futurist *serate*, which can be seen as the origin of Performance
Art in general. Futurism may not have reconstructed the universe, but
it's hard to exaggerate the role it played in the shaping and propaga-
tion of twentieth-century experimental aesthetics.

Despite his manifesto commitment, Marinetti did his utmost
throughout the interwar years to keep his movement alive in however
compromised, attenuated a form, and to align it, as far as possible,
with the nationalist ideals of Fascism. In the teeth of his virulently
expressed hatred of all institutions, he agreed to act as Secretary of
the Union of Fascist writers, and to join the newly formed Academia
d'Italia. Mussolini's invasion of Ethiopia in 1936 was welcomed as
yet another opportunity to express the Futurist belief in the "moral
hygiene" of war, and although over sixty, Marinetti instantly enlisted
as a volunteer. During the Second World War he accompanied Italy's
beleaguered troops during their disastrous Russian campaign on the
Don. He died soon after his return, in December of 1944 in Bellagio,
the last refuge of the Fascist hierarchy, who can't have been much
comforted, as the Allies steadily advanced, by his late Futurist poems
hymning the achievements of the Black Brigades. His state funeral in
Milan was one of the last public ceremonies of the doomed regime.

London Review of Books, May 2004: Review of *F. T. Marinetti: Selected Poems and Related Prose*,
selected by Luce Marinetti and translated by Elizabeth R. Napier and Barbara R. Studholme
(Yale University Press, 2002).

That Goddam Ginsberg

It's over thirty years since the angry drumbeat of *Howl* first assembled the dissatisfied tribes of an expanding American subculture, and gave them a name and a voice. The first reading took place at the Six Gallery in San Francisco on the 7th of October, 1955. Michael McClure, who also read that night along with Gary Snyder, Philip Whalen and Philip Lamantia, describes the poem's impact in *Scratching the Beat Surface* (1982):

> I hadn't seen Allen in a few weeks and I had not heard *Howl* – it was new to me. Allen began in a small and intensely lucid voice. At some point Jack Kerouac began shouting "GO" in cadence as Allen read it. In spite of all our memories no one had been so outspoken in poetry before – we had gone beyond a point of no return – and we were ready for it, for a point of no return.

Ginsberg himself was in tears, "driving forward", as he recalled in his third-person memoir of the event a couple of years later, "with a strange ecstatic intensity", "surprised at his own power", and in the process restoring to American poetry "the prophetic consciousness it had lost since the conclusion of Hart Crane's *The Bridge*".

From the first *Howl* had a kind of totemic significance, partly as a result of its trial for obscenity, and partly because it drew so clearly and cleverly the lines of battle between the hips and the squares, the holy bums and the Establishment's "scholars of war" and "fairies of advertising" with their "mustard gas of sinister intelligent editors". And when it finally came out in book form in 1956, it attracted exactly the kind of denunciatory press in the leading academic journals that was guaranteed to increase its underground following. It was Ginsberg's old Columbia colleagues, John Hollander, Norman Podhoretz and Louis Simpson, all cutting their teeth in the New York literary scene under the approving auspices of Lionel and Diana Trilling, who led the charge against the Beats. "It is only fair to Allen Ginsberg to remark on the utter lack of decorum of any kind in his dreadful little volume", began Hollander in *Partisan Review*. Podhoretz's was a more general attack on the know-nothing bohemians of *On the Road*: "This is the revolt of the spiritually underprivileged and the crippled of soul – young men who can't think straight and so hate anyone who can." Among others who leapt to the defence of culture as they knew it were Donald Hall, Herbert Gold, Delmore Schwartz, Truman Capote (on Kerouac: "that's not writing, that's type-writing"), Robert Brustein and James Dickey *("Howl* is the skin of Rimbaud's *Une Saison en Enfer* thrown over the conventional maunderings of one type of American adolescent, who has discovered that machine civilisation has no interest in his having read Blake"). Riding the waves of this kind of adverse publicity, the Beats broke through to an enormous audience extraordinarily quickly. Within a few years, long articles had appeared in *Time* and *Life* depicting them as savage, anarchistic *enfants terribles,* but they were soon repackaged for national consumption more as whacky misfits than existential destroyers; up-to-date hostesses could rent-a-Beatnik to spice up their parties, and, without upsetting its audience at all, a popular soap-opera introduced a bearded, sandal-wearing dope loosely modelled on media images of Ginsberg. By 1958 Ginsberg was even well enough known to earn a magisterial put-down from Edith Sitwell in the course of a reading tour in America. "My, you *do* smell bad, don't you?" she is supposed to have said on being introduced. "What was your name again? Are you one of the Action Poets?"

Ginsberg, Kerouac and Burroughs weren't the only ones alert to the repressions simmering within the Cold War mentality of the "tranquillised Fifties", as Lowell called them. Mailer's "The White Negro", for instance, features a Faustian hipster jealous of the black man's intenser and more frequent orgasms and scornful of the puritan virtues of self-containment: "A stench of fear has come out of every pore of American life, and we suffer from a collective failure of nerve." Ginsberg and Kerouac, too, tended to idolise blacks without really knowing many, and jazz was obviously the seminal influence on the development of their "spontaneous bop prosody". "Blow as deep as you want to blow" is No. 7 on Kerouac's list of "The Essentials of Spontaneous Prose", and Ginsberg discovered in this advice the necessary impetus for *Howl*. "I realise how right you are", he wrote to Kerouac in a letter accompanying the manuscript: "that was the first time I sat down to *blow.*"

Nonetheless, looking back on the lives of the Beats and their heroes in the Forties and early Fifties, and on the "crazy" feats which they performed and which *Howl* and *On the Road* immortalise, one is most struck by how very literary they all were. Ginsberg arrived at Columbia wanting to be a labour lawyer who would fight for blue-collar rights, but under the influence of Burroughs and Lucien Carr he soon began to see himself as a *poète maudit* and Nietzschean transgressor. Burroughs handed out reading-lists that included Gide, Rimbaud, Dostoevsky and Lautréamont, and introduced into their set as a live existentialist hero the low-life Herbert Huncke – a 42nd Street junkie, pusher and small-time thief in and out of Riker's Island for much of his life. Jack Kerouac one night wrote out his undying dedication to the novelist's art in his own blood. Even Neal Cassady wasn't immune. "I'm not the N.C. you know", he wrote to Ginsberg. "I'm not N.C. anymore. I more closely resemble Baudelaire."

From time to time these literary fantasies lurched disastrously into reality. In 1944, for instance, Lucien Carr made their fantasies of romantic doomed youth come true by stabbing to death his homosexual admirer Dave Kammerer. "His sense of himself and his friends as Nietzschean outlaws was confirmed", Kerouac later commented in *Vanity of Duluoz*. Arrested and brought to book, Carr went into court with a copy of Rimbaud's poetry and Yeats's *A Vision* under his arm. The following year Ginsberg himself was suspended for a year from Columbia for writing "Fuck the Jews" and "Butler has no balls" in the grime on his window pane. ("But he is a Jew", the Dean puzzled.) He was only allowed back with a note of clearance from his psychiatrist.

A couple of years later, in 1949, Ginsberg found himself sharing his East Side apartment not only with Huncke, who had shown up on his doorstep one night fresh out of jail, his "shoes full of blood", but with Huncke's partners Little Jack Melody and Priscilla. As the rooms rented in his name slowly filled up with stolen goods, Ginsberg grew nervous, and finally insisted they move them. On their way to Long Island Little Jack took a wrong turn down a one-way street; he was chased by the police and crashed the car. When they'd all been arrested, the *Daily News* ran a large picture of them entering court on its front page. "The whole thing was transformed from the hermetic, cosmic, nebulous Dostoevskian thing that it was, with like *real* people involved, into this total stereotype of a giant robbery operation – six-foot marijuana-smoking redhead, three-time loser pariah criminal, boy-wonder mastermind", Ginsberg was later to complain.

While the others went to jail, Ginsberg pleaded insanity and went to Columbia Psychiatric Institute where he met Carl Solomon. Solomon was heavily under the influence of Gide and Artaud, and had been committed for various *actes gratuits* which he perpetrated after reading *Lafcadio's Adventures*. He stole a sandwich from a cafeteria and showed it to a policeman. In what he called a Dadaist "illustration of alienation" he threw potato salad at the novelist Wallace Markfield while he was lecturing on Mallarmé, and he often used to pretend he was Auden, and sign autographs in Auden's name. A worthy disciple of Artaud, he even demanded his own lobotomy. Their meeting at Columbia Psychiatric Institute is now legendary. Solomon was being wheeled through the ward as he emerged from an insulin-shock coma. "Who are you?" he asked Ginsberg. "I'm Prince Myshkin", said Ginsberg. "I'm Kirilov", Solomon replied.

Most of Ginsberg's poetry of this period isn't particularly interesting, but it illustrates well the deathly effect of the New Critical orthodoxies on a free spirit like his. A lot of it is in the pastiche Metaphysical vogue which was popular in the academies, with archaic spelling and rhyme ("I may waste my days no more / pining in spirituall warre"), and these clash disastrously with the burning guilts and desires which anxiously lurk beneath the poem's surface, desperate to be confessed. It wasn't until he met Williams in 1950 that he realised poetry could be written in everyday English, and then he immediately went to the opposite extreme, writing flat monochrome slabs describing New Jersey sewage works and factories. Williams showed these to Marianne Moore and she thought them "terribly depressing".

Ginsberg was a long time finding both his poetic voice and his "real self". Throughout his twenties, working in New York as a copyboy, a market-researcher, in advertising, and still not fully out of the closet, he was oppressed by a "Kafkian sordidness of self", as he put it in a letter he wrote, but never sent, to Wilhelm Reich, whose orgone boxes were all the rage in the Village. He had soul-shattering visions of Blake in which the Master's spirit appeared in his room in East Harlem and declaimed "The Sunflower" and "The Sick Rose" in an unearthly voice. A lot of people thought he'd gone mad. As late as 1952 he was hoping a new analyst would "cure" him of his homosexuality and help him integrate into society. But in 1954 he moved to San Francisco where he found a new type of analyst who advised him to do exactly what he wanted. He met Peter Orlovsky and they exchanged lovers' eternal vows. He gave up his girlfriend and his job, started taking heavier doses of peyote and began to trust the messianic stirrings in his soul.

"The only poetic tradition is the voice out of the burning bush. The rest is trash and will be consumed", Ginsberg wrote soon after finishing *Howl,* but the notes and appendices published along with this facsimile of the working sheets reveal a much cannier awareness of the poem's methods. *Howl* is a unique mishmash, as much mock-heroic as epic, or to use Ginsberg's own words in his note to the first "crucial" revision (changing "mystical" to "hysterical" in the first line): "The poem's tone is in this mixture of empathy and shrewdness, the comic realism of Chaplin's *City Lights,* a humorous hyperbole derived in part from Blake's *The French Revolution.* 'If you have a choice of two things and can't decide, take both', says Gregory Corso." Ginsberg of course takes his own prophetic denunciations absolutely seriously ("Moloch! Moloch! Nightmare of Moloch! Moloch the loveless! Mental Moloch! Moloch the heavy judger of men!") and under the right conditions these can seem powerful and even wise, but the poem's appeal rests much more on the wild picaresque of its anecdotes and phrasing. In the same way, nothing Dean Moriarty says ever makes much sense, but we respond strongly to his exploits and endless rambling speech. "Everyone in Ginsberg's book is hopped up on benzedrine, reefers and whisky, and is doing something as violently and loudly as he can, in 'protest' or 'fulfilment'", Dickey remarked sourly, but *Howl* is one of those poems that seem to soar on the wings of a collective fantasy beyond the reach of this kind of responsible criticism, even though, or perhaps especially because, these are the visions of a single individual. It might be argued that something similar happens in early Auden, or the infinitely more self-conscious myth-making of Yeats.

Consider Ginsberg in full flight:

who chained themselves to subways for the endless ride
    from Battery to holy Bronx on benzedrine until the noise
    of wheels and children brought them down shuddering
    mouth-wracked and battered bleak of brain all drained of
    brilliance in the drear light of Zoo,
who sank all night in submarine light of Bickford's floated
    out and sat through the stale beer afternoon in desolate

Fugazzi's, listening to the crack of doom on the hydrogen
jukebox,
who talked continuously seventy hours from park to pad to
bar to Bellevue to museum to the Brooklyn Bridge,
a lost battalion of platonic conversationalists jumping down
the stoops off fire escapes off windowsills off Empire State
out of the moon ...

The lines have an obvious charm and seem grounded in an authentic innocence – which transforms what were probably dreary incidents in real life into an intense and glamorous myth. (Bickford's, for instance was a 42nd Street cafeteria where Ginsberg was mop-boy for a season.) When *Howl* first came out people were upset by lines like "who let themselves be fucked in the ass by saintly motorcyclists, and screamed with joy, / who blew and were blown by those human seraphim, the sailors, caresses of Atlantic and Caribbean love" (supposed to be a reference to Hart Crane), "who balled in the morning in the evenings in rosegardens", and the offending words were bowdlerised in various reprints of the poem. Yet all this is closer to the realms of pastoral inconsequence than it is to real sex or obscenity. Ginsberg is like his great precursor, Whitman ("a mountain too vast to be seen", he often wrote in letters), in whose work sex is similarly Orphic and unerotic, more like a healthy purge.

Howl pays its own price for walking naked in its peacock-way, but its vulnerabilities register less in the form of reprimands from the society its heroes defy than as a kind of organic exhaustion, like coming down from a trip, or burning oneself out. In a similar way Ginsberg exhausts his own store of anecdotes, expanding each one in a single driving line to its moment of vision "eluding the last gyzym of consciousness", before moving on. The poem's effect is cumulative rather than structural, and although – to the disgust of Kerouac, who believed a writer should never revise – Ginsberg wrote innumerable drafts of the different sections (there are 18 for Part II alone), the drafts themselves are largely interchangeable. He continually sharpened the focus of the poem, rearranging the order and improving the wording, but there are no decisive interventions like Pound's in *The Waste Land* manuscript. It's all pretty much as he wrote it in single bursts of inspiration during the summer and early autumn of 1955.

The appendices added here include various accounts of the poem's reception, a bizarre compilation of "sources" ranging through Smart and Shelley to Kurt Schwitters and Lorca, much of Ginsberg's correspondence from the mid-Fifties, and a history of *Howl's* ludicrous trial for obscenity in the San Francisco courts – the best the prosecution could muster was a private English tutor called Gail Potter who attested: "You feel like you're going through the gutter when you have to read that stuff." Ginsberg is mainly in triumphant mood, playing off the costive disapproval of the squares – Trilling: "I'm afraid I have to tell you I don't like the poems at all. I hesitate before saying that they seem to me quite dull" – against his own copious justifications of his work, including an excerpt from the brilliant letter he wrote in self-defence to Hollander, which is quoted in full in Jane Kramer's *Allen Ginsberg in America* (1969). In the textual notes he shows painstakingly how he arrived at elliptical formulations like "hydrogen jukebox" or "total animal soup of time" via haiku and Cézanne. Carl Solomon, who wasn't particularly happy at his vicarious rise to fame, is given a say at last, but his comments on the individual lines aren't always enlightening. "Crap", one of them begins. "Sorry Allen. Also 'heterosexual dollar' is crap; much of our literature is crap. And so on ad infinitum. *Howl* is a good poem but poetry isn't life." Also published here for the first time are the absurdist letters they wrote together from Columbia Institute to T.S. Eliot and Malcolm de Chazal.

The fall-out from *Howl* was immense, and not entirely benign. For a start, the San Francisco renaissance that had been quietly brewing for several years under the watchful guidance of Rexroth and Duncan suddenly became a New Yorker's one-man show, though Ginsberg

himself was tireless in promoting his fellow "break-through artists".
Squabbles broke out. Rexroth lost not only his status as West Coast
King of the Cats, as Yeats would have put it, but his girlfriend as
well, to Robert Creeley, who, along with other Black Mountain poets, quickly arrived, wanting in on the kill. Ginsberg himself shipped
out as a Merchant Marine to the Antarctic for a few months, and
then travelled around Europe with Peter Orlovsky on his earnings,
and over much of the globe: Central America, South America, Is-
rael, where they met with Martin Buber, and then India and the Far
East in search of more forthcoming gurus. Ginsberg had become a
household name – the *Daily Mail* called him "one of the most vi-
cious characters in America" – and his quests for enlightenment, as
related in the voluminous Journals he has published from these years,
show a certain kind of public spirit: Ginsberg as the arrowhead of a
generation that has conclusively rebelled, but has yet to find a permanent alternative base on which to establish itself. Whereas Kerouac
was emotionally destroyed by the first breath of fame and hostility,
Ginsberg managed to accept with humour and courage his role as
public spokesman, creating a relationship with his colossal audience
comparable only to Kipling's this century. Unlike Kipling, however,
he was taken to be as much catalyst as reflector of social change, and
there were plenty of people ready to lay the numerous casualties of
the Sixties at his door. On phone-ins middle-aged women would ring
up only to scream: "Ginsberg, you're nothing but a douche-bag." His
poetry after *Kaddish* mellowed, even sagged in many places, perhaps
because, as he laments in a poem in his new volume *White Shroud,*
he became "a prisoner of Allen Ginsberg". From his middle years, the
work inspired by the Vietnam War is always moving, and there are
occasional jewels like "Eclogue" and *Bixby Canyon to Jessore Road,* but
few would deny there are also huge trackless wastes in *Collected Poems*
(1984), "a panorama of valleys and plateaus with peaks of inspiration
every few years", as he engagingly puts it in his introduction. Well,
those peaks are fewer and further between than ever now, but *White*

Shroud contains at least one or two good poems to set alongside his best.

Ginsberg's involvement in Eastern religions during the Sixties and since has been one of his most publicised and intriguing idiosyncrasies. When he visited Pound in Rapallo in 1967, he not only insisted on playing him the latest Dylan and Beatles albums, but chanted Hare Krishnas at the silent sage for hours on end. He got a more positive response when leading the sit-down at the Democratic Convention in 1968, and claims to have defused the confrontation between police and protesters simply by chanting his favourite mantras over and over again. More recently, he co-founded, with the Tibetan lama Trungpa, the Jack Kerouac School for Disembodied Poetics at Naropa, the only accredited Buddhist college in the Western world. But for all that, and the tranquillity of "undifferentiated consciousness" which his poetry so proudly displays, there is, as Bellow's Shawmut points out in the story "Him with his Foot in his Mouth", something irreducibly Jewish about Ginsberg, an inescapable urge for "comic self-degradation" which none of his conversions can disguise.

A rich and famous Buddhist schlemiel? That's the impression *White Shroud* conveys, even though quite a few of the poems present him in extremely enviable circumstances, as a fêted celebrity in China – where he goes down with bronchitis – or putting the boot into the Moral Majority, or in bed with one of the adoring golden-haired disciples who come to pay homage to their "poetry master". In this last genre, there are no more fantasies of the "Please, Master" or "Sweet Boy, Give me Yr Ass" kind, but descriptions, both pathetic and obscurely touching, of events that obviously happened exactly the way he says they did:

> I enter slow, he's soft
> no pain, he raises his behind
> no hard on, hips aloft
> I push, he doesn't mind.

> My trouble is, I'm old
> and tho this young kind boy
> gives me a chance for joy
> I'm not hard enough to be bold.

Before it was plastic dildos: now he can't get it up. Bellow sees in this kind of thing a "crazy simplemindedness" but also an affinity with the traditional Jewish role of humorous self-abuse found in his own novels, and those of Roth, Heller, Malamud and so on. In *White Shroud* this is best exploited in the delicate balance achieved in the title poem between, on the one hand, Ginsberg's sense of his own present success, and, on the other, the more deeply ingrained fear of victimisation he inherited from, among other sources, his mother's prolonged and painful insanity.

Diana Trilling, in her supercilious account of the Beats' reading at Columbia in 1959, attributes all to Naomi's madness: "This was the central and utterly persuasive fact of this young man's life." Ginsberg himself has suggested almost as much – for example, in the preface-note accompanying the publication in 1976 of another long letter about *Howl* from the mid-Fifties, this time to Eberhart. "What I didn't say to Eberhart: *Howl* is really about my mother, in her last years at Pilgrim State Hospital – acceptance of her, later inscribed in *Kaddish* detail." Two poems here directly confront this theme, both using a dream form. It was Ginsberg himself who finally signed the papers authorising Naomi's lobotomy and in "Black Shroud" this guilt surfaces in a nightmare narrative in which he decapitates her in the bathroom: society, mindful of his "Collected Works", exonerates him. The much more powerful "White Shroud" has him revisiting a bustling West Bronx full of street dogs, baby carriages, shoppers at Macy's, "mankind thriving in their solitudes in shoes". Here he stumbles on a bag-lady living in "a niche between buildings with tin canopy / shelter from cold rain", surrounded by pots and pans and plates, on her head a "motheaten rabbit-fur hat", her teeth no more than "hard flat flowers" arranged around her gums. Of course it is Naomi, and he launches into a fantasy of domestic bliss: with this the dream fades and he wakes up back in Boulder, Colorado, with Peter Orlovsky downstairs watching the early-morning News.

Ginsberg's own sanity is more strongly marked in *White Shroud* than ever, and perhaps this is why so many of the poems in it are so low-key, even dull. Throughout his career Ginsberg has appealed to the world as a heroic eccentric, and it is hard not to think that it is the absurdity of his enterprise that has taken him so far. For, where at the heart of Lawrence there is an unassailable spiritual dignity, or of Blake an almost deadly clarity of intent, something much slushier and less interesting is at the centre of Ginsberg's achievement. As a prophet he has fathered no self-sustaining vision or system – which is obviously why he fails to win a pedestal in Bloom's pantheon of anxious repressives. In a sense, Ginsberg is far too healthy, even too saintly, to be a great poet. His poems divulge their secrets automatically, without asking. If the publication of the *Howl* drafts is intended to evoke a comparison with *The Waste Land,* then Ginsberg is way out of his depth. While Eliot's reticence and privacies grow more compelling and elusive with each reading, Ginsberg's impact depends on an awesome lack of ambiguity. While Eliot plumbs the "cunning passages" of literature and history, Ginsberg abolishes them altogether. He does so in the name of the present, of "raw beauty", unable even to assume the chuckling deceptiveness of Whitman, who once described himself, in the third person, as "*furtive,* like an old hen". Ginsberg, on the other hand, is always making remarks like the one he made to Mark Van Doren in his Columbia years: "I want to be a saint, a real saint when I am still young, for there is much work to do." This kind of upfrontness has been found both embarrassing and liberating, and it is in complete opposition to the deep "quarrel with ourselves" which activates so much of the great poetry written since the Romantics. The emotional pressure behind *Howl* and *Kaddish* makes them his most inspired and energetic performances, but it's also true they happen all at once: probing beneath their surfaces reveals nothing.

It is this lack of deviousness which has made Ginsberg such a success. When he visited the analyst who encouraged him to break free from convention in 1955, he couldn't help asking him: "But what if I get old?" "Oh, don't worry, there will always be people who will like you", the analyst replied. No prediction could have come truer. Perhaps the most accurate testimony to Ginsberg's qualities comes from Terry, a follower of Sonny Barger, president of the Oakland Hell's Angels. Hunter S. Thompson relates how the Angels were planning to stomp a peace march Ginsberg and the flower-power children of Berkeley had organised against the Vietnam War. Ginsberg, hearing of this threat, went to plead with Barger – they had already met at Ken Kesey's – and won a promise that this time the marchers would be left alone. Terry was outraged:

> That goddam Ginsberg is gonna fuck us *all* up. For a guy that ain't straight at all, he's about the staightest son of a bitch I've ever seen. Man, you shoulda been there when he told Sonny he loved him ... Sonny didn't know *what* the hell to say.

London Review of Books, 1987: Review of Allen Ginsberg's *"Howl": Original Draft Facsimile* (Viking, 1987) and *White Shroud: Poems 1980-1985* (Viking, 1987).

The Well-Wrought Ern

Australia's most celebrated Modernist poet was born on the 14th of March, 1918, in Liverpool. His father, wounded in the war, died in 1920, and soon after that the family moved to Australia, settling in Sydney where his mother had relations. He left school at 14, and worked over the ensuing years at a random series of jobs, as a garage mechanic, an insurance salesman, a watch repairer. Most of his brief adult life was spent in Melbourne, where he was, in the words of his elder sister Ethel, "fond of a girl" but "had some sort of difference with her", a difference movingly reflected in such lyrics as "Perspective Lovesong".

He was something of a loner, "always a little strange and moody", to quote his sister again. In his early twenties he contracted Graves Disease, a horrific – though very rarely fatal – illness which causes sleeplessness, irritability, diarrhoea, muscular tremors, bug eyes and excessive sweating. His perverse reluctance to seek medical help aggravated his condition, and after a sudden collapse he gradually lost strength. He died at his sister's house in Sydney on 23rd of July, 1943. He was 25 years and four months old, the same age at death as the most famous of all doomed Romantics: "Yet we are as the double almond concealed in one shell", he broods in "Colloquy with John Keats", going on to predict his own equally untimely demise in harsh demotic terms – "Look! My number is up!" After his cremation at Rookwood Cemetery Ethel opened his trunk and set about disposing of his pitiably meagre possessions; in the process she came across a yellowing sheaf of typed papers bound together and titled *The Darkening*

Ecliptic. For the first time it dawned on her that her brother had been a poet.

It is fifty years since the death of Ern Malley, and his "fidgety ghost" – the phrase comes from one of his *Pericles*-inspired poems, "Young Prince of Tyre" – still haunts Australian poetry. One pictures the poet lugging a battered second-hand typewriter from flea-pit hotels to temporary lodgings, watching through sleepless mosquito-plagued nights ("Now / Have I found you, my Anopheles!") under a single naked electric bulb; acidly noting the complacent routines of the city's masses, "mechanical men posting themselves", yet conscious that he is himself a mere phantom in their midst; taciturnly observing a faulty carburettor, but never quite meeting the customer's eye. Corrosive despair at the impossibility of making his "obsessions intelligible" alternates with a sardonic compulsion to puncture his own effusions. Like a Conrad outcast, he constantly questions his own reality, though even these doubts can only be voiced in a "No-Man's-language appropriate / Only to No-Man's-Land". What existentialist ever interrogated the authenticity of his own being with such resonance?

> And now out of life, permanent revenant
> I assert: the caterpillar feet
> Of these predictions lead nowhere,
> It is necessary to understand
> That a poet may not exist, that his writings
> Are the incomplete circle and straight drop
> Of a question mark ...

In the 18th century Paley deduced the reality of God from a watch: Malley, who, Ethel reports approvingly, "made a fair amount of money repairing watches", is his dark modern opposite, uncertain even of his own existence. Like Odysseus in the Cyclops' cave he can declare only that he is no one.

The fact that Malley really didn't exist has only increased his fascination in the Postmodern era. It's some time since Roland Barthes announced the death of the author, insisting that all texts should be seen merely as a "multi-dimensional space in which a variety of writings, none of them original, blend and clash". No texts could illustrate this idea of literature more neatly than those of Ern Malley, whose complete works were concocted in a single afternoon and evening by two young Australian poets, James McAuley and Harold Stewart, as part of a plot to expose the obscurantism and meaninglessness of what passed for poetry under the aegis of Modernism. The Malley œuvre was composed, they were later to reveal,

> with the aid of a chance collection of books which happened to be on our desk; the *Concise Oxford Dictionary*, a *Collected Shakespeare, Dictionary of Quotations* etc. We opened books at random, choosing a word or phrase haphazardly. We made lists of these and wove them into nonsensical sentences. We misquoted and made false allusions. We deliberately perpetrated bad verse, and selected awkward rhymes from *Ripman's Rhyming Dictionary*. The alleged quotation from Lenin in one of the poems, "The emotions are not skilled workers" is quite phoney. The first three lines of the poem "Culture as Exhibit" were lifted, as a quotation, straight from an American report on the drainage of breeding-grounds of mosquitoes.

Their principles also stipulated that there "be no coherent theme, at most, only confused and inconsistent hints of a meaning", and that no care be taken "with verse technique, except occasionally to accentuate its general sloppiness by deliberate crudities".

At the time of the hoax McAuley and Stewart were both in their mid-twenties. They had attended the same high school in Sydney, and were now working together in an army think-tank in Melbourne. Each had flirted with Modernism before renouncing all experimental

art, from Picasso to Joyce, and metamorphosing into ardent tradi-
tionalists. They especially despised Surrealism, reserving particular
contempt for the New Apocalypse school (Dylan Thomas and Co),
whose influence was just beginning to register on the Australian literary scene, mainly thanks to the only avant-garde journal of the time,
Angry Penguins.

Angry Penguins was edited by Max Harris, a student at Adelaide
University, and John Reed, who was 10 years Harris's senior and lived
just outside Melbourne. Independently wealthy, Reed was committed
to sponsoring any form of artistic originality that caught his eye; on
meeting the 22-year-old Harris, who was already carving a reputation
for himself as the *enfant terrible* of Australian letters, he declared: "he
may be egocentric, bombastic, but it just so happens that if he isn't a
genius, he is certainly about as near to being one as Australia has yet
produced."

By no means all of Australia's contemporary belletrists would have
agreed with the verdict. Harris's Surrealist novel *The Vegetative Eye*
– known to many as *The Vegetable Pie* – was issued in December
1943 by the newly-formed Reed and Harris publishing house, with
an outrageously self-praising blurb comparing the author with Rilke
and Kafka. "The plain fact is that Mr Harris cannot write", A.D.
Hope observed, before going on to charge the young firebrand with
plagiarism: "We have a Zombie, a composite corpse, assembled from
the undigested fragments of authors Mr Harris has swallowed without chewing."

It was to Harris in Adelaide that McAuley and Stewart dispatched
a selection of the most enticing Malley poems and a covering letter
from his sister. Ethel's epistolary style, which the hoaxers later claimed
demanded far more literary skill than the poems themselves, brilliantly
captures the bewildered sceptical tone of a narrow-minded philistine
doing her duty by her incomprehensible, improvident brother, but
with no great relish for the task: "I am not a literary person myself,"
she explained, "and I do not feel I understand what he wrote, but I

feel that I ought to do something about them. Ern kept himself very much to himself and lived on his own of late years and he never said anything about writing poetry. He was very ill in the months before his death last July and it may have affected his outlook."

It's not hard to imagine the impact on the suggestible young editor of the contrast between Ethel's wooden prose and the dazzling authority and scope of "Dürer: Innsbruck, 1495", or "Documentary Film". Obsessed with the difficulties of forging an international avant-garde so far from the capitals of Western art, Harris must have thrilled to the vision of the Australian artist struggling to express himself only to find that all has been said before:

> Now I find that once more I have shrunk
> To an interloper, robber of dead men's dream,
> I have read in books that art is not easy
> But no one warned that the mind repeats
> In its ignorance the vision of others. I am still
> The black swan of trespass on alien waters.

The lines echo the description by A.D. Hope – much revered by McAuley and Stewart – of Australia as

> a vast parasite robber-state
> Where second-hand Europeans pullulate
> Timidly on the edge of alien shores

but translate this standard antipodean dilemma into less stable, aesthetically personal terms cunningly calculated to appeal to Harris's notions of poetic subjectivity. Instantly intoxicated, he wrote to Reed with news of his "terrific discovery" and to Ethel requesting the rest of her brother's manuscripts, details of his artistic enthusiasms, and as much biographical information as possible.

He was even more excited on receiving the rest of the Malley œuvre, 16 typed poems in all, and one unfinished fragment called "So Long" written in an uncertain, death-bed hand, scored through with a smudgy "No" scrawled in the top margin. They had exotic titles such as "Sonnets for the Novachord", "Baroque Exterior", "Egyptian Register", "Sybilline", and the least of them revealed an awesomely confident poetic talent, a master manipulator of a stunning variety of idioms; they were by turns Expressionist, Surrealist, High Romantic, one moment tipping the wink to Eliot ("The evening / Settles down like a brooding bird / Over streets that divide our life like a trauma"), the next indulging in some knock-about Elizabethan pastiche, before suddenly soaring on outstretched wings through the Symbolist ether:

> The solemn symphony of angels lighting
> My steps with music, o consolations!
> Palms!
> O far shore, target and shield that I now
> Desire beyond these terrestrial commitments.

In her accompanying letter the comically obtuse Ethel struggled to field Harris's demands for information about her brother's intellectual development ("I wouldn't have thought Ern was interested in architecture and art as you say") but did at least reveal that he was "a great reader" and "often used to go to the public library at night". Those solitary hours of study were evident everywhere in *The Darkening Ecliptic*: Blake, Shakespeare, Freud, Pound, Lenin, Longfellow, Baudelaire, Mallarmé (of whose name his own is a not so earnest comic diminutive), Dylan Thomas, Marlowe, Rimbaud, Hart Crane, all had been absorbed with startling authority into the richly-layered texture of Malley's poetics. But the young bard wasn't simply shooting from the hip: Ethel had also forwarded an excruciatingly dense and contorted hand-written "Preface and Statement" that outlined the aesthetic theories behind the work. Harris must have been both puzzled and reassured by Malley's terse, gnomic declarations of intent: "There are no scoriae or unfulfilled intentions ... Every poem should be an autarchy ... Simplicity in our time is arrived at by ambages." Pound himself couldn't have devised a more impressive, or less revealing, manifesto. On one point Malley was particularly firm, and absolutely truthful: "There is no biographical data."

The Ern Malley Issue of *Angry Penguins*, published in the autumn of 1944, was a sumptuous affair, a fit setting for the poems it was unveiling. Harris had furnished an uninhibited critical introduction and a prose poem of his own, "Elegiac for Ern Malley", written in inspired homage to his newly-discovered hero. The young Sidney Nolan, a close friend of the Reeds, had been fired by Malley's work and had produced for the cover a dreamy painting that both illustrated and incorporated some of Ern's most affecting lines from the sequence's final poem, "Petit Testament":

> I said to my love (who is living)
> Dear we shall never be that verb
> Perched on the sole Arabian tree.

Only the strongest of poets can steal with such aplomb from Shakespeare. Nolan's painting figures himself and Reed's wife, Sunday, with whom he was deeply involved at the time, naked together in a tree silhouetted against the Australian outback. "All those lovely baby garments which Maxie knitted for his foundling child!" Harold Stewart cooed in a letter to the painter Donald Friend when, after a nine-month wait, he at last saw his and McAuley's handiwork irrevocably in print.

The hoaxers' gaff was blown much too early. Their longer-range plans had included involving internationally known defenders of the Modernist faith, particularly Herbert Read, chief apologist for the New Apocalyptics and, in McAuley's words, "a dead sucker for any gross rubbish that came his way". Foxing the likes of Harris and Reed, editors of a not exactly universally respected magazine with a tiny print run, was, he felt, simply "taking lollies from children". However, in a fit of ebullience some months before, Harold Stewart had let a young trainee journalist friend of his in on the secret, and on seeing the issue on sale she assumed the hoaxers had achieved their ends and a major scoop was hers.

The speed with which the Ern Malley story caught fire, and the gleeful vehemence with which it was pursued in the Australian media and then around the globe – *Time, Newsweek*, the *New Yorker*, the *Spectator*, the London *Times* each ran the story, while the *New York Times* even devoted an editorial to it, and all this in the middle of the Second World War – took the hoaxers themselves aback. Called upon to explain themselves, they cobbled together a rather high-flown defence of the scheme as "a serious literary experiment"; and Malley's work, conceived as "a wonderful jape" that would "absolutely slay Max Harris", was now presented as an honest rearguard action directed at the totalitarian might of Modernism. On the other side the embattled Penguins took and held the line that McAuley and Stewart wrote better than they meant or knew, and were immensely heartened to receive support in this from Herbert Read, who boldly cabled from London: "Hoaxer hoisted by own petard has touched off unconscious sources inspiration work too sophisticated but has elements genuine poetry." They even received a cautious blessing from the highest priest of all: T.S. Eliot, it seems, was "extremely interested, but this was not for publication in any way".

In the popular Australian press, however, Harris in particular suffered a merciless battering. Although he consoled himself that in time the affair would serve to "produce a deepening & even more honestly naked quality" in his own poetry, his immediate experience consisted of more or less constant public humiliation. And just as the worst seemed to be blowing over, he was visited by two policemen at the magazine's offices in Adelaide; they informed him that, as editor and distributor of the Ern Malley issue of *Angry*

Penguins, he was to be prosecuted under South Australia's obscenity laws.

A more farcical trial would be difficult to dream up. In front of a packed court Harris spent more than twenty hours in the dock defending work by a non-existent author expressly devised to make him look a fool. Chief witness for the Crown was Detective Vogelesang. An unconventional literary critic, he was keen to bring wisdom he had learnt on the beat to the interpretation of Malley's suggestive images. He was most suspicious of the couple who enter a park at night in the last two stanzas of "Night Piece":

> The symbols were evident,
> Though on park-gates
> The iron birds looked disapproval
> With rusty invidious beaks
>
> Among the water-lillies
> A splash – white foam in the dark!
> And you lay sobbing then
> Upon my trembling intuitive arm.

He felt the disapproval of the iron birds to be an important clue to the couple's "immoral" behaviour, and knew from his experience on the Force that "people who go into parks at night only go there for immoral purposes". The trials of *Ulysses*, Ginsberg's *Howl*, *Lady Chatterley's Lover*, all had their comic moments, but none achieved the level of sustained surreal hilarity occasioned by the indictment of Ern Malley. Harris was dragged line by line through the entire corpus and called upon to defend his phantom prodigy against charges of both obscenity and unintelligibility – equally heinous crimes in the eyes of the prosecuting counsel. Despite his valiant and increasingly ingenious feats of practical criticism, the judge ruled against him. He was fined £5 and ordered to pay costs of £21 and 11 shillings.

Over the half-century since his birth, life, death and meteoric rise to fame, Ern Malley has continued to provoke virulent debate. Michael Heyward's shrewd and funny book not only provides full social and literary contexts for the affair, but explores Malley's almost equally intriguing afterlife. Much to the dismay of his two inventors, he was no sooner invented than he cut loose and set about forging his own way in the literary world: Heyward's book is itself a symptom of his enduring appeal. In the teeth of their attempt to establish once and for all that *The Darkening Ecliptic* is "utterly devoid of literary merit as poetry", Malley's work has never lacked supporters, or general readers either. There have been six separate editions of the poems, and in a radio programme made in 1960 a librarian recorded Malley's œuvre as being among the most popular on the poetry shelves, though many borrowers had no doubt gone to it in pursuit of a snigger. At the other end of the spectrum Malley has been championed by the New York poets John Ashbery and Kenneth Koch, who printed a selection of his work in 1961 as part of a special "collaboration" number of *Locus Solus*, a magazine they edited with Harry Mathews and James Schuyler. (It was here that I first came across Malley's poems, nestled up against an audacious collaboration between Frank O'Hara and the French language.) Both Ashbery and Koch have included Malley in the curricula of their university poetry courses. At exam time Ashbery would present his students with two unattributed poems, one from *The Darkening Ecliptic* and one from Geoffrey Hill's *Mercian Hymns*; candidates were asked to guess which was a hoax, and give reasons for their choice. Half the students, Ashbery reports, picked the Malley poem, and half picked the Hill.

As Heyward points out, seen through the lens of the New York avant-garde Malley becomes a wholly different figure, a Postmodern *avant la lettre* fabricating a provisional identity from whatever material lies to hand but never fully convinced by his own fictions. The wildly unstable tone, the sudden shifts of idiom, the incorporation of different kinds of diction (that report on the draining of mosquito-breeding grounds), the penchant for bathos, pastiche, false quotation, the use of elusive narratives, have all become standard techniques in the experimental poetry of the last decades. Malley's mockery of the notion that some kind of authenticity is inherent in language is also in line with much recent thinking. His ludic verse habitually thwarts the reader's search for a single stable source of authority, while teasingly assuming prophetic tones that have long been exposed as untenable. It is this acute self-awareness, a pervasive doubt even about his own existence, which generates the poems' correspondingly extreme freedom to play with the symbols of the universe:

> I have arranged the interstellar zodiac
> With flowers on the Goat's horn, and curious
> Markings on the back of the Crab. I have lain
> With the Lion, not with the Virgin, and become
> He that discovers meanings.

Malley's relationship to the giants of Modernism also prefigures that of many later poets. His allusions to Eliot and Pound register as a quizzical, though not unsympathetic, critique of their quest for new dispensations. The more fatalistic Malley can muster no such confidence in poetry's powers of renewal, or in the originality of his own vision:

> But in time the fading voice grows wise
> And seizing the co-ordinates of all existence
> Traces the inevitable graph ...

It was Malley's Postmodern mutation which returned to Australia, via the New Yorkers, to strike a chord with a younger generation of poets such as John Forbes, Robert Adamson and John Tranter, who included the entire sequence in the *Penguin Book of Modern Australian Poetry* (co-edited with Philip Mead (1992)). In their introduction to the volume they argue that "these unsettling works of the imagination may be seen as early examples of the Post-Modernist technique of bricolage". They survive as "radical, intriguing challenges to traditional ways of writing and reading".

McAuley and Stewart would have none of this, fortunately, for a certain element of Malley's charm has always depended on his creators' disavowal. Had either ever conceded that the stuff wasn't, after all, so bad, the unique frisson that readers experience in discovering they admire *The Darkening Ecliptic* would have vanished. In time the two men found widely differing solutions to the moral, political and aesthetic chaos they were satirising in the figure of the neurotic, alienated Malley. McAuley drifted steadily to the right, developing into one of Australia's fiercest Cold Warriors. More dramatically, he converted to Catholicism in 1952, and much to the dismay of those who had admired his wonderfully vivid and intelligent early poetry, the rituals and history of the Church and the decadence of modern society began to bulk large as themes in his work. At all stages of his career McAuley was capable of exquisitely chiselled and convincing poems, but his reputation has come to rest mainly on such brilliant early pieces as "The Blue Horses" (inspired by Franz Marc), and some of the agonised late lyrics recording his spiritual despair. He died of cancer in 1976.

McAuley was always a pugnacious figure on the Australian poetry scene. Harold Stewart, by contrast, found the publicity attendant on the hoax so distasteful that he resolved to withdraw once and for all from the literary world. Besides, he soon lost even his scornful interest in 20th-century Western poetry, immersing himself instead in the sacred arts and writings of Asia. After several visits to Japan, he settled permanently in Kyoto in 1966, converted to Pure Land Buddhism, and developed into a leading authority on Japanese literary and religious traditions. His own poetry is serenely oblivious of all contemporary debates and developments: in 1981 he published *By the Old Walls of Kyoto*, 12 books of regularly rhymed pentameters that intertwine jewelled, but absolutely accurate, descriptions of certain locations in and around the city with his own spiritual progress in the Buddhist faith. When I visited him in late July of 1993 he was on the point of finishing an even longer epic, begun 14 years ago, based on a Chinese legend of the T'ang Dynasty. A charming, extremely eloquent man now in his mid-seventies, he chuckled briefly at the memory of *The Vegetable Pie* and enraged Penguins, but explained that the hoax itself had rapidly become a bore. When I asked him why he thought the egregious Ern has so triumphantly survived the ravages of time, he put it down to the blankness of Australia's cultural memory: "Ned Kelly, Phar Lap and Ern Malley – that's all that's ever happened there."

Michael Heyward also ponders the issue of Malley's longevity, and finally attributes it to the entrancing uniqueness of his poetic identity; though Malley borrows freely, he is, in a bizarre way, a poet "exactly himself", to use a phrase of Wallace Stevens's. That this should be so still seems incredible, not quite explicable even when all the facts have been thoroughly marshalled. Needless to say, the prescient Malley was fully aware of his own impending immortality, but realised also how much it was the pure anomaly of his non-existence that would consummate his fame. For the poet who breaks all the rules there can be no limits. In his own final words: "I have split the infinitive. Beyond is anything."

London Review of Books, 1993: Review of Michael Heyward's *The Ern Malley Affair* (Faber & Faber, 1993).

André Breton is Passing By

The first recorded use of the word "surrealist" occurs in some programme notes written by the poet Guillaume Apollinaire for Jean Cocteau's 1917 ballet, *Parade*, an all-star affair performed by Diaghilev's Ballets Russes on sets designed by Picasso to music composed by Erik Satie. A month later Apollinaire sub-titled his own play *Les Mamelles de Tiresias* [*The Teats of Tiresias*] "a surrealist drama", and offered this explanation of the term: "When man tried to imitate walking he created the wheel, which does not resemble a leg. He then performed an act of Surrealism without realising it."

Les Mamelles de Tiresias is in fact a pretty silly burlesque, but its stormy one-off performance proved of crucial significance to the future "Pope of Surrealism", André Breton, at this point 21 and a medical orderly in the Army. The play, which was three hours late getting underway, was jeered and heckled throughout the first act. In the interval a riot broke out, and Breton spotted his friend Jacques Vaché, dressed as an English officer, waving a loaded pistol and threatening to fire on the crowd. Breton rushed forward to soothe his irascible friend, but secretly thrilled to his display of exemplary recklessness. The defiantly gun-toting Vaché, Breton later declared, "cut the figure of an enlightener".

Breton was never content himself, however, with the mere acting out of his extreme fantasies of confrontation and nonconformism. Breton genuinely believed the Surrealist enterprise would revolutionise all aspects of existence – aesthetic, political, social – by liberating the unconscious processes of the mind. "Surrealism", he explains in his first *Manifesto* of 1924, "is based on the belief in the superior reality of certain forms of previously neglected associations, in the omnipotence of dreams, in the disinterested play of thought. It tends to ruin once and for all all other psychic mechanisms and to substitute itself for them in solving all the principal problems of life." Breton's vast and varied writings – from the scattiest poetic word cluster to the most thunderous of his polemics – are uniformly driven by his desire to develop a belief-system based entirely on the latent patterns of connection that the rational mind ignores or suppresses. Only by attending to illogic, coincidence, and chance can one hope to escape the reason's deathly stranglehold – first imposed, Breton argues, by Graeco-Roman culture – and enter the realm of the marvellous and beautiful: "Beauty will be CONVULSIVE," as he famously declared at the conclusion of *Nadja* (1928), "or will not be at all."

Breton's most interesting texts (*Nadja, Communicating Vessels* (1932), *Mad Love* (1937), *Arcane 17* (1944)) are not themselves works of convulsive beauty so much as commentaries on the irruption of convulsive beauty into his own life, each time in the shape of a woman to whom he found himself irresistibly attracted. Breton worshipped writing that might be described as convulsively beautiful through and through – Lautréamont's *Maldoror*, the poetry of Rimbaud, de Sade's *120 Days of Sodom* – but was himself as concerned to interpret convulsive experience as to present it. Breton examines each meeting or episode like a detective searching for clues, fanatically scrutinising the slightest memory or allusion for evidence of the uncanny and inexplicable. In *Mad Love*, for instance, he realises that a poem ("Sunflower") written over a decade earlier is wholly *"prophetic"* of the affair on which he has just embarked; he unearths in it specific references to places and people the couple observed on their first night walk together, and it even mentions swimming: at the time he met her, Jacqueline Lamba (who became Breton's second wife) worked as a nude underwater dancer at a large Montmartre music hall.

Breton's obsession with discovering relations of this sort governs not only his autobiographical writings, but his entire sense of his identity. He was born on February 19, 1896, yet later amended his birthday to February 18, a date that allowed him to claim significant astrological links with two of his major literary heroes, Rimbaud and Gérard de Nerval. His pursuit of what he called the "circumstantial-magical" always involved a rigorous screening out of who or whatever failed to contribute to his own conception of Surrealist liberation. Group members who disagreed with or challenged their leader were swiftly expelled. Conversely, chance finds such as the large wooden spoon with a small shoe carved at the tip of its handle described in *Mad Love*, or the "irregular, white, shellacked half-cylinder" of *Nadja*, or Nadja herself, become for Breton suddenly replete with intense mysterious significance, treasures whose appeal he ponders at inordinate, portentous length.

The dense streams of association and exposition prompted by such *trouvailles* are intended to embody the inexhaustible richness of the mind's powers of connection when properly unleashed, yet Breton's compulsive cross-referencing also suggests a buried fear of the kinds of experience that refuse all transmutation, of the "empty moments" – to use his own phrase – that remain stubbornly unmagical. His millennial claims for the powers of Surrealism never wholly disguise the personal anxieties motivating his quest for the Philosopher's Stone.

In the 1924 *Manifesto of Surrealism* Breton argued that "it is perhaps childhood that comes closest to one's 'real life'... Thanks to Surrealism, it seems that opportunity knocks a second time." His very occasional references to his own desperately lonely early years suggest though that he wouldn't have much relished reliving them. "For a long time," he tells his eight-month old daughter in the touching letter with which he concludes *Mad Love*, "I thought it was the gravest insanity to give life. In any case I held it against those who had given it to me." The only child of a police ledger clerk and a former seamstress, Breton was born in Normandy, but grew up mainly in Pantin, a drab industrial suburb of Paris. He particularly loathed his mother, whom he figures as a caricature petit bourgeois shrew, "authoritarian, petty, spiteful, preoccupied with social integration and success". Although disdainful of their social aspirations, Breton performed well in school, and on passing his *baccalauréat* reluctantly opted for a medical career, yet as early as his late teens he began seeking out the leading literary figures of the day – Valéry, Apollinaire, Reverdy. Poetry offered Breton not only an escape from "the walls of the real that enclose us", as an early poem puts it, but a means of forming the friendships his childhood lacked. His fellow Surrealist Philippe Soupault once described Breton as "a solitary man who could not live alone". Parallelling Breton's hunger for the marvellous was his hunger for the group – preferably one formed and presided over by himself.

Certainly Breton spent the decade preceding the official launch of Surrealism in 1924 gathering disciples in almost Christ-like fashion – first Soupault, then Louis Aragon, Paul Eluard, Benjamin Péret, Robert Desnos, Antonin Artaud... Initially his programme was largely determined by the dandyish Jacques Vaché's nihilist concept of "umour" (i.e. humour without the *h*), which Vaché glossed in one of his War Letters to Breton as a sense of "the theatrical (and joyless) futility of everything". Vaché was nearly three years at or near the Front, and his bitterly absurdist epistles to Breton anticipate the derangements of Dada and early Surrealism. Vaché haughtily disdained the "tainted charms" of literature, and these letters are his only surviving writings. On January 6, 1919, Vaché and a soldier friend were found dead of a drug overdose in a hotel room in Nantes. "His death was admirable," Breton later wrote, "in that it could pass for accidental." Breton believed, what's more, that Vaché had concealed from his friend the likely effects of so much opium, and thus committed one last wholly characteristic *"humorous deception"*.

Much as he approved of Vaché's heroic indifference, Breton seems not to have seriously contemplated suicide himself, though it was intended that his drama *If You Please*, written in collaboration with Philippe Soupault, would end with one of its authors, picked at random, blowing his brains out on stage. Neither in the event felt up to the challenge. It was with Soupault also that Breton first began experimenting with automatic writing: over a period of eight days in the summer of 1919 they set about composing "as rapidly as possible without any intervention on the part of the critical faculties". The resulting text, *The Magnetic Fields*, is a beautiful, often hilarious stream of images, by turns plangent, despairing, mysterious, outraged. Breton found the process of spontaneous composition dangerously intoxicating, and even began to fear for his sanity. "Hallucinations lay in wait", he later confessed; "I don't believe I'm exaggerating when I say that it couldn't go on any longer."

The Magnetic Fields is dedicated to Jacques Vaché, and its headlong rush towards "The End of Everything" (the title of the final chapter) figuratively emulates Vaché's suicidal impetus. Casting around for less destructive ways of fulfilling the ideals of umour, Breton turned to Dada's chief spokesman, the gleefully anarchic Tristan Tzara, who arrived in Paris in early 1920, and at once began organising Dadaist demonstrations calculated to attract as much publicity as possible. Breton was excited by Tzara's brazen iconoclasm, yet felt the events, in many of which he participated, were tedious and silly. He also disliked being twitted and overruled by the rambunctious Tzara, who seemed to him motivated more by love of scandal than revolutionary fervour. He finally denounced Tzara as a "publicity-mongering impostor" and began prospecting for other means of undamming the subversive energies of the unconscious.

Similar to the process of automatic writing were the group's "sleeping fits", initiated by the poet René Crevel in 1922. Under seance-like conditions Crevel discovered himself able to slip into a hypnotic slumber during which he improvised gruesome *Maldora*-ish narratives and pronounced terrifying Gothic curses. Breton was exhilarated – "A dazzling new day is dawning" he declared – and instigated sleeping fit sessions each evening. Unable to enter the state of trance himself, Breton took dictation and printed the results in the group's current magazine, the ironically titled *Littérature*. The sleepers soon took to expressing their dreams in actions as well as words. On one occasion Breton discovered Crevel preparing to hang himself from a coat-rack, while Robert Desnos had to be restrained after chasing Paul Eluard across the lawn with a knife. Alarmed, Breton terminated the experiment; as he had discovered before with automatic writing, the thinnest of thin lines separated liberation from madness.

Breton was never averse, though, to impressing his enemies with the violent dimension of his revolution. Incensed by a slur on Picasso's name at one of Tzara's final Dada events, the Surrealists swarmed on stage, pinioned the offender, and ordered him to leave the theatre; when he refused Breton swung at him with his cane and fractured his arm. Group members were forever disrupting cultural events they disapproved of, attacking performers, being beaten up by stage hands, returning to the fray. Their most notorious sabotage occurred at an official banquet for the Symbolist poet Saint-Pol-Roux, which coincided with the outbreak of the Rif War in Morocco. The Surrealists circulated a pamphlet denouncing France's involvement, and began chanting anti-patriotic slogans. In the ensuing melee Soupault, swinging from the chandelier, hurled crockery about the room, while below Desnos, Aragon, and Breton did battle to the utterance. This particular protest inspired united and widespread condemnation in the press. Though Breton, the group's master strategist, now despised Tzara, he had undoubtedly learned from him the value of scandal to a nascent artistic movement.

In his various manifestoes, on the other hand, Breton attempted to present Surrealism as an all-embracing philosophy capable of healing the major dichotomies of Western Civilisation. Despite his hatred of all institutions, he was keen to organise the group on an official basis, and even opened a Bureau of Surrealist Research. Attendance at weekly café meetings was compulsory. As his concerns grew increasingly politicised, Breton attempted to establish links with the French Communist Party, in the hope that Surrealism might become the dominant aesthetic mode of a post-revolutionary Communist world order. Years of fencing between the two basically incompatible groups ensued. Breton finally denounced Stalin at the time of the Show Trials, deciding he had become "the great negator and principal enemy of the proletarian revolution, and the most inexcusable of murderers."

If Breton's political involvements and his authoritarian style of leadership betray his urge to control people and wield power, his erotic entanglements repeatedly reveal the opposite impulse, his desire to cast himself upon the ineffable waters of chance. Much of the appeal of Nadja or X (Suzanne Muzard) of *Communicating Vessels* lies in their elusiveness and unpredictability, their refusal – or inability – to behave according to the dictates of common sense. Nadja in particular incarnated for Breton the principle of "total subversion", rather as Jacques Vaché had done some ten years earlier. Driving back to Paris one night, she "pressed her foot down on mine on the accelerator, tried to cover my eyes with her hands in the oblivion of an interminable kiss, desiring to extinguish us, doubtless forever, save to each other, so that we should collide at full speed with the splendid trees along the road. What a test of life, indeed!" Needless to say, Breton declined the pact, but declared the experience the perfect image of true love. In fact Breton found the "eccentricities" of the original of Nadja more elating in theory than in practice. He soon cut off all relations with her, and the following year she was committed to a psychiatric hospital in southern Paris, where she was visited by Aragon and Eluard, but not by Breton. Towards the book's conclusion he adduces the "well-known lack of frontiers between *non-madness* and madness", yet his behaviour again suggests how acutely aware he was of the gap between his own self-possession and the derangements he celebrated in others.

Breton was himself to be betrayed – or so he thought – by nearly all of his early comrades-in-arms in the Surrealist movement: from the Thirties on its history reads like one long internecine feud, an endless succession of trials, defections, suicides, expulsions, and recriminations. By the time of the Second World War, which he spent in New York, Surrealism had effectively – though he could never admit this – escaped Breton's grasp, and begun to modify the world's expressive means in styles Breton neither foresaw nor approved. To borrow Auden's phrase, it had become its admirers. On his return to Paris he set about reconvening the group which he now hoped would play a major role in the reconstruction of Europe, only to find the Existentialists determining the post-war cultural agenda. Breton and his admiring entourage of young but not especially talented "new generation" Surrealists found themselves increasingly marginalised. Movements ranging from the New York Abstract Expressionists to the Parisian Tel Quel group paid homage to Surrealism's decisive impact on their own development, but Surrealism itself – or at least Breton's purist version of it – had become part of the history books.

This excellent biography is the first full-length account of Breton's life and achievement to be published in English. It is both a remarkable work of scholarship and a superbly controlled narrative feat. Polizzotti skillfully braids together Breton's highly individual intellectual development, his complex relationships with Surrealist friends such as Aragon, Eluard, and Soupault, and his turbulent emotional history. In addition Polizzotti reveals the extent to which for Breton these distinctions scarcely existed; always open about his affairs, he frequently prided himself on living as if in "a glass-house", and his best writing continually insists on the indivisible nature of all experience.

It has become customary to think of Breton's influence on other artists as somehow outweighing his own colossal *œuvre* – the first two volumes of Gallimard's complete edition run to almost 2,000 pages each, and two more are projected. Under his aegis artists as varied as Yves Tanguy and Aimé Césaire, René Magritte and Luis Buñuel, found themselves discovering new aesthetic resources and freedoms of expression. Breton of course tended to revile any who later became successful, or at least earned any money. He anagramatically transformed Salvador Dali into Avida Dollars, and even the more Surreal that thou Max Ernst was booted out of the group in 1954, for winning the grand prize at the Venice Biennale. Oddly, given his oft-avowed intention of "killing art", Breton ended up perhaps the most significant aesthetic catalyst of the twentieth century.

His own writings, though, have proved less assimilable than those he enabled. Breton despised all existing literary genres, and his wholly original amalgams of autobiography, polemic, photographs, art criticism, alchemy, philosophy, dream-analysis, *que sais-je encore!* – defy easy categorisation. Inevitably Breton has been recuperated into the French literary tradition he so opposed – as the Gallimard project and this biography alike testify – but exactly what niche he should occupy in it still seems as ambiguous as the enigmatic communication he receives at the conclusion of the *"prophetic"* "Sunflower":

> And yet the cricket that sang in the ashen hair
> One evening near the statue of Étienne Marcel
> Aimed a nod of recognition at me
> André Breton it said is passing by.

New Republic, 1995: Review of Mark Polizzotti's *Revolution of the Mind: The Life of André Breton* (Bloomsbury Press, 1995).

Elizabeth Bishop at the Water's Edge

One of Elizabeth Bishop's earliest short stories, "The Sea & Its Shore" (1937), describes the peculiar life of a man called Edwin Boomer. Boomer's job is to keep a large public beach clean. He is given a stick with a nail at its end, a sack, a large wire basket in which to burn whatever litter he finds, and, since his beach-cleaning takes place at night, a lantern. He is also provided with a small wooden beach-hut (four by four by six feet) in which he spends much time sitting and reading the miscellaneous fragments of newspapers and magazines he collects on his nightly rounds. Edwin Boomer, Bishop writes, "lived the most literary life possible. No poet, novelist, or critic, even one who bends over his desk for eight hours a day, could imagine the intensity of his concentration on the life of letters". He separates the articles he gathers into three categories: extracts of writing which seem to refer directly to his own life and occupation, or contain some advice or instructions relevant to his own future; stories of celebrities whose lives interest him; and items of which he can make no sense at all. Boomer's absorption of so much print has its effect on the way he views the world:

> Either because of the insect armies of type so constantly besieging his eyes, or because it was really so, the world, the whole world he saw, came before many years to seem printed, too.
>
> Boomer held up the lantern and watched a sandpiper rushing distractedly this way and that.

It looked, to his strained eyesight, like a point of punctuation against the "rounded, rolling waves". It left fine prints with its feet. Its feathers were speckled; and especially on the narrow hems of the wings appeared marks that looked as if they might be letters, if only he could get close enough to read them.

The sandpiper is another haunter of beaches. Around the same time Bishop wrote "The Sea & Its Shore" she drafted a prose fragment entitled "The Sandpiper's Revenge", which, twenty-five years later, she transformed into the five quatrains of "Sandpiper". Her wading bird, like Boomer, seems to be searching for vital clues in the sand: "His beak is focussed; he is preoccupied, // looking for something, something, something".

Bishop clearly identified with these denizens of the coast: the lonely beachcomber shares the poet's initials, and his second name was Bishop's mother's maiden name. Like Bishop he is prone to alcoholism, and, when drunk, is something of an artist: he models busts and animals out of sea-soaked wads of newspaper, which he then dries and burns. But on nights when he is very drunk, the sea seems to him to have metamorphosed into gasoline:

> He glanced at it fearfully over his shoulder between every sentence he read, and built his fire far back on the beach. It was brilliant, oily, and explosive. He was foolish enough then to think that it might ignite and destroy his only means of making a living.

In around 1959 Bishop began work on a poem she never completed entitled "A Drunkard" in which she related the origins of her own alcoholism to a fire that broke out in 1914 near the Bishop family's summer home in the seaside resort of Marblehead, Massachusetts. Although Bishop was only three at the time, the inferno appears to have made an indelible impression on her:

> the red sky was filled with flying moats [sic],
> cinders and coals, and bigger things, scorched black burnt
> The water glowed like fire, too, but flat ...
> The beach was strewn with cinders, dark with ash –
> strange objects seemed [to] have blown across the water
> lifted by that terrible heat ...

The morning after, walking with her mother along the beach, she marvels at the way furniture, boats and clothes have been reduced to "blackened boards, shiny black like black feathers", just as Boomer's conflagrations in his wire basket leave piles of ashes that resemble a "bundle of grey feathers like a guinea hen's". Out of curiosity she picks up a woman's black stocking, and is sharply rebuked by her mother – *"Put that down!"* "Since that day, that reprimand," she broods, "I have suffered from abnormal thirst."

Bishop's "abnormal thirst" was not just for alcohol but for ways of controlling the panic that lies beneath the scrupulously accurate surface of her poems. Under the influence of drink and his scavenged texts Boomer sees the whole world as "printed", and thinks even the marks on the sandpiper's features are actually letters. One of Bishop's favourite poets was Baudelaire, and she seems here to be slyly alluding to the opening lines of "Correspondances": "La Nature est un temple où de vivants piliers / Laissent parfois sortir de confuses paroles". Conversely, on windy nights the newspaper pages that litter the beach take flight and appear to the inebriated Boomer like strange kinds of bird he must pursue and kill. The letters themselves seem to fly from the paper on which they are printed:

> He raised his lantern and staff and ran waving his arms,
> headlines and sentences streaming around him, like a man
> shooing a flock of pigeons.

When he pinned them through with the nail, he thought
of the Ancient Mariner and the Albatross, for, of course, he
had run across that threatening poem many times.

If Boomer is threatened by Coleridge's parable of transgression and
guilt, Bishop's sandpiper is pictured as questing after another kind of
Romantic vision, one that, like Baudelaire's conception of "correspondances" makes the world legible:

> The roaring alongside he takes for granted,
> and that every so often the world is bound to shake.
> He runs, he runs to the south, finical, awkward,
> in a state of controlled panic, a student of Blake.

In his "Auguries of Innocence" Blake celebrated the ideal of seeing
"a World in a Grain of Sand / And a Heaven in a Wild Flower": for
Bishop's sandpiper, too, there is "no detail too small"; like Boomer,
however, he is figured as oscillating between chaos and vision, between
fear of the sea (which is again presented as potentially combustible
– "the beach hisses like fat"), and an obsessive absorption in random
minutiae which may or may not be significant: he runs "watching his
toes" while water "glazes" (a word that suggests firing, as in a kiln) his
"dark and brittle feet":

> As he runs,
> he stares at the dragging grains.
> The world is a mist. And then the world is
> minute and vast and clear.

The poem does more than invite us to explore the nature of the poet's
identification with the bird, it positively forces us to respond to what
Seamus Heaney has called its "hint of self-portraiture":

Poor bird, he is obsessed!
The millions of grains are black, white, tan, and gray,
mixed with quartz grains, rose and amethyst.

We know the sandpiper is searching for food rather than the rainbow-hued transfiguration of Bishop's final line, and yet accept the analogy between poet and sandpiper as an example of what Wallace Stevens called "the poem of the mind in the act of finding / What will suffice": the poem is itself about controlling panic in the face of elemental, indifferent, potentially overwhelming forces, the Atlantic as it "drains / rapidly backwards and downwards". It wryly congratulates both bird and poet on their power to survive in the rich but dangerous place where sea and land meet, and to find there, even if only momentarily and in minute quantities, "what will suffice".

In Bishop's work coasts are often figured as the space where the contest between different systems of meaning can be most fully and rewardingly staged. "Yes," she ruminated in 1976 in her acceptance speech for the *Books Abroad* / Neustadt International Prize for Literature, "all my life I have lived and behaved very much like that sandpiper – just running along the edges of different countries, 'looking for something'. I have always felt I couldn't *possibly* live very far inland, away from the ocean; and I *have* always lived near it, frequently in sight of it." And she describes herself as having spent most of her life, like her sandpiper, "timorously pecking for subsistence along coastlines of the world". In this she was following in the footsteps of her mother's ancestors, the Boomers or Bulmers, as she explained in a letter of 1963 to Anne Stevenson: "That line of my family seems to have been fond of wandering like myself – two, perhaps three of the sea-captain's sons, my great uncles, were Baptist missionaries in India". One of these ancestors painted the "Large Bad Picture" considered in the poem of that title. Bishop was drawn to "bad" or faux-naïf or primitive art because it allowed her to ignore the endless "roaring alongside" and to escape into a realm of singular, precise, enticing de-

tail and liberatingly haphazard shifts of perspective. The coastal scene
of "Large Bad Picture" is, like that glimpsed by the sandpiper between
his toes, "minute and vast and clear":

> Receding for miles on either side
> into a flushed, still sky
> are overhanging pale blue cliffs
> hundreds of feet high,
>
> their bases fretted by little arches,
> the entrances to caves
> running in along the level of a bay
> masked by perfect waves.

Bishop's language plays off the sublime against the naïve, the picture's
attempt to suggest the soaring and illimitable ("receding for miles ...
hundreds of feet high") against details that are homely and reductive:
the painter's scrupulously "perfect waves" and "little arches" fretted
in "pale blue" cliffs, and the poem's use of clunking full rhymes, alike
serve to undermine the picture's drive for the transcendent. The sea
itself is figured in terms that suggest a room in which a child plays
with a set of miniature ships:

> On the middle of the quiet floor
> sits a fleet of small black ships,
> square-rigged, sails furled, motionless,
> their spars like burnt match-sticks.

The burnt match-sticks again evoke the threat of fire that, paradoxically, invades so many of Bishop's seascapes. Here, though, the
comically childish aspects of the large bad picture seem to license an
equivalently childish comedy in the poem as well:

In the pink light
the small red sun goes rolling, rolling,
round and round and round at the same height
in perpetual sunset, comprehensive, consoling,

while the ships consider it.

Like a child's magic lantern, the little red sun consoles, as the analogously faux-naïf perspective momentarily shared by painter and poet consoles by screening out whatever it is the poet needs consoling *for*. Unlike the painting, however, the poem is insistently aware of its *un*comprehensiveness, of what it allows itself to exclude, and the repetitions of "rolling" and "round" (words emphasised also by Boomer), and the fantasy of the ships considering the sun, as if they too were mini-naïve artists, are savoured as final indulgences just before poem and painting part company:

Apparently they have reached their destination.
It would be hard to say what brought them there,
commerce or contemplation.

Bishop may be remembering here the gap between the aesthetic or wondrous and the imperatives of commerce dramatised by Auden at the end of "Musée des Beaux Arts", published some three years before she wrote her poem:

the expensive delicate ship that must have seen
Something amazing, a boy falling out of the sky,
Had somewhere to get to, and sailed calmly on.

But vocational anxiety and family history, on her mother's mother's side, suffuse the lines also. The picture was painted by George W. Hutchinson, her grandmother's younger brother, who, as Bishop recorded in a brief biographical sketch written in the early 60s, "at the age of 14 started painting portraits of sailing ships for the shipbuilders then flourishing in Nova Scotia; he grew up to be an academic English painter" (not, as "Large Bad Picture" informs us, a schoolteacher). George Hutchinson also painted the view near Great Village commemorated in Bishop's late "Poem", where again their "visions" coincide – no, not visions, Bishop corrects herself, "our looks, two looks". The painter's father, Robert Hutchinson, was a "master-owner of a bark in the West Indies trade. He also wrote a small text book on navigation. He was lost at sea, with all hands, off Sable Island, in a famous storm". Bishop visited Sable Island in the summer of 1951, in the hope of writing a travel article about it, which she never completed, "and maybe", as she revealed in a letter to Lowell, "a poem or two". The island is "cheerfully known", she informs Lowell, "as 'the graveyard of the Atlantic'", and she wonders if she is not about to "fulfil [her] destiny and get wrecked too".

It would be interesting to know exactly what kind of "commerce" great-grandfather Hutchinson was involved in – probably part of the sugar trade that linked the West Indies plantations to Canada, America and Britain. The effect of the word in the poem is to shatter the good-humoured, half-mocking dialogue on aesthetics between poet and painter by reminding us not only of the role of ships in the colonization of the world and the formation of empires, but of the possible relationships of art to the ideology of expansion. "Large Bad Picture" was in fact written in 1943 when Bishop was living in militarised Key West. Shortly after Pearl Harbour she had written to Marianne Moore that the once easy-going, raffish resort she had settled in some three years earlier was "no place to be unless one is of some use". Yet she spent most of the war there, and even in an attempt to be "of some use" took a job in the binoculars department of the U.S. Navy Optical Shop. This, her one foray into the working world of non-literary "commerce", lasted only five days because the cleaning fluids inflamed her eczema and the eyestrain made her sick. Her description of the military site to Marianne Moore reveals a struggle between the faux-naïvely aesthetic and the practical that greatly resembles that enacted in "Large Bad Picture":

> The "shop" was very nice, open across one end and right on the edge of the water, where hundreds of ships, subma-rines and all kinds, are coming and going, being repaired and painted, all day long. The water is jade green, the gray ships looked bright blue against it, and of course I could spend a lot of time – had to – watching everything through magnificent optical instruments of every kind, including periscopes.

Observation, experimenting with perspectives, is motivated here not only by aesthetic curiosity but by the needs of the job. But she goes on to complain to Moore that her fellow workers, though "polite and kind and helpful", lack "imagination":

> not one of them had any idea of the *theory* of the thing, *why* the prisms go this way or that way, or what "collimate" and "optical center" really mean, etc. – and of course I kept fussing and fuming because I was so sure certain things could be done better in some other way, or that some very simple change would make it all easier.

A little "contemplation", Bishop felt, and a proper understanding of words and the larger picture, would have accelerated this aspect of the war effort. Bishop's poetry is routinely commended for – to quote her own praise of Darwin – its "endless, heroic observations", yet, bizarre-ly, in the Optical Shop she is the one exasperated by minutiae and detail: "I was infinitely impressed with the patience of those men *fid-dling* day after day with those delicate, maddening little instruments. I don't think I could do it, even if it hadn't made me sick."

Her poetic work, though, involved a different kind of *"fiddling"*, draft upon draft upon draft testifying to her compulsion to "make the casual perfect", to quote from Lowell's sonnet on her compositional methods; it also, however, involved an awareness that – as Marianne Moore famously put it in "Poetry" – "there are things that are important beyond all this fiddle". But where, then, between the poles of commerce and contemplation, between the brute facts of war, empire, the history and politics of trade, and the too-optimistic "consolations" of the aesthetic, can the poem stand? The place where land and water meet initiates many of her most complex figurations of this conflict.

"Land lies in water", begins the first poem of her first book, *North & South* (1946). Cartography makes possible a stylised, panoramic view of the globe's surface, yet in fact the first verse of "The Map" presents coasts as unstable and open to all kinds of speculation and interpretation:

> Shadows, or are they shallows, at its edges
> showing the line of long sea-weeded ledges
> where weeds hang to the simple blue from green.
> Or does the land lean down to lift the sea from under,
> drawing it unperturbed around itself?
> Along the fine tan sandy shelf
> is the land tugging at the sea from under?

The lines posit a number of different, almost contradictory ways of construing the relationship between land and sea. Sea-weeds are envisaged as somehow linking blue and green in a kind of entranced suspension verbally mimed by Bishop's use of a series of near-homonyms: shadows, shallows, edges, ledges, sea-weeded, weeds. Yet the word "simple" can't help implying its opposite. Any map – even the one dreamed up by Borges and Bioy Casares which is as large as the country it charts – must be a simplification; Bishop's use of the word alerts us to the way the map, like the large bad picture, licenses a dreamy, whimsical simplification of the complexities of existence. "What one seems to want in art," as she put it in her letter on Darwin, "in experiencing it, is the same thing that is necessary for its creation, a self-forgetful, perfectly useless concentration." This state seems to have been a prerequisite for Bishop's creativity, yet she was also acutely aware that art is never really "useless"; it may originate in contemplation, but exists in the end only because it enters the world of commerce, is published, paid for, and consumed. And the "concentration" itself is likely to be motivated by forces or tensions or fears the artist cannot control in any other way – by the need to forget one's self.

Words like "simple" or "unperturbed", then, also evoke their opposites, the state of "controlled panic" in which the sandpiper runs south. Bishop began "The Map", her biographer Brett Millier records, on New Year's Eve of 1935, and the actual map that she contemplated was of the North Atlantic – the Canadian Maritime Provinces, Greenland, Iceland, Scandinavia. The poem does not mention her mother's home-town, Great Village, Nova Scotia, where Bishop spent various periods of her childhood in the care of the Boomer or Bulmer family, but the image of the land "leaning down to lift the sea from under, / drawing it unperturbed about itself" seems itself to draw on the early memories of her mother recorded in "In the Village" (1952). Gertrude Bishop suffered a mental collapse shortly after her husband's death from Bright's disease eight months after their only child was born; she spent the next five years in and out of mental institutions, before being diagnosed as permanently insane and hospitalised in a sanatorium in Dartmouth, Nova Scotia, where she died in 1934. "In the Village" describes Gertrude Bishop's final visit to her daughter in 1916. She is being fitted for a purple dress that is to signify her coming out of her protracted mourning:

> She wasn't at all sure whether she was going to like the
> dress or not and she kept lifting the folds of the skirt, still

unpinned and dragging on the floor around her, in her
thin white hands, and looking down at the cloth.
  "Is it a good shade for me? Is it too bright? I don't know. I
haven't worn colors for so long now ... How long? Should it
be black? Do you think I should keep on wearing black?"

The child watches and hears, while the dressmaker fusses, the beautiful sound of the village blacksmith's hammer on his anvil:

> *Clang.*
> The pure note: pure and angelic.
> The dress was all wrong. She screamed.
> The child vanishes.

In contrast, in "The Map" the maternal land is pictured as leaning
down and gently lifting the sea which she then draws "unperturbed"
around herself. There is no scream or commotion, as the poem's adjectives keep insisting: "The shadow of Newfoundland lies flat and still";
"We can stroke these lovely bays, / under a glass as if they were ex-
pected to blossom"; "Mapped waters are more quiet than the land is".
The quietness is of noise subdued, of motion stilled, like the scream
which is present and absent at once: "No one hears it; it hangs there
forever, a slight stain in those pure blue skies". Other images in the
poem, however, suggest threats to this stillness, or the perils of "emotion too far exceed[ing] its cause"; the land is pictured as "tugg[ing]"
at the sea rather as Bishop's mother is shown "twitching the purple
skirt with her thin white hands", before bursting into a wail. Like the
sandpiper, "Norway's hare runs south in agitation", and the printed
"names of seashore towns run out to sea", challenging the illusion of
stasis the map induces. Underlying the whole "dreamy divagation",
to borrow a phrase from "The Moose", is an awareness that although
the map-makers' colours may seem more "delicate" than those of historians, the antithesis is essentially as false as that between commerce

and contemplation: maps not only made possible the conquest of the globe, but the national boundaries they chart are the result of infinitely complex historical processes, and liable at any moment to be redrawn. And like the "magnificent optical instruments" she handled while working for the Navy at Key West, maps are supremely "useful": they make whoever owns them very much "favorites" in the struggle for territorial or economic advantage.

This tension between a naïve, "self-forgetful", whimsical absorption in quirky detail and slightly absurd speculation, and a more responsible, at times unendurable, knowledge of what she calls in a 1964 letter to Robert Lowell "grimness and horrors of every sort", animates many of Bishop poems. She treats it most directly in "Seascape", written in 1941 in Key West, but initially inspired by a tapestry based on a Raphael cartoon of the miraculous draught of fishes, which she saw in the Vatican in November of 1937: "the shallow blue water, reflections, the birds feathers – very Florida-like and calm", she observed in her notebook. The first thirteen lines of the poem present a "celestial seascape" in which the natural features of the Florida coastline are infused with an idealizing, religious iconography:

> This celestial seascape, with white herons got up as angels,
> flying as high as they want and as far as they want sidewise
> in tiers and tiers of immaculate reflections.

Even the mangrove roots suggest Gothic arches, while white bird-droppings on green leaves are compared to a religious manuscript's "illumination in silver". This "cartoon by Raphael for a tapestry for a Pope", Bishop asserts, "does look like heaven". This is "embroidered nature", to quote the epigraph to "Brazil, January 1, 1502", drawn from Sir Kenneth Clark's *Landscape into Art*, "tapestried landscape", or in this case seascape. But Raphael's cartoon, however entrancing and magical, could not be called "useless", or an act of disinterested contemplation. "I never had so clear an idea before", Bishop also observed in her notebook while in Rome, "of the vast commerce, the *tides of gold*, of the church, and I never disliked it so much". That doesn't mean that she agrees with the stern Puritanical skeletal lighthouse who dominates the last ten lines of the poem, who "lives on his nerves" and insists

> that hell rages below his iron feet,
> that that is why the shallow water is so warm,
> and he knows that heaven is not like this.
> Heaven is not like flying or swimming,
> but has something to do with blackness and a strong glare ...

"Seascape" illustrates very obviously the polarities of north and south that structure Bishop's first volume, and translates them also into a sectarian argument between Protestant and Catholic, or low and high church. As a Northerner Bishop is delighted to find Florida's languorous coastline seems to allow her to escape the weight of guilt and responsibility, of living on her "nerves", of her fear of the blackness and strong glare which dominate drafts of "A Drunkard". Poems such as "Pleasure Seas", "Florida", and "Little Exercise" evoke a world of enchanting inconsequence. The warm seas disperse obsessions and commitments, indeed the very idea of depth, to create a sense of endless *jouissance*:

> The sea is delight. The sea means *room*.
> It is a dance-floor, a well ventilated ballroom.
> From the swimming-pool or from the deck of a ship
> Pleasures strike off humming, and skip
> Over the tinsel surface: a Grief floats off
> Spreading out thin like oil. And Love
> Sets out determinedly in a straight line,
> One of his burning ideas in mind,
> Keeping his eyes on

The bright horizon,
But shatters immediately, suffers refraction,
And comes back in shoals of distraction.

A sense of the provisional, the weightless, and the self-delighting permeates Bishop's descriptions of the Florida shore-line: the whole state
is seen as floating "in brackish water, / held together by mangrove
roots"; pelicans "coast for fun on the strong tidal currents / in and
out among the mangrove islands", and the white spray thrown up by
waves breaking on the coral reef is imagined as "dancing happily by
itself". "Little Exercise" figures a storm breaking over the "unrespon-
sive" mangrove keys as growling "like a dog looking for a place to
sleep in". Like the Audenesque abstractions Grief and Love in "Pleasure Seas", it is dispersed before it can wake the human sleeper with
whom the poem ends:

Now the storm goes away again in a series
of small, badly lit battle-scenes,
each in "Another part of the field."

Think of someone sleeping in the bottom of a row-boat
tied to a mangrove root or the pile of a bridge;
think of him as uninjured, barely disturbed.

The sleeper's northern equivalent is the corpse with which "Love Lies
Sleeping" ends, in whose open unseeing eyes the city (clearly New
York) lies "distorted and revealed". In the city excess – "emotion too
far exceed[ing] its cause" – leads to stupor and even death, but down
in the forgiving Florida Keys there are no revelations, no reprimands,
no need to sleep, like Bishop's unbeliever (in the poem of that name)
"on the top of his mast / with his eyes closed tight". Even the unbeliever's dreams reflect his anxiety:

"I must not fall.
The spangled sea below wants me to fall.
It is hard as diamonds; it wants to destroy us all."

In the "careless, corrupt" tropical south, on the other hand, death is freed from ideas of guilt and regret and judgement. The mangrove skeletons and turtle skulls and dead trees that strew the coast in "Florida" are simply a part of the region's eco-system, haphazard features of what she described in a notebook as "the detailed flatness of Key West". In "The Bight" even the ocean is presented as pure surface or flatness, indeed as not even wet:

At low tide like this how sheer the water is.
White, crumbling ribs of marl protrude and glare
and the boats are dry, the pilings dry as matches.
Absorbing, rather than being absorbed,
the water in the bight doesn't wet anything,
the color of the gas flame turned as low as possible.
One can smell it turning to gas; if one were Baudelaire
one could probably hear it turning to marimba music.

"Sheer" in the first line – meaning "transparent" as in "sheer stockings" – evokes once more the scene of transgression on the beach at Marblehead. Here again the water seems on the point of conflagration, yet the random, permissive disorder of the scene, and of Florida generally, allows the threat of fire to be tamed, by being domesticated and, implicitly, feminised – as the image of peninsulas taking "the water between thumb and finger / like women feeling for the smoothness of yard-goods" feminises the sea in "A Map". Bishop's reference to Baudelaire serves to distinguish her low-key, quotidian aesthetic of accurate observation from his exotic High Symbolism, but the allusion also establishes a link between the two: is it any odder to compare the sea to the flame of a gas-stove than to think one can hear it turning to marimba music? Poets, like everyone else, interpret reality according to their psychic or imaginative configurations and moment of cultural history. The randomness of any individual's responses, whether they be Bishop or Baudelaire, is of a piece with the random clutter of the bight – the term itself suggests the indefinite and shapeless: a bight is less distinctive than a bay or a port, merely a curve or indentation on what she calls in "Florida" "the monotonous, endless, sagging coast-line".

While at work on "The Bight" Bishop wrote to Lowell that she was trying to finish a couple of "not very serious" poems about Key West, "& then I hope I won't have to write about the place anymore". Part of the appeal for Bishop of Key West – where she spent the best part of a decade – was its lack of seriousness, the extent to which it allowed her to "let go", as she lets go of the fish at the end of her best-known poem. But this letting go could involve slipping into inconsequential idleness and loss of vocational purpose. "The Bight" was inspired by dredgers at work in Garrison Bight in Key West observed by Bishop in January of 1948, her last full winter there. She wrote to Lowell:

> The water looks like blue gas – the harbor is always a mess, here, junky little boats all piled up, some hung with spong-es and always a few half sunk or splintered up from the most recent hurricane. It reminds me a little of my desk.

The birthday the poem commemorates was her thirty-seventh, and Bishop had begun to worry about her rootless existence, "the dis-tractions of travelling – that rarely offers much at all in respect to work", as she put it earlier in the letter to Lowell, who was at the time consultant to the Library of Congress, and hence in the thick of "intellectual life":

> I guess I have liked to travel as much as I have because I have always felt isolated and have known so few of my

"contemporaries" and nothing of "intellectual" life in New York or anywhere.

"The Bight" is about not belonging, about missed opportunities, about failed relationships, about time passing, about fear of chaos and meaninglessness and not achieving anything, but it is also about how to struggle on in the face of all these threats to one's sense of self, about how a "joking voice" can make bad bilingual puns even when faced with what looks "like disaster":

> Some of the little white boats are still piled up
> against each other, or lie on their sides, stove in,
> and not yet salvaged, if they ever will be, from the last bad
>   storm,
> like torn-open, unanswered letters.
> The bight is littered with old correspondences.
> Click. Click. Goes the dredge,
> and brings up a dripping jawful of marl.
> All the untidy activity continues,
> awful but cheerful.

The poem's last line became something of a talisman for Bishop. She decreed the words be inscribed on her headstone, clearly feeling they best summed up her attitude to life. She seems also to have used the phrase as a mantra: the year after writing the poem she sent a copy to Dr Anny Baumann, who began treating her for her various ailments and addiction to alcohol in 1947. "If I can just keep the last line in mind," she wrote after one of her periodical binges, "everything may still turn out alright". The paradox of the "awful but cheerful" has come to pervade most accounts not only of the way Bishop's poems work, but of her troubled life and radiant sense of humour. Take, for example, this anecdote told by James Merrill, who visited her in 1970 in Brazil, at her house in Ouro Prêto where a young Brazilian painter was also staying:

> Late one evening, over old-fashioneds by the stove, a too re-
> cent sorrow had come to the surface; Elizabeth, uninsistent
> and articulate, was in tears. The young painter, returning,
> called out, entered – and stopped short on the threshold.
> His hostess, almost blithely made him at home. Switching
> to Portuguese, "Don't be upset, José Alberto," I understood
> her to say, "I'm only crying in English."

If, in the main, Key West and the Florida coast furnished Bishop with
scenes and characters – such as Jéronimo, Faustina, or the naïve painter Gregorio Valdes – that allowed her to emphasise the cheerful side
of her epitaph, her poems set on the North Atlantic seaboard tend to
be explorations of the "awful", sublime or other impossible aspects of
existence. These cold northern seas are presented as hostile, "bearable
to no mortal", as embodying a harsh destructive truth to be ignored
at one's peril. Along the sprawling Florida coastline land and sea over-
lap and interact until it is hard to know which is which: the water is
thick with sediment, on it float "weightless mangrove island[s]" on
which oysters flourish in clusters; palm trees seem like "limp fish-skel-
etons", and the shallow sea-bed seethes with vegetation: "Clay-yellow
coral and purple dulces [a kind of sea-weed] / And long, leaning,
submerged green grass". Wading at Wellfleet, Massachusetts, on the
other hand, is like being attacked by Assyrian chariots whose wheels
have been fitted with sharp scimitars:

> This morning's glitterings reveal
> the sea is "all a case of knives."
>
> Lying so close, they catch the sun,
> the spokes directed at the shin.
> The chariot front is blue and great.

> The war rests wholly with the waves:
> they try revolving, but the wheels
> give way; they will not bear the weight.

The sea cannot usurp the land, as it does in Florida, and it brings to mind not Raphael's sumptuous cartoon for a Pope, but the self-scrutinising Protestant theology of George Herbert – Bishop's all-time favourite poet – from whose "Affliction IV" her quotation comes. To the shore-bound observer of "Cape Breton" the ocean seems not so much antagonistic, as occluded and impossible to predict or interpret:

> The silken water is weaving and weaving,
> disappearing under the mist equally in all directions,
> lifted and penetrated now and then
> by one shag's dripping serpent-neck ...

The attempt to figure the sea's currents in terms of a woman weaving a silken cloth – or stocking? – breaks down as the mist descends and the water disappears "equally in all directions". The narrator of this poem is not content with the mysteriously shifting perspectives created by the mist; she longs to lift and penetrate, like the serpent-necked shag, to delve beneath surfaces and discover what has been held back. Turning her attention to "the mainland", she finds it equally inaccessible:

> The road appears to have been abandoned.
> Whatever the landscape had of meaning appears to have been
>   abandoned,
> unless the road is holding it back, in the interior,
> where we cannot see,
> where deep lakes are reputed to be,
> and disused trails and mountains of rock
> and miles of burnt forests standing in gray scratches

like the admirable scriptures made on stones by stones –
and these regions now have little to say for themselves ...

The journey into "the interior" seems also a journey into prehistory, into mute regions from which the poet is cut off. Cape Breton is the northern tip of Nova Scotia, and Bishop spent six weeks there in the summer of 1947. The previous summer she had returned to Great Village for the first time in almost 15 years – a trip that resulted in "At the Fishhouses" and – eventually, 26 years later – "The Moose". An oblique, bracing determinism seems to drive these poems, perhaps best summed up by the peculiar affirmative described in "A Moose":

> "Yes ..."
> A sharp, indrawn breath,
> half groan, half acceptance,
> that means "Life's like that.
> We know *it* (also death)."

"Cape Breton", "At the Fishhouses" and "The Moose" all explore the relationship between lost origins and the sense of the sublime, between the contingencies and speculations of the present and the mysterious elemental forces the poet is driven to encounter or investigate:

> The thin mist follows
> the white mutations of its dream;
> an ancient chill is rippling the dark brooks.

In the course of her 1946 trip north Bishop visited Lockeport Beach on the Atlantic, and observed in her notebook: "Description of the dark, icy, clear water – clear dark glass – slightly bitter (hard to define). My idea of knowledge. this cold stream, half drawn, half flowing from a great rocky breast" [the last four words crossed through]. Despite the deletion of "a great rocky breast" she decided in the end to use the image in "At the Fishhouses", though Lowell, for one, felt it "too much". The entry develops the motto the unnamed narrator of "In Prison" – a more sophisticated version of Boomer who longs to be incarcerated for life – declares the ultimate truth: "'Freedom is knowledge of necessity'; I believe nothing as ardently as I do that." In the poem the abstract idea becomes a physical experience:

> I have seen it over and over, the same sea, the same,
> slightly, indifferently swinging above the stones,
> icily free above the stones,
> above the stones and then the world.
> If you should dip your hand in,
> your wrist would ache immediately,
> your bones would begin to ache and your hand would burn
> as if the water were a transmutation of fire
> that feeds on stones and burns with a dark gray flame.
> If you tasted it, it would first taste bitter,
> then briny, then surely burn your tongue.
> It is like what we imagine knowledge to be:
> dark, salt, clear, moving, utterly free,
> drawn from the cold hard mouth
> of the world, derived from the rocky breasts
> forever, flowing and drawn, and since
> our knowledge is historical, flowing, and flown.

The "marl" of "The Bight" surely evokes the "burning marl" of Hell in *Paradise Lost*. Milton's description of Hell's "inflamèd sea", its "fiery deluge, fed / With ever-burning sulphur unconsumed", seems latent also in Bishop's most apocalyptic and "awful" vision of the pains of "knowledge" that she, like Eve, is compelled to "taste". After persuading Adam to eat, Eve's eyes dart "contagious fire", and their "love's disport" is "of their mutual guilt the seal". Lowell's flinching at Bishop's use of the word "breast" is intriguing in this context; did he find

it "too much" that in the midst of this confrontation with grand elemental absolutes an image of such disquieting female intimacy should
appear – rather as Bishop's mother had rebuked her for picking up a
woman's stocking in the face of so much destruction on the beach at
Marblehead?

The knowledge Bishop imbibed with her mother's milk was of
death, absence, madness and abandonment. The poem deliberately
subverts *The Prelude's* vision of beneficent Nature fulfilling parental
roles in the care and instruction of gifted orphans; Bishop once described herself as a "minor female Wordsworth", but the "cold stream"
of the notebook entry could hardly be further from the amiable Der-
went, the "fairest of all rivers", who

> loved
> To blend his murmurs with my nurse's song,
> And from his alder shades and rocky falls,
> And from his fords and shallows, sent a voice
> That flowed along my dreams.

Bishop's personification works the other way, to indict her mother for
being as indifferent as the cold, hard, rocky coast and bitter, icy sea.

This knowledge, the poem's last line insists, is "historical" – always
in process, and hence always eluding our grasp. There is finally no
perspective possible that can quell or control this endless flowing, no
means of representation that can offer more than a temporary illusion
of escape from the forces of history. But Bishop is here pushing up
against the limits of a genre much less crudely stylised than the inept
bad picture or the mass-produced map; it is a measure of the poem's
ambition that its conclusion makes use of an elevated vocabulary and
diction that recall Whitman at his most incantatory and death-haunt-
ed in *Sea-Drift* poems such as "Out of the Cradle Endlessly Rocking"
and "As I Ebb'd with the Ocean of Life" ("Ebb, ocean of life, (the
flow will return,) / Cease not your moaning you fierce old mother"),

or lines such as those from Keats's "Bright Star" that Edwin Boomer quotes in the context of the cleaning of beaches:

> The moving waters at their priestlike task
> Of pure ablution round earth's human shores ...

The human shore of "At the Fishhouses" is brilliantly depicted in the poem's opening section: the Wordsworthian old man netting in the gloaming, the silver sea and silver benches, the fish tubs lined with herring scales, the wooden capstan

> cracked, with two long bleached handles
> and some melancholy stains, like dried blood,
> where the ironwork has rusted.

While the clutter of "The Bight" creates a sense of the haphazard and inconsequential, the details picked out in "At the Fishhouses" are made to seem precious and vulnerable, imbued with meaning because under threat. The old man embodies for the poet a glimpse of ancestral continuity – "He was a friend of my grandfather". They discuss the "decline of the population", and she marvels at his gutting knife:

> He has scraped the scales, the principal beauty,
> from unnumbered fish with that black old knife,
> the blade of which is almost worn away.

Bishop often locates meaning in use; Crusoe's knife, for instance, in "Crusoe in England", on his island "reeked of meaning", but once he no longer needs it he finds its "living soul has dribbled away". The old fisherman's "almost worn away" blade, his "shuttle worn and polished", dramatise the heroic, everyday struggle to survive in difficult, probably worsening conditions; indeed the concept of use unifies the scene very much as the silver of the herring scales visually connects "the benches, / the lobster pots, and masts, scattered / among the wild jagged rocks", the fish tubs, the flies and the old man's vest and thumb. From the shore the sea also seems silver and "opaque", but "at the water's edge" the poem's vision and perspective pivot. In the central paragraph – which consists of a single sentence – "thin silver / tree trunks" laid on the ramp induct the poet almost hypnotically into the unfathomable mysteries of the "element bearable to no mortal", the "cold dark deep and absolutely clear" sea.

"Here is a coast; here is a harbor" begins "Arrival at Santos", the first poem of Bishop's third book, *Questions of Travel* (1965). Bishop is heralding her *vita nuova* in Brazil, her return from the infernal freezing flames of isolation and alcoholism, and her discovery of what often seemed like an earthly paradise: "I feel I must have died and gone to heaven without deserving to", she wrote to Anny Baumann some eight months after moving into Lota de Macedo Soares's spectacular house-in-progress in Petrópolis, 60 miles inland from Rio. This was the "interior" anticipated in the final line of "Arrival at Santos", and once settled there she felt stable enough to revisit her childhood in prose pieces such as "Gwendolyn", "In the Village", "Memories of Uncle Neddy", "Primer Class", and "The Country Mouse", and in poems such as "Sestina", "Manners", and "First Death in Nova Scotia"; there, for a while at least, Bishop found a way, to adapt a line from "Questions of Travel", to "dream [her] dreams / and have them, too".

Five years before she died, however, Bishop published her final ode to the Eastern seaboard. "The End of March" – in many ways a companion piece to "At the Fishhouses" – describes a walk taken with her last partner, Alice Methfessel, along the beach at Duxbury, Massachusetts, in a freezing cold late winter wind, while the tide is out. Unlike the "swelling", "swinging" sea of "At the Fishhouses", the ocean here seems "shrunken" – the adjective perhaps borrowed from Hardy's "The Darkling Thrush" ("The ancient pulse of germ and birth / Was shrunken hard and dry ..."):

91

Everything was withdrawn as far as possible,
indrawn: the tide far out, the ocean shrunken ...

Even in such unpropitious circumstances Bishop can imagine life in
a beach-hut like Boomer's way out on the dunes, where she'd lead the
life dreamed of by the narrator of "In Prison":

I'd like to retire there and do *nothing*,
or nothing much, forever, in two bare rooms:
look through binoculars, read boring books,
old, long, long books, and write down useless notes,
talk to myself, and, foggy days,
watch the droplets slipping, heavy with light.
At night, a *grog à l'américaine*.
I'd blaze it with a kitchen match
and lovely diaphanous blue flame
would waver, doubled in the window.

The "useless notes" would never end up as poems circulating in the
world of commerce; Bishop, at this point, was a creative writing in-
structor at Harvard, and so for the first time in her life making a living
out of her poetry. The lighted *grog à l'américaine* she'd enjoy there
fuses the imagery of flames, sea-shore and alcohol that she struggled
unsuccessfully with in the drafts of "A Drunkard", but which unite
so many of her coastal scenes. Even the relatively benign description
of the Nova Scotia tides and shore at the opening of "The Moose"
includes "burning rivulets". Here they no longer threaten because the
fantasy is so clearly just that – "perfect! But – impossible". That day
at the end of March the wind is so cold the walkers don't even get far
enough to glimpse Bishop's "proto-dream-house", but they do follow
a set of animal prints as large as a lion's to a final – and this time male
– version of the forbidden black stocking, "lengths and lengths, endless, of wet white string, / looping up to the tide-line, down to the

water, over and over". This "thick white snarl, man-size, awash", must be "a kite string? – But no kite". On the way back the sun momentarily appears:

> For just a minute, set in their bezels of sand,
> the drab, damp, scattered stones
> were multi-colored,
> and all those high enough threw out long shadows,
> individual shadows, then pulled them in again.
> They could have been teasing the lion sun,
> except that now he was behind them
> – a sun who'd walked the beach the last low tide,
> making those big, majestic paw-prints,
> who perhaps had batted a kite out of the sky to play with.

Like the rose and amethyst discovered by the sandpiper, or the "rainbow rainbow rainbow" of her victory over the fish, or the "rainbow-bird" of "Sonnet", the "multi-colored" stones dramatise a sense of life as suddenly – if only briefly – radiant with possibility. Knowledge here is awareness of the fictive nature of our imaginings, of the scope for play within a given history. Bishop finds herself led by her tangled kite string to a vivid apprehension of how her creativity emerges from and figures forth the interplay of elements – and of the poetic prints her own work will end up leaving on the literature of the sea and its shore.

Essays in Criticism, 2003

Harry Mathews and the Oulipo

The Oulipo, or Ouvroir de littérature potentielle, was founded in 1960 by Raymond Queneau and François Le Lionnais. The group's initiatory text was a sequence of ten sonnets written by Queneau entitled *Cent mille milliards de poèmes*: these sonnets all use the same rhymes, and are grammatically constructed so that any line in any sonnet can be replaced by the corresponding line in any of the other nine sonnets. Each sonnet in the original edition was cut into 14 strips, enabling the curious reader to construct a poem which began, say, with line 1 from sonnet 7, took its line 2 from sonnet 3, its line 3 from sonnet 10, and so on. This novel procedure allowed Queneau's 140 lines to generate, potentially, 100 million million (10^{14}) poems, which would take, he later calculated, someone reading 24 hours a day around 190,258,751 years to peruse in their entirety.

But most Oulipian texts astonish not by their powers of expansion, but by their self-imposed laws of constraint. The best known of these is Georges Perec's lipogrammatic *La Disparition* (1969), composed without once using the letter *e*, and his *Les Revenentes* (1972), which contains no vowels except *e*. Over the years Oulipians have developed or recovered all manner of demanding exercises: "snowballs", popular in Classical times, in which each word is one letter longer than its predecessor ("I am the text which begins sparely, assuming magnitude ..."), "isograms", in which no letter appears more than once, tautograms, in which all words must begin with the same letter ("Oulipians ordinarily operate out of ostensibly oddball overproportion ..."), palindromes (the longest of which, by Perec, is over 5,000 letters long), and *"ulcérations"* (in French) and "threnodials" (in English) which employ only the eleven most common letters of the language. As Jacques Roubaud, one of the group's most gifted practitioners, observed in 1991: "An Oulipian author is a rat who himself builds the maze from which he sets out to escape."

Harry Mathews is the only American member of the Oulipo, to which he was introduced by Georges Perec in 1972. He soon invented what came to be known as "Mathews's algorithm", a formula for arranging material based on the principle of permutation first illustrated by Queneau's *Cent mille milliards de poèmes*. Both Mathews's algorithm and Queneau's sonnets are examples of what the Oulipo call "combinatorial literature", which might be defined as the business of applying mathematical concepts to uses of language. Oulipian texts often derive their forms – or perhaps that should be formats – from the permutations generated by a particular concept or set of equations, which provide the author with a set of pre-determined elements or themes which must all feature in a given chapter or section. Secret mathematical formulations underpin texts as diverse as Italo Calvino's *If on a Winter's Night a Traveller* (1979), Jacques Roubaud's ∈ (1967), Georges Perec's *Life: A User's Manual* (1978), and Harry Mathews's *Cigarettes* (1987).

Cigarettes depicts the world of affluent East Coast respectability into which Mathews was born in 1930. He has not disclosed the law of permutation that governs its intricate set of intertwined plots, but we learn in an epilogue that the novel is in fact the work of one of its characters, Lewis Lewison, an aspiring writer (his first poems are published in *Locus Solus*, "a little magazine whose reputation was unrivalled"), and a no-holds-barred masochist. In one episode the ill-fated Lewis arranges to have himself crucified by a circle of S and M devotees, only to have the police – accompanied by journalists – raid the event just after he's been nailed to the cross and hoisted aloft. To the consternation of his parents, a photograph of their son as aspirant Christ appears on the front page of the next morning's papers. In another, Lewis's sadist lover, the art-critic Morris, coats him in quick-drying cement, and harangues him in campy slang:

> "Even if I don't like reading you the stations, I won't spread jam. So please, Louisa, get it and go. You're a mess, a reject, a patient – I could go on for days. And don't tell me – I have your nose wide open. I'm sorry. Spare me the wet lashes, it's all summer stock. Because the only one you've ever really been strung out on is your own smart self, and you always will be. Think I'm going to stick around and watch the buns drop? And for what – to keep catching my rakes in your zits? Forget it, Dorothy. This is goodbye. Remember one thing, though. No matter what I've said to you, no matter how I've turned you out, the truth is" – Morris's eyes become wet; he turns a surprising shade of red – "the truth is, and I'm singing it out: I lo— ..." Morris is staring past Lewis as his voice breaks off. Has he stopped because the telephone is ringing? His color veers from red to gray. He turns to lean on the back of a chair, except that no chair is to be found where he leans: he sinks to his knees before lying face down on the floor.

Lewis eventually manages partially to shatter his concrete shell and telephone for help, but it arrives too late to save Morris, who has suffered a fatal heart-attack. Poor Lewis has no trouble, however, in completing Morris's final unfinished sentence: "The truth is, I loathe you."

Mathews's "Autobiography" (also published in 1987), suggests a number of links between himself and Lewis – for instance, as children both used thieving as a way of securing their mothers' exclusive love. Lewis's quest for extreme sensations perhaps mirrors his creator's impatience with the complacencies of the WASP milieu in which he grew up (private schools in Manhattan and Massachusetts, followed by Princeton and Harvard, from which he graduated with a BA in music). He too scandalized his parents, though rather less dramatically: when he was 19, and on a mid-college tour of duty with the Navy, he went AWOL so as to elope with a woman he'd met on a train, Niki de Saint Phalle.

His parents tried to have the marriage annulled, which precipitated a family rift. In 1952 Mathews and de Saint Phalle and their one-year old daughter set sail for Europe. For a while they lived in Deyà, Mallorca, where Mathews came under the influence of Robert Graves, whose *The White Goddess* lurks behind some of the arcane mystic lore that turns up in the plot of his first novel, *The Conversions* (1962). A much greater influence on his early fiction, however, was Raymond Roussel, to whose work he was introduced by John Ashbery in 1956: Roussel's "sovereign genius", Mathews later declared, "demonstrated to me that psychology was a dispensable fashion, that the moral responsibilities of writing did not lie in a respect of subject matter, and that the writing of prose fiction could be as scrupulously organized as Sir Philip Sidney's double sestina." Both *The Conversions* and *Tlooth* (1966) present the reader with a cornucopia of improbable inventions, bizarre artefacts, linguistic riddles, and mind-boggling discoveries, all recounted in a studiedly neutral tone that is at once lucid, precise, and wholly unrevealing of its author's "psychology". Like Roussel's, Mathews's multifoliate narratives seem designed to defy paraphrase or explication: the opening chapters of *The Conversions*, for example, feature a ritual adze engraved with seven cryptic scenes relating to the life of a medieval female saint; a race between three worms whose progress is accompanied by ascending notes blown on ancient serpents; an inset narrative relating the struggle for survival of three enthusiastic amateurs of old German music stranded in the Arctic, where they sing *Ein fester Burg ist unser Gott* in Schütz's harmonization; and a competition between the narrator and the chief of a group of Long Island gypsies which requires each to hold a terracotta jar filled with boiling water and describe as quickly as they can the scene moulded on its lid:

> Of a group of nine men on their knees, clubs laid aside,
> I said: Victorious Yankees pray for humility.
> The chief: From the dead God's eye swarm fat swine.
> My next scene showed two men, one of them looking in
> amazement at the other, who was chiseling at the bust of
> an old man set in the middle of a fence. I said of it: Con-
> founding Brunelleschi, Donatello carves a venerable God
> from a fencepost.
> The chief: Cool drink in hand, Somerset Maugham is
> gently toothdrilled.

This particular contest offers a *mise en abyme* of Mathews's early prose style: streams of arcane information are fiercely compressed into the fewest possible words; fabulously baroque vignettes succeed each other according to some severe logic of correspondences one can never quite fathom. Both novels make use of comically simple overall plots; the protagonist of *The Conversions* has to discover the meaning of the scenes on the adze in order to claim an inheritance left him by the enormously wealthy Mr Wayl, while the narrator of *Tlooth*, once a violinist, seeks revenge on a surgeon who amputated the index and ring fingers of her left hand. Her first attempt occurs in the course of a baseball match at a Siberian concentration camp, where both are imprisoned: as Evelyn Roak, the surgeon, steps to the plate, the narrator, who is catcher, substitutes for an ordinary baseball one with a small bomb concealed in it; the first three pitches are foul, at the fourth Roak swings and misses, and the fifth flies way over the plate, and disappears "irretrievably, and with an abysmal liquid reverberation, into a drain". Much of both *Tlooth*'s and *The Conversions*'s comedy derives from Mathews's ingenuity in fusing the *outré* and the banal.

The Conversions was first published in instalments in the short-lived little magazine *Locus Solus* (1961-62) edited by Mathews himself (who also funded it with a legacy inherited from his grandfather), Ashbery, James Schuyler and Kenneth Koch. Like most avant-garde magazines, *Locus Solus* (named after Roussel's second prose novel, published in 1914, and with an epigraph from his final long poem, *Nouvelles Impressions d'Afrique* (1932)) was founded primarily as a forum for the work of the editors and their friends. Unlike most other avant-garde magazines, however, *Locus Solus* was much too cool to bother with manifestoes or justifications of its editors' aesthetic criteria: it neatly sidestepped the poetry wars raging between the "cooked" (i.e. the academic and formal) and the "raw" (i.e. the bardic and beat) then fissuring American poetry, instead suggesting by example the ways in which American experimental writing could incorporate foreign models without being overwhelmed by them. Issue Two, for instance, was devoted to the principle of literary collaboration, and included, alongside in-house co-productions by its editors, poems jointly written by Fletcher and Shakespeare, by Kakei and Basho, by Coleridge and Southey, by Eluard and Péret, by Cowley and Crashaw, by Breton and Tanguy, as well as two of the finest works of Ern Malley. "La poésie doit être faite par tous", as Lautréamont, one of Mathews's favourite writers once declared.

Like many bilingual authors, Mathews is particularly fascinated by the kinds of collaboration involved in attempts to convert one language into another. Translation figures again and again in Mathews's work because it fuses the business of reading and writing, and foregrounds the reader's part in the creation of whatever experience a novel makes possible. Indeed for Mathews, creation, translation and collaboration are more or less interchangeable terms. This conviction is most fully and elaborately embodied in his third novel, *The Sinking of the Odradek Stadium* (1975), which is made up of letters exchanged by a married couple, Zachary McCaltex, a lapsed Catholic American librarian, and Twang Panattapam, a business-like Buddhist from a Montagnard hill tribe. The ostensible plot concerns their attempts to recover a treasure trove from a galleon wrecked off the coast of

Florida in the sixteenth century; while Twang burrows into archives in Italy, Zach hunts for clues in and around Miami. Twang writes a peculiar hybrid English which makes special demands on her correspondent – and the reader: "To raed this has need, not idees but a tenshn (to-trans-late of Twang)", as she explains in her first epistle. Piecing together her reports on her researches into Florentine politics and history is a bit like working through a history of the Medici as rewritten by an Asian James Joyce. The novel's eccentric form and use of culturally diverse protagonists allows Mathews to dramatize the sheer messiness of collaborating and translating, the tangents, cross-purposes, and missed meanings involved in interacting with another in a partially-shared language. As they close in on the map that will lead to the treasure, their investigations begin to throw up all kinds of rarefied epistemological questions, especially when Twang starts reading Wittgenstein.

A short story from around this period reprinted in Mathews's collected stories, *The Human Country*, presents the relationship between languages in even more antithetical terms. "The Dialect of the Tribe" (a phrase of Mallarmé's appropriated by T.S. Eliot in "Little Gidding") is in the form of an academic article in which an unnamed Professor discusses a small New Guinea tribe whose peculiar language has no content, but instead somehow enacts the process of translation itself. Every Pagolak sentence embodies the "magic of changing" in a manner that renders elusive the thing being changed. Pagolak is all process, like an abstract expressionist canvas, or like the pure "mode of intention" that Walter Benjamin envisioned linking the different languages of the world in his 1923 essay, "The Task of the Translator". This of course makes Pagolak untranslatable – indeed any version of a Pagolak sentence in a foreign language will actually conceal rather than reveal the original's meaning. By the end of the story the Professor has abandoned his native tongue altogether, and is haranguing his readers in Pagolak, insisting that if only they'd pay due attention, then "tak nalaman namele Pagolak kama – ".

Another story from the Seventies, "Remarks of the Scholar Graduate", features an even more ingenious linguist who is able to decode
the puzzling script of very early Bactrian civilization, despite the fact
it consists simply of seven vertical lines. These lines, he persuasively
reasons in a lecture delivered at his old school, are the written version
of the Bactrian mantra, "God copulates with the soul of mother",
which is in fact the cardinal meaning of all Bactrian declarations. Later
Bactrian scripts and dialects, indeed perhaps modern languages also,
are all a corruption of this all-purpose, all-signifying sentence. The
lecturer propagates his *idée fixe* with numerous sideswipes at the theories of his arch rival, Gartner, and with a conviction and intensity that
has us doubting his sanity. Like so many of Mathews's obsessive first
person narrators, the scholar graduate evokes the deranged exegetes
who populate the fiction of Kafka and Nabokov, while the fiendish
speculations of such as Borges and Bioy Casares seem an influence
on Mathews's enquiries into the nature of language. Both Bactrian
and Pagolak recall the mysterious *Ursprache* of Borges's Tlön, which
contains no nouns but only impersonal verbs, and in which famous
poems consist of a single enormous word.

The mysteries of Pagolak were initially revealed by an Australian
scholar, Ernest Botherby, who on his anthropological travels in New
Guinea in the 1890s also came across two tribes who lived two days
journey apart, but were seemingly oblivious of each other. The Ohos'
language, is even more limited than that of the Bactrians; indeed it has
only three words which Botherby translates as "Red makes wrong",
while that of the Uhas he found to be equally rudimentary, its only
phrase being "Here not there". On his return from the Uhas to the
Ohos Botherby is eager to inform the tribal chiefs of the existence of
their neighbours; his gestures are readily understood, but he pauses
before discussing the Uhas' language:

How do you render "Here not there" in a tongue that
can only express, "Red makes wrong?"

Botherby did not hesitate long. He saw, as you of course
see, that he had no choice. He grasped at once what all
translators eventually learn; a language says what it can say,
and that's that.

This parable serves in the title essay of Mathews's collection of non-
fiction pieces to introduce a discussion of translation and the Oulipo.
Oulipian methods are not, Mathews concedes, likely to appeal to
commercial editors, focusing as they do, like Pagolak, on the act of
conversion itself. Phèdre's famous lament, *C'est Vénus toute entière à
sa proie attachée* emerges from the *ouvroir* in a variety of barely recognizable forms: "I saw Alice jump highest – I, on silly crutches" (each
French word replaced by an English word with the same number of
letters); "Save our news, toot, and share as uproar at a shay" (a phonetic transliteration – which can then be expanded into a mini-narrative
about someone creating pandemonium by bellowing as a one-horse
carriage passes); "Look at Cupid's mom just throttling that god's
chump" (demotic and no e's); "At this place and time exists the goddess of love identified with the Greek Aphrodite, without reservation
taking firm hold of her creature hunted and caught" (each word given
its dictionary definition). For Mathews the point of such exercises is
the way they force writer and reader into unfamiliar realms, and make
us acknowledge language as an ongoing continuum rather than a stable set of agreed truths, just as the word "truth" itself is morphed into
the nonce-word "tlooth" in the title of Mathews's second novel – a title the book's French translator, Georges Perec, oulipianly rendered as
Les verts champs de moutarde de l'Afghanistan. "If we think of writers as
translators," Mathews argues, "what they must translate is not something already known but what is unknown and unpredictable. The
writer is an Oho who has just heard what the Uhas say." In a further
twist he also insists that it is only by venturing into the unknown that
writer and reader can hope to make provisionally legible whatever
narratives lie buried within, for one's own life's story is as mysterious

as the kaleidoscopic permutations of language: a great book, as Proust once asserted, is never "invented by a great writer – it exists already inside him – but it has to be translated by him".

The persevering Maltese of the essay's title refers to a painting in Venice by Carpaccio known as "The Vision of St. Augustine": the saint has just been informed by a miraculous voice of the death of St. Jerome, to whom he was about to write a letter. To the left, bathed in celestial light, sits an alert and expectant Maltese dog, who seems to be asking of his astonished master, "What next?" Oulipian constraints, Mathews suggests, help liberate the kind of open-ended curiosity embodied by Augustine's pet, and needed by a writer to bring to light inner obsessions and private habits of connection.

It was only, for instance, after he had devised an elaborate formal scheme for *Cigarettes* that the novel's characters and situations were able to emerge "from nowhere", as it seemed, though in fact that nowhere was the world of his childhood. *Cigarettes* is to my mind one of the most brilliantly original – and underrated – novels of the 20th century, a dazzling mosaic of interlocking stories which combine to create an intricate and mesmerising portrait of a particular society in a particular era. The book's complexities are all in its structure and patterning. Mathews allows himself none of his early fiction's linguistic high jinks: the style of *Cigarettes* – which we must assume to be Lewis's – is unremittingly purposeful and direct, concerned wholly with the business of character and story-telling. It's a novel, the reader should be warned, that can prove as addictive as its title promises; but though I have read it many times, I never feel I have quite plumbed the "mysteries of construction" (to use a phrase of Marianne Moore's) that underlie it.

Cigarettes features thirteen characters; each of its chapters presents a pairing, (Lewis and Morris, Morris and Walter, Lewis and Walter, and so on) in the fictional equivalent of a round dance or game of tag. Several plot strands that involve a portrait and a racehorse link many of the stories, but each chapter is also as complete and satis-

103

fying in itself as a perfectly wrought short story. Perhaps the most moving of these describes the tribulations of Lewis's sister, a young painter called Phoebe, who is afflicted – as Niki de Saint Phalle was – by hypothyroidism, a glandular disease which causes depression and hallucinations. Her case is misdiagnosed, and she finds herself swept into vertiginous cycles of self-loathing and ecstasy, paranoia and visionary exaltation. Mathews brilliantly traces the precise contours of her mood swings, their pace and imagery, their irrational, irresistible force. One moment she sees herself in the mirror as a skinned rabbit's head, the next she is overwhelmed by an all-consuming radiance:

> She rose to meet and savour it, gliding through rings of splintery light, up, up. Where was she going? Higher, she found or mentally assembled webs of incandescence out of which the flakes came sprinkling. She guessed, she *knew* what they were: stars. The teetering stars had spilled into the gloom of her mind. She had no strength to resist that shower or the spidery filaments above it that sucked her in.

She is haunted by a set of letters, b.s.t.q.l.d.s.t, which, as in some kind of Oulipian torture, she must wrestle into an expression of her oscillating states: "Beasts stalk the question lest demons sever trust", perhaps, or "But soon the quest lured drab saints thither". On a train the letters seem to signify the noise of the wheels and engine, but then momentarily dissolve into the formula:

> Cigarettes, tch, tch
> Cigarettes, tch, tch.

Phoebe's collapse is in no sense symbolic or presented as part of some necessary artistic *via negativa:* the reduction of her life to eight random consonants, however, which then metamorphose into a nonsense phrase which in turn furnishes the book's title, does mime the primary alchemical processes of verbal disintegration and recombination to which Mathews frequently draws attention in explanations of how he writes his books. His collection of non-fiction, for instance, includes worksheets for the composition of a poem called "Birth" which shows his fondness for Rousselian procedures such as homophony (twelve hundred metres > Delft under Demeter) and polysemy (Apostles [twelve] cento [hundred] meters [as in prosody]); the random elements are then divided and combined (For Demeter, cento meters / Delft under the Apostles) and used to generate lines which describe the "prodigious pastiche prosodies" that greet the arrival of the goddess of marriage, and missionaries walking down corridors of blue-and-white tiles.

This deliberate "prospecting" in language, to use Roussel's term, involves jettisoning the idea that creativity has to be spontaneous to be authentic. *Cigarettes* concludes with a celebration of inauthenticity, and a complex meditation on the struggle between the forces of determinism and the powers of play. Lewis notices at a train station a perfectly dressed man who seems on his way to some glamorous event:

> A blazer of not-quite-navy blue followed the slope of his shoulder and the fall of his slack right arm with uncluttered smoothness. Above the flattened collar of the jacket appeared a neat ring of off-white crepe de chine shirting, its points drawn together with a glint of gold beneath a rep tie of plum and pewter stripes, whose mild bulge was nipped by a more visible clasp of gold above the open middle button of the blazer. From a gently cinched waist fell pleated trousers of dove-gray flannel – my mental fingertips fondled their imagined softness, confirmed by the delicacy with which they broke, an inch above their cuffs, against the insteps of brown-and-amber saddle shoes. To complete

the array, the man in his left hand held a high-crowned, pale-yellow Panama hat, using it to fan – so solemnly I wondered any air was displaced – his sweatless head.

Lewis later learns his immaculately attired fellow traveller is in fact an unsuccessful professional actor who supplements his income by escorting single women to fashionable parties. The imperious way the actor invents his own presence prompts Lewis to brood on the unfathomable layerings of identity, and the extent to which we are shaped by forces wholly beyond our control, rough-hew them how we will: nevertheless, we persist in our absurd, stubborn conviction that "you are only you, and I I". " I sometimes think", Lewis continues:

that only the residual strength of the dead beings inside me gives me power to survive at all. By that I mean both the accumulated weight of the generations succeeding one another and, as well, from the first of times, when names held their objects fast and light shone among us in miracles of discovery, the immortal presence of that original and heroic actor who saw that the world had been given him to play in without remorse or fear.

London Review of Books, 2003: Review of Harry Mathews's *The Human Country: New and Collected Stories* (Dalkey Archive Press, 2002) and *The Case of the Persevering Maltese: Collected Essays* (Dalkey Archive Press, 2003).

Genius in Its Pure State:
The Literary Manuscripts of Raymond Roussel

The French writer Raymond Roussel was fifty-six years old when he left Paris for Sicily in the early summer of 1933. It seems clear he had no intention of ever returning to France. His theatrical extravaganzas, legendary generosity, and eccentric lifestyle had consumed the bulk of his colossal fortune. He was addicted to drugs. One morning in his hotel in Palermo he opened a vein in his wrist in the bath, but immediately summoned help. "How pleasant it is to die", he was heard to remark. Eleven days later he was found dead of an overdose of barbiturates.

Roussel's writings are full of hidden treasures suddenly come to light, and particularly the discovery of lost and unlikely manuscripts – a sonnet composed by the youthful Milton on an egg-shell in which he declares his love for the consumptive girl next door, a very peculiar version of *Romeo and Juliet* in Shakespeare's own hand, a Racine letter describing a play he hopes to write about a third century Corsican tight-rope walker. On occasions Roussel took active steps to preserve his own literary papers, depositing various manuscripts with his financial advisor, Eugène Leiris (father of Michel Leiris), not all of which have come to light. By the time of his departure for Sicily in 1933, however, Roussel seems to have lost interest in his literary career. Though he tidied up many personal affairs, including the execution of a new will, he left no instructions concerning the thousands of pages of rough drafts, fair copies, typescripts, and proofs left behind in the apartment he rented in the family house on Rue Quentin Bauchart. Boxed up and placed in storage in a furniture warehouse, these papers were only disinterred when the removals company itself moved premises in 1989.

These manuscripts now form the *fonds Roussel* at the *Bibliothèque Nationale* in Paris, and have recently become available for consultation on microfilm. For years a dedicated Rousselian, I finally decided to write a book exploring his life, work, and influence on a variety of artists ranging from Marcel Duchamp to Michel Foucault, from John Ashbery to Georges Perec. Accordingly, I spent the summer of 1996 working my way through this enormous archive in the stately gloom of the ornately carved *Salon de Manuscrits* on the first floor of the *Bibliothèque Nationale*, just down from the *Bourse* where Roussel senior earned the huge fortune which was to fund his son's literary activities. Initially I felt I was trespassing into the heart of some unfathomable French mystery, the sort not even the French have time for. "You write", Marcel Proust told Roussel on receipt of his first book, *La Doublure*, "without losing breath, a hundred verses as another writes ten lines." I felt the full weight of Proust's not entirely complimentary observation: Roussel's texts seemed to proliferate, like some tropical rainforest, in every direction. I soon came to understand that his bizarre compositional methods were devised not to stimulate his creativity, but to curb this delirium of excess.

Roussel's unique imaginative world is most fully embodied in his two novels, *Impressions d'Afrique* (1910) and *Locus Solus* (1914). Both present a dazzling array of virtuosos and freaks, artworks and inventions, performances and discoveries. The opening chapter of *Impressions d'Afrique*, for instance, includes a description of a life-sized statue of a helot – a Spartan slave – clutching at a sword plunged into his heart. The statue is fashioned out of black corset whalebones, and is fixed to a trolley – also of corset whalebones – whose wheels rest on two rails made of a coarse, red, gelatinous substance that turns out to be calves' lights, that is the gastronomic delicacy made from the lungs of young cows; statue, trolley, and rails are in turn mounted on a platform bearing the inscription DUAL, followed by a bracket and two forms of an Ancient Greek verb. When a carefully trained magpie activates an internal spring with its beak the platform slowly tilts, and trolley and statue are set gently in motion.

This elaborate creation, we later find out, is the handiwork of Norbert Montalescot and his sister Louise; Louise has been imprisoned by the African king Talou VII for having had an affair with his chief enemy, Yaour, and her release depends on the Montalescots' accomplishment of this and a number of other appallingly difficult tasks. The statue of the helot alludes to a story, supposedly to be found in Thucydides, in which a recalcitrant student-slave is required to learn, on pain of death, the conjugation of various auxiliary verbs. Called to the front of the class, he soon makes a gross mistake in the dual of the aorist, and instantly suffers the threatened punishment.

During his lifetime, despite the howls of derision his work regularly inspired, Roussel steadfastly refused to offer either explanation or justification of his writings. Some time before his death, however, he sent to his publisher a short essay to be issued posthumously entitled *"Comment j'ai écrit certains de mes livres"*, in which he outlines the *"procédé très speciale"* underlying the composition of his novels and plays.

> I chose a word and then linked it to another by the preposition *à* [with]; and these two words, each capable of more than one meaning, supplied me with a further creation ... 1st. *Baleine* (whale) *à ilot* (small island); 2nd. *baleine* (corset whalebone) *à ilote* (helot); 1st. *duel* (combat between two people) *à accolade* (embrace, as when two adversaries are reconciled after the duel); 2nd. *duel* ("dual" as in Greek grammar) *à accolade* (typographical bracket); 1st. *mou* (spineless individual) *à raille* (here I was thinking of the raillery directed towards a lazy student by his comrades); 2nd. *mou* (lights of a slaughtered animal) *à rail* (railway line).

Hence the Montalescots' extraordinary sculpture. Roussel declares it his duty to disclose this secret method, so that future writers may benefit from his innovations.

Though the essay reveals, with a multitude of examples, *how* Roussel wrote certain of his books, it doesn't attempt to explain *why* he developed and adopted such singular procedures. He directs our attention to the psychologist Pierre Janet's account in *De l'angoisse à l'extase* of a nervous crisis the young author suffered when still in his teens for which Janet treated him, but offers nothing himself on the relationship between his life and work, beyond the "curious fact" that though he has travelled all around the world he has never used a single detail from these voyages in his books: "It seems to me that this is worth mentioning, since it clearly shows just how much imagination accounts for everything in my work."

Roussel's immense wealth enabled him to publish his writings in luxurious editions at his own expense, to hire the most prestigious theatres, actors, directors, and set-designers for his plays, and to mount massive publicity campaigns for each new production or publication. He hoped to become as popular as Pierre Loti or Jules Verne, and was dismayed when his lavishly presented work encountered only "an almost totally hostile incomprehension". Janet records the young Roussel predicting that his glory would one day outshine that of Victor Hugo or Napoleon, that he felt himself the equal of Dante and Shakespeare. His final testament more modestly hopes that, "*faute de mieux*", his books may one day gain some measure of posthumous recognition.

It was while composing *La Doublure*, which he always believed his ultimate masterpiece, that Roussel was irresistibly seized by a conviction of his own greatness. "Everything I wrote", he told Janet, "was surrounded by rays of light; I would close the curtains for fear the shining rays that were emanating from my pen would escape through the smallest chink; I wanted to throw back the screen and suddenly light up the world. To leave these papers lying about would have sent out rays of light as far as China and the desperate crowd would have flung themselves upon my house... No doubt, when the volume appeared, the blinding furnace would be revealed and illuminate the entire universe ..." Published in 1897, *La Doublure* sank without trace, and Roussel was plunged into a profound nervous depression. The skin of his entire body erupted in a red rash, and he felt he'd "plummeted to earth from the prodigious summits of glory". Nevertheless, this crisis seems not to have fundamentally weakened his faith in his own destiny. On recovery he spent some years "prospecting", as he calls it in *"Comment j'ai écrit..."*, exhaustively seeking new ways of revealing his genius. "This prospecting tortured me," he records, "and usually ended with my rolling around on the floor, raging against my failure to attain those sensations of art for which I had strived."

La Seine and *Claude et Luce,* the two most startling additions to the Roussel canon discovered among his papers, both derive from this period. *La Seine* (probably composed between 1900–1903) is one of the strangest plays ever written. Its opening act suggests a wholly standard domestic drama: Raoul suddenly decides to leave his wife and child for his mistress Jeanne, whom he has rescued from life on the streets. The enormous second act, almost 5,000 lines long, presents an evening the couple spend at the Moulin Rouge. They are, however, by no means its sole concern; Roussel introduces character after character, and the act unfolds as a seemingly endless series of new people, new conversations, new stories, from grisly murders to mild flirtations, from aesthetic theories to unsettling dreams. In all the play offers over 400 speaking parts, and would take the best part of a day to perform. Act III, set in the Bois de Boulogne, is just as discursive. Only in Act IV does Roussel think to return to his narrative: Raoul, now abandoned by Jeanne and tortured by jealousy, hurls himself from a bridge into the Seine. A related fragment, *La Tonsure*, projects a different outcome; here Raoul has become a Trappist monk, and a remorseful Jeanne arrives at his monastery to beg his return.

La Seine runs to around 7,000 lines. *Claude et Luce* is much longer, nearer 20,000, and even so far from complete. It's harder to date than *La Seine*, but was certainly composed before Roussel evolved his *procédé* around the age of 30. It exists in various states of transcription, from sketchy worksheets to revised fair copies, and presents a number of editorial difficulties. Hundreds of pages of Acts II and III of its final section, are only roughly drafted; many consist of a few scattered words per line, and some of not much more than rhyme words jotted down the right hand side of the page. There follows an extended, densely written plot outline, and then a final plan detailing further narrative developments. The whole cycle consists of around 2,900 pages of manuscript, not all of it easily legible.

Its main plot is not, however, any more complex than that of *La Seine*. Claude works in a bookshop and Luce as a seamstress. One Easter Monday they take a trip on a pleasure boat to the Bois de Vincennes. Parts I and II both consist of crazily minute descriptions of every aspect of this outing. Roussel devotes pages and pages, for example, to charting the progress of a series of soap-bubbles blown by a young boy on the terrace of a café where the couple stop for a drink. As in *La Seine*, Roussel's obsession with circumstantial detail continually overwhelms the story-line's all but arrested progress. Part II breaks off late at night in the wood with Luce seemingly on the point of succumbing to Claude. A fragment appended to this section presents a different evening that ends more explicitly, with Claude and Luce embracing behind the locked door of her room. A rough outline suggests that Roussel intended the poem to end, like *La Seine*, tragically: Claude has left to take up a job in Africa, Luce is pregnant, dismissed from her job, homeless, and preparing to sleep rough "*à la belle étoile*". Yet another drafted ending would have the abandoned and visibly pregnant Luce confronting Claude, now accompanied by a new girl friend, at the Moulin Rouge.

The third part of the poem, however, turns away from its principals. "*A l'Ambigu*" (a now defunct Parisian theatre) describes a gruesome melodrama attended by Claude and Luce in which a gang of criminals attempt to blackmail the wife of a dissolute rake found murdered in the Bois de Boulogne by making public her son's illegitimacy – or at least this seems the main narrative, but others proliferate around it with furious abandon. In addition, he makes use of the play's intervals to offer us the young lovers' impressions of the performance they're witnessing. One thinks of Henry James's remark in the Preface to *Roderick Hudson* of the artist's need to draw a circle around relations that really stop nowhere: the young Roussel seems unaware of this need. Texts like *La Seine* or *Claude et Luce* might continue forever, mesmerically in thrall to the world's banality and open-endedness.

Yet they failed to deliver those "sensations of art" Roussel craved. It was only through the *procédé*, which converts all words into double entendres, that Roussel was able to fuse narrative and language. His first experiments in this direction were the stories posthumously collected under the punning title *"Textes de Grande Jeunesse ou Textes-Genèse"*. The first and last phrases of these stories are identical except for a single letter, but each major word is used in a different sense. *"Parmi les noirs"* ("Among the Blacks"), for example, begins: *"Les lettres du blanc sur les bandes du vieux billard"* (The letters [as of the alphabet] in white [chalk] on the cushions of the old billiard table), and concludes: *"... les lettres du blanc sur les bandes du vieux pillard"* ("the letters [i.e. missives] sent by the white man about the hordes of the old plunderer"). "The two phrases found," Roussel comments, "it was a case of writing a story which could begin with the first and end with the second." *"Parmi les noirs"* opens with the narrator composing a cryptogram on the cushions of a billiard table as part of a country-house parlour game; this cryptogram in turn alludes to a novel by one of the guests concerning a white man held hostage in Africa who manages to send letters to his wife by carrier pigeon, in which he relates the exploits of his aged captor and his plundering hordes. It was by extending the principle of such double meanings that Roussel evolved the word-games that generate the narratives of *Impressions d'Afrique* and *Locus Solus*, both the *baleine à ilot* type, and the more complex deformations also described in *"Comment J'ai écrit ..."* based on a random phrase or line of poetry broken down into discrete phonetic units. Contrary to expectations, one learns nothing of the development or deployment of the *procédé* from the manuscript versions of these two novels.

Impressions d'Afrique greatly expands the narrative suggested by the *billard / pillard* rhyme of *"Parmi les noirs"*. It concerns a group of passengers shipwrecked on their way to Buenos Aires, and held hostage on the west coast of Africa. While waiting for the arrival of the ransom money demanded by the sovereign Talou VII, they form a club called *Les Incomparables* and prepare a gala to celebrate the day of their release. The performers include, among many others, the marksman Balbet, who shoots away the white of a distantly placed soft-boiled egg without disturbing the yolk, the colossally mouthed Ludovic, capable of singing all four parts of *"Frère Jacques"* simultaneously, a worm who has been trained to play Hungarian melodies on the zither, the one-legged Lelgoualch who performs Breton airs on a flute carved out of his own tibia, the sculptor Fuxier who creates miniature tableaux within the pulp of white grapes...

The intensively worked manuscripts of *Impressions d'Afrique* contain a number of events and characters missing from the published novel, but in general it is much less ruthlessly edited that its successor, *Locus Solus*, from which Roussel removed a whole series of fully developed episodes. The successive versions of *Impressions d'Afrique* reveal Roussel's writing becoming richer, more surprising, less easy to absorb. King Talou, for instance – originally Bangoja – is presented in the early drafts as a stereotypical savage chieftain. When one of the European artistes appears riding a bicycle and brandishing a racket in each hand with which he bats four shuttlecocks in the air, Bangoja interrupts and attempts the feat himself, only to fall instantly sprawling in the dirt. Talou is a much purer embodiment of the Rouselian than his primitive prototype, as his first appearance in the book makes strikingly clear: he arrives at the head of his troops dressed as a music-hall chanteuse, in a blue dress with a low neckline, on which the figures 472 are sewn in black. On his head he sports a woman's wig of magnificent waved golden hair.

The gala is won in the published text by the ten year old Marius Boucharessas, owner of a troop of cats who, at a word of command, execute a thrilling game of prisoners' base. In early versions this act is more original still: the cats arrive, each wearing a schoolboy's cap, in a small chariot pulled by two clams, stimulated into motion by a few drops of a corrosive liquid. As a further embellishment the star of the group, an Angora named Tito, leafs through an atlas and puts his paw on any town or region the young impresario – here called Roger Danglès – asks him to find. Many other performances and experiments are similarly refined by Roussel's revisions, and on occasion the effect they produce is completely reversed. The drafts, for example, portray the historian Tinglet – who becomes Juillard – as an arrogant lecherous boor and his interminable lecture on a variety of literary and historical topics is greeted by an enraged audience with hoots and stones. By the final version he has metamorphosed into a brilliant speaker whose lucid and witty account of the history of the Electors of Brandenburg holds his listeners utterly spellbound.

The baroque fecundity of *Impressions d'Afrique* contrasts sharply with the severe, almost classical rigour of Roussel's next work, *Locus Solus*. The later book's formal elegance was achieved, it now emerges, only after numerous reshapings; Roussel quarried its seven self-contained chapters from a vast sprawling draft almost twice as long as the published version. This involved discarding both further adventures of characters, such as the sybil Felicity, who do appear in the final text, and a number of wholly new story-lines. Nearly all the excised material is as lively and inventive as the episodes Roussel finally chose to retain.

Locus Solus (in Latin "a solitary place") is the name of the spacious estate on the outskirts of Paris where the *savant*, Martial Canterel, conducts his researches. One Thursday in early April he invites a select group of friends to admire his unique *objets d'art* and various works in progress. Roussel probably began work on *Locus Solus* soon after his mother died in 1911. Her sudden death disrupted performances of his theatrical adaptation of *Impressions d'Afrique* – one typescript version of which has happily turned up among the rediscovered papers – and Roussel was so grief-stricken he had a glass pane inserted in her coffin so he could gaze on her beloved features up to the very moment of her internment. *Locus Solus* is Roussel's most disturbing and moving work; its cornucopia of stories – many of which feature violence and trauma – refract a profound, unreachable melancholy. The episodes omitted embody equally elaborately the desire for some impossible restitution, the need to recover and reanimate by any means possible tokens or simulacra of the irretrievably lost.

The most complicated of these involves an apparatus capable of recording and reproducing the winds, a harp whose strings are made from wax tears shed by the wives of fifteen brothers, Shakespeare's second left rib, hollowed out, the cracked chime of a London clock, and an engraved zinc flower. A friend of Boudet's (as Canterel is here called), one Isaac Zabulon has learned from the papers of a Biblical ancestor of a drug which, taken orally, converts a weeper's tears into wax. These wax tears, once solidified, possess strange acoustic powers, as the Biblical Zabulon discovered when he fitted them to an Aeolian harp which he placed in a windy desert. He also found that if each string were made from a wax tear shed by women married to brothers, the music emitted became more intoxicating still. Together Boudet and Zabulon reconstruct this unique auditory experience, with the help of fifteen wax tears shed by the fifteen Madames Pelognes, and a specially built wind machine for which a friend based in North Africa has recorded a raging simoom. The resulting sounds induce in the listeners an unimaginable ecstasy.

Boudet then thinks to expand the experiment further. He has recently come into possession of Shakespeare's second left rib, plundered from the bard's grave by the eighteenth century English lord Albert of

Dewsbury. Dewsbury was obsessed by the need to discover the precise location of the seat of the soul within the body, and spent many years travelling the world comparing the opinions of different peoples and cultures on this matter. Not until reaching the west coast of Australia did he find a satisfactory answer to the mystery: there he stumbled across a tribe called the Terani who believed the soul to be lodged in the second left rib. This bone was accordingly removed from each recently deceased body, carefully hollowed out, and affixed to a stake planted in a vast field, each rib facing into the east wind. Visiting this unique burial ground, Dewsbury was amazed to hear the sound of the wind through each bone form, if not exactly a language, a number of different vowels, easily construed by the Terani into words of advice or consolation. Exhilarated, Dewsbury returned to England where he conceived – and carried out – the mad scheme of stealing Shakespeare's left rib and attempting to coax from it some sort of communication. Dewsbury's experiments – which involved coordinating, for extra resonance, the sound of the wind through the rib with both the chimes of a cracked church bell and music performed on a violin so expertly made that anyone could play it like a maestro – proved only partially successful, but before his sudden death in a riding accident the rib did produce "a human, conscious moan", and the clearly distinguishable vowels, *e, i,* and *a*. Dewsbury kept the rib, and a manuscript explaining his researches, in a secret hiding place in the library of his castle on the banks of the Thames, where it remained buried until chanced upon one day by the property's current owner, the Italian tragedienne, Adinolfa. She in turn passed the precious bone on to Boudet for further investigation, who, substituting the harp for the violin and continuously reproducing the cracked chime of the church clock by the complex use of electromagnets, eventually also manages to derive from the rib the syllables *e, i,* and *a*. As a final flourish, he has the vowels projected against a flower which has been grafted with the metal zinc, and on which a jeweller has engraved the three scenes which eventually appear as the bas-reliefs introducing the second story in the first chapter of *Locus Solus*; the petals unfold in response to the syllables, and thus on *a* all three images are disclosed. Roussel's stories often fit together like so many Chinese boxes, but lead nowhere beyond their own implausible recoveries and conjunctions. The recorded simoom blows through the harp and the hollowed out rib, the clock chimes, the bone produces the syllables *e*, *i*, or *a*, according to the wind's strength, and in turn a scene engraved on the zinc flower is revealed or covered up. Some random word-pattern is narratively fulfilled at unimaginable cost – "I shed blood over every phrase", Roussel once told Janet – but the writing's inner motivations and ulterior purposes remain obscure. Each experiment is pursued for its own sake, within its own terms, its applications confined rigorously to the requirements of the story. Another episode cut from *Locus Solus* concerns a formula for a *"gaz évolutif"* capable of making young aquatic life-forms instantly adult. This formula was divulged by a young monk Gur... (Roussel often left names incomplete) to the Emperor Constantine in the presence of Saint Eusèbe. The horrified Emperor has the monk put instantly to death, but Eusèbe decides to preserve the dangerous secret through a cleverly encoded cryptogram, for which he employs the bizarre lower lip of a friend of his called Lao.... On a pilgrimage to the Holy Land Lao... had stopped by a spring to rest and been tempted by the fruit of a tree growing nearby. That evening he fell ill with a fierce fever and his lower lip became both enormous and terribly scarred. Eusèbe recalls an old story relating a similar distention and malformation of the lower lip afflicting ten neophytes who also ate the fruit of this alluring tree, and is able to establish that in each case the pattern traced by the scarring was identical. Eusèbe copies the letters of the formula on a piece of parchment using the zig-zag shadows cast by the scars of Lao...'s lower lip as a grid; to make the mystery harder to solve, he doesn't disclose at what time of day he made this transcription – hence at what angle the sun shone through the lip – and he incorporates the 137 letters strewn across the parchment into an elaborate description of Constantine's burning of the piece of paper on which Gur... had written his discovery. Eusèbe includes this account in his *Vie de Constantin*, but the page-long parchment on which the formula is encrypted he has buried with him in a casket in his tomb. Centuries later an intrepid alchemist, R..., retrieved this manuscript from the grave and cracked the code, only to be condemned to death at the stake as a sorcerer. Boudet happens to have purchased R...'s copy of the *Vie de Constantin* in the binding of which he finds an account of R...'s researches hastily written just before his arrest. Boudet accordingly makes a number of manuscript copies on different sizes of paper of the passage describing the burning of the manuscript, while his friend Fra... sets off for the desert, finds the tree, eats the fruit, and develops the vast cicatrized lower lip which enables Boudet eventually to piece together the formula of *"gaz évolutif"*. A young tadpole released into water infused with this gas almost immediately develops into a mature frog.

The grid of Lao... and Fra...'s lower lips is one of dozens of strange encoding and decoding processes to be found in Roussel's writings. A number of French critics have suggested his work conceals some secret system of correspondences which, once brought to light, would explain the motives behind his procedures. André Breton, for instance, was convinced Roussel was concealing esoteric alchemical messages relating to the search for the *Grand Oeuvre* or Philosopher's Stone. Nothing in his recovered papers lends credence to this hypothesis, nor points to the existence of some ultimate key to the Rousselian. His fanatically worked manuscripts demonstrate, rather, an intense, almost Flaubertian obsession with the *mot juste*, a wholly single-minded quest for those "sensations of art" on which he felt his existence depended. He seems never to have considered the *procédé* as in itself a justification of his writing, only as a catalyst. "It is essentially a poetic method," he observes in *"Comment j'ai écrit ..."*; "just as one can use rhymes to compose good or bad verses, so one can use this method to produce good or bad works."

The excellence of so much of the material Roussel chose not to publish does, however, lead one to question his critical judgment. In *"Comment j'ai écrit ..."* he rather dismisses the superb *L'allée aux lucioles*, begun just after *Locus Solus* but interrupted by mobilisation for World War I. Episodes from this unfinished work exist in several revised typescripts: it is set mainly in the summer court of Frederick II, and features a new chapter of *Candide*, a game which involves fireflies enclosed in dice and a manual written by a Spanish boatman, an attempt by Don Juan to seduce an Abbess, a cure for baldness, the invention of a weightless cloth called *lin d'Icare*, and unmelting ice figurines that keep wine cool in hot weather without diluting it, much to the delight of young Frederick and his famous guest, Voltaire.

It is not clear why Roussel abandoned this enchanting prose work to begin the composition of a long poem to be called *Nouvelles Impressions d'Afrique* in which he planned to describe a tourist's souvenir of Egypt, a miniature pair of opera glasses which, held up to the eye, show photographs of a Cairo bazaar on one side and of the Nile at Luxor on the other. After some years of labour Roussel renounced this project too, and began work on another poem also to be called *Nouvelles Impressions d'Afrique* which – aside from eighteen months spent writing his two plays, of which no manuscripts exist – absorbed him for the remainder of his creative life. This poem again presents various Egyptian scenes, but this time fractured by innumerable brackets, so one has to read the first and last lines of its four cantos first, and then work one's way back and forth through the canto connecting the disjointed sentences. The manuscript pages of the final *Nouvelles Impressions d'Afrique* that have been preserved present – unsurprisingly given the excruciating difficulties inherent in the poem's methodology – an almost illegible morass of erasures and revisions; despite its bewildering disjunctions each canto rhymes perfectly throughout, and even the footnotes are in alexandrines. Roussel estimated each of its lines cost him fifteen hours of work.

Of course literary manuscripts form only a part of the ten thousand or so pages that make up the *fonds Roussel*; also discovered were numerous photographs, hundreds of letters received, a diary of a trip to Egypt in 1906, documents relating to the patent Roussel applied for in 1922 for a new method of vacuum insulation he'd invented, ruinous ruinous bills, endless laundry lists, a notebook recording all his dedications (to such as Mussolini – hailed in a copy of *La Poussière de Soleils* as a *"moderne Jules César"* – Proust, Colette, Robert Desnos, Pierre Loti *"dont on ne doit prononcer le nom qu'à genoux"*), self-promoting publicity handouts, details of his extravagant theatrical ventures, press clippings describing his *roulotte*, a luxury caravan he had custom built and of which he was so proud he tried to have it driven into the Vatican to show the Pope. This mass of material exponentially augments our knowledge of Roussel's social milieux and activities, his family, his travels, and his finances, yet his life and work lose none of their power to intrigue and confound. Admirers of Roussel may be relieved to learn that he seems likely to remain as enigmatic and unassimilable as ever, a radiant paradigm of what Cocteau once called "genius in its pure state".

London Review of Books, 1997

Mina Loy

As the conventional accounts of Modernism shift and totter, all sorts of neglected early twentieth-century writers are being led from the shadows and into the limelight. During her lifetime Mina Loy – anything but a wallflower – seems to have been the magnetic centre of whatever milieu in which she happened to find herself, but her refusal to construct an œuvre or literary career has meant that until recently she normally figured in critical discussions of the period as a beautiful footnote to the doings of others. Over the past few years, however, Loy studies have gained considerable momentum, and her elliptical writings are now frequently championed as the missing voice of feminist Modernism.

Loy's five decades or so of obscurity seem to have been at least partly the result of her own diffidence. "I never was a poet", she remarked to her publisher Jonathan Williams as he prepared to issue a selection of her work in 1958. Though she knew she had written a handful of brilliantly original poems, she hated the idea of aspiring to the status of a professional, and after around 1930 didn't even bother to send new pieces to interested magazines. One thinks of the poet in Cocteau's *Orphée*, who, when asked his deepest wish, replies, "*Écrire, sans être écrivain.*"

Loy's dilettantish approach to the various arts that appealed to her – she was not only a poet but a painter, a *collagiste*, a novelist, and a commercially successful designer of lampshades – makes assessing her work a hazardous business. In a review printed in *The Dial* in 1926 Yvor Winters, of all people, claimed Loy's poetry offered "a solid foundation in place of Whitman's badly aligned corner-stones, a foundation which is likely to be employed, I suspect, by a generation or two." It's hard to think of a less appropriate image for Loy's capricious poetics than that of architecture. In her best work a mordant self-awareness constantly ironizes the quest for some metaphysical grounding beyond the mutabilities of "serial metamorphosis", to borrow a phrase from her late poem, "Ephemerid". Her unfinished autobiography was to be called *Islands in the Air*, and in a late prose text made up of a sequence of spiritual meditations she reaches only the throw-away conclusion that "Being alive is a queer coincidence."

Loy's indifference to the grand narratives and cultural anxieties that structure much Modernist writing is at once refreshing and disarming. Though her idiom is frequently as impacted as Hart Crane's, her relentless internal rhymes and intensive use of alliteration and assonance suggest that it is only some haphazard, ineffable acoustic pattern that is holding the poem together. The satirical and the lyrical dissolve each other to form some unstable new compound. "Lunar Baedeker", the title poem of her 1923 collection, ostensibly mocks decadent literary projections of the sublime onto the moon, yet the dazzling, icy web of the poem's language itself seems bathed in a mysterious lunar light:

> A silver Lucifer
> serves
> cocaine in cornucopia
>
> To some somnambulists
> of adolescent thighs
> draped
> in satirical draperies

In his comments on Loy in an essay in *The Little Review* Ezra Pound applied his highest term of approval to such effects, which he saw as illustrating "logopoeia" – "the dance of the intelligence among words and ideas."

Loy was not herself disposed to advance aesthetic theories that might justify or explain her work, and seems to have been unbothered by the sporadic nature of her interest in writing. Poetry, like being alive, was a "queer coincidence", more a symptom of her liberation from repressive conventions than the means of her escape. In a striking poem composed in 1919 entitled "O Hell" she most clearly endorses Pound's injunction to "Make it new", but unfettered desire rather than high culture or spiritual truth seems the dominant element in her imagined Utopia:

> Our person is a covered entrance to infinity
> Choked with the tatters of tradition
>
> Goddesses and Young Gods
> Caress the sanctity of Adolescence
> In the shaft of the sun.

The lines conjure up an almost Blakean vision of innocent sexual congress nurtured by potent, benevolent solar rays.

The "tatters of tradition" inhibiting Loy's own energies derived from a repressive late Victorian upbringing and the miseries she suffered as a result of her parents' unhappy marriage. In the caustic long poem *Anglo-Mongrels and the Rose* (1923–25), Loy anatomized in savage detail the failure of her mother and father's relationship and the effect of their mutual hatred on her development. Sigmund Lowy (Loy dropped the *w* soon after leaving home) was a Hungarian Jew who emigrated to London in his early twenties and soon became a prosperous tailor. By calling him Exodus in the poem, Loy implies that he never really felt at home in his adopted nation. One day walking in the country Exodus meets an English rose "simpering in her / ideological pink" whom he foolishly plucks and marries. The English rose (Alice or Ada in the poem) turns out to be anti-Semitic, rabidly class-conscious, and a fierce champion of her "divine right of self-assertion". Loy's mother attempted to offset the uncertainties of their social status by a fanatical adherence to social propriety. Loy – who was born in 1882 – and her two younger sisters were brought up on a severe diet of pious texts, lumpy porridge, and insistent self-mortification. Loy records in her autobiography how her mother greeted the first signs of puberty in her eldest daughter with a violent tirade against the body: "Your vile flesh," she screamed, "you'll get no good out of it. Curse you."

Loy felt herself to be "a mongrel girl / of Noman's land", a hybrid stranded in limbo. In her late teens she attended art schools in London and Munich, and then in Paris, producing overblown, parodic homages to the clichés of Decadent art. It was in Paris that she met her loathed first husband, Stephen Haweis, caricatured in *Anglo-Mongrels and the Rose* as a ridiculous, self-obsessed aesthete, and witheringly compared to her second, the magnificent Colossus, a.k.a. Arthur Cravan. Haweis dabbled in a number of arts without much success, but for a while earned a reasonable living as Rodin's official photographer. He also attempted to market his pictures of Loy herself, swooning, soft-focused studies in which she is transformed into an enigmatic, supremely desirable *objet d'art*. In one she leans alluringly forward, balancing a small Rodin sculpture on the palm of her hand, while her half-closed eyes and half-parted lips suggest the onset of some aesthetic or erotic trance.

Loy and Haweis only married to save appearances – she was four months pregnant at the time of their wedding – and within a few years both were involved in other relationships. Their first child died, and her second was the result of an affair with her doctor. Notwithstanding their many differences, in 1907 they moved together to Florence, and only separated permanently in 1913.

Loy's interest in literature – hitherto dormant – was fomented by three crucial relationships she established during her time in Flor-

125

ence. In 1911 she met Gertrude Stein, whom she later eulogized as a "Curie / of the laboratory / of vocabulary", capable of extracting "a radium of the word." In *The Autobiography of Alice B. Toklas* Stein relates showing Haweis and Mina Loy the manuscript of *The Making of Americans*. Haweis pronounces himself fascinated, but begs her to introduce some commas to help clarify her writing, while Loy, "equally interested was able to understand without the commas. She has always been able to understand."

Stein's linguistic experiments certainly underlie the equally comma-free dissections of Loy's early poems, but her more intimate relations with the twin figure-heads of Futurism, F.T. Marinetti and Giovanni Papini, provided the immediate catalyst for her sudden development into a poet in her early thirties. The Futurists promised to liberate not only Italy but all of Europe from the suffocations of its overbearing cultural inheritance. "Burn the museums!" they urged; "Let's murder the moonlight." It was the Futurists who first developed the tactics that were later deployed by practically every revolutionary avant-garde of the century, from the Dadaists to the L=A=N=G=U=A=G=E poets. The charismatic Marinetti's outrageous pronouncements and confrontational stage-antics generated a furious *succès de scandale* wherever he appeared. In Florence in December of 1913 a huge audience arrived armed with eggs, dried pasta, and rotten fruit and vegetables, but Loy for one was impressed by his attack on the *passatisti* (those locked in the past) whose only argument, Marinetti scornfully declared after cleanly catching an egg hurled by an enraged spectator, was "a horde of dirty vegetables".

Loy was exhilarated by Marinetti's verve and energy, and soon produced her own "Aphorisms on Futurism", complete with hectoring capitals and italics:

> BUT the Future is only dark from outside.
> *Leap* into it – and it EXPLODES with *Light*.

FORGET that you live in houses, that you may live in
yourself –

But Loy's "Aphorisms" refuse to ratify one central tenet of the Futurist revolution – *disprezzo della donna*. Marinetti's virulent misogyny was an essential aspect of his determination to release the primal masculine energies stifled by conventional *mores*. In "Sketch of a Man on a Platform" Loy shrewdly satirizes the self-important, technologically advanced Futurist boldly asserting himself in matters of love and war:

> Your projectile nose
> Has meddled in the more serious business
> Of the battle-field
> With the same incautious aloofness
> Of intense occupation
> That it snuffles the trail of the female
> And the comfortable
> Passing odors of love

Nevertheless, Loy found herself inspired by Futurism's promise of a brave new world, and attracted by Marinetti's preposterous bravado. By the end of their appropriately whirlwind affair Loy at least felt convinced, after years of depression and uncertainty, that "THE Future is limitless – the past a trail of insidious reactions." Though fully aware of Marinetti's many failings and prejudices, Loy candidly acknowledged in a letter of 1915 that she was "indebted to M. for twenty years added to my life from mere contact with his exuberant vitality."

Her relations with Papini were more complex and confusing, as her "Songs to Joannes" so vividly illustrates. Giovanni Papini was Marinetti's Futurist opposite and antagonist: shy, intellectual, married, spectacularly ugly, gnawed by self-doubt, Papini at first cautiously resisted Loy's advances, and then, once he'd succumbed, vacillated and squirmed and retreated. In "The Effectual Marriage, or the Insipid Narrative of Gina and Miovanni" – a poem extravagantly praised by both Eliot and Pound – Loy figures the unhappy lovers in their gender-prescribed spheres, Miovanni with his ego in the library, Gina in the kitchen among the pots and pans, and bitterly notes:

> To man his work
> To woman her love
> Succulent meals   and an occasional caress

The series of poems that make up "Songs to Joannes" provide, however, a more nuanced account of their relationship. How strange that this *tour de force* of intelligence and sophistication, of sexual directness and spiralling self-consciousness, is still absent from most anthologies of Modernist poetry. Like so many early Modernist texts, from Eliot's "Prufrock" to Stevens's "Sunday Morning", "Songs to Joannes" embodies a devastating critique of outdated rhetorical conventions and ossified belief-systems, but it also anticipates the decentering fluidities characteristic of Postmodern poetics. Loy is deliberately vague about the circumstances of the love affair the poem describes, allowing the images themselves to function as units enacting an indecisive, though charged, erotic pursuit:

> Spawn of Fantasies
> Silting the appraisable
> Pig Cupid   his rosy snout
> Rooting erotic garbage
> "Once upon a time"
> Pulls a weed white star-topped
> Among wild oats sown in mucous-membrane

This notorious opening stanza provocatively confounds distinctions between imagined and actual sex. The Classical god of love is reduced to a phallic, porcine snout rooting among the dreck of fantasies and possibilities for some adequate object to appropriate. The first four sections of the poem appeared in Alfred Kreymborg's *Others* in 1915 and aroused, Kreymborg later recalled, a "violent sensation", the critics complaining that Loy was either incomprehensible or pornographic, or both. In fact the poem's mixture of the indeterminate and scabrous constitutes an extremely effective charting of the nebulous terrain of the erotic, in which excitement and disillusionment succeed one another to form an endless series of repetitive cycles. Loy's thirty-four poem sequence revolves episodes of rapture and despair, of lust and hurt, of intimacy and disgust, without either reaching conclusions or developing a clear narrative. "Love — ", she muses in the one-line final section, "the preeminent litterateur". It is Loy's awareness of the provisional or merely literary nature of her formulations that enables the poem to unfold with such compelling linguistic buoyancy. If not "*the* best since Sappho", as she jokingly claimed in a letter, the sequence does exude a certain Sapphic freshness and swagger.

The failure of Loy's relationship with Papini was matched by a general souring of her attitude to Florence and Italy. Some of her best early poems, such as "Costa Magic" or "Virgins Plus Curtains Minus Dots", reflect upon the hapless situation of young Italian women imprisoned indoors, allowed only to squeak and flutter, "Wasting our giggles / For we have no dots" [i.e. dowries]. In her energetic "Feminist Manifesto" of 1914 Loy called for the "*unconditional* surgical *destruction of virginity* throughout the female population at puberty", as a first step to liberating women from the only two roles then available to them, "*Parasitism & Prostitution*". Her friendship with the free-living Mabel Dodge encouraged Loy to believe that in America she might at last cast aside her moral inhibitions once and for all. She set sail for New York in 1916, leaving her two children Joella and Giles, at this point aged nine and seven, in the care of their saintly Italian nurse. Though Loy courageously insisted in her manifesto that "every woman has a right to maternity", regardless of her marital status, she seems to have been less concerned about the mother's obligations to her offspring. In the event Loy was not to see her children again for almost three years.

Loy's poetry had already been published in a number of New York's emergent avant-garde magazines, and she quickly established herself in New York's various Modernist salons. Only two months after her arrival she performed in a one-act play by Kreymborg called *Lima Beans* with a love-struck William Carlos Williams, and had become friends with such as Marcel Duchamp, Francis Picabia, and Man Ray. She was even declared "a clever and a sound philosopher" by the fastidious Marianne Moore, whose poem "These Various Scalpels" is generally interpreted as a portrait of her glamorous rival. Moore admiringly evokes the cosmopolitan magnificence of Loy's appearance and manner, but hints at some disjunction between the sophistication of her "weapons" and the banality of surrounding circumstances: "But why", Moore wonders, "dissect destiny with instruments / more highly specialized than components of destiny itself?"

This mismatch was to end, but oh so briefly, when she met Arthur Cravan in 1917. Cravan, who became the Dadaists' ultimate hero, was born Fabian Avenarius Lloyd in Switzerland in 1887. His father, Otho Lloyd, was Oscar Wilde's wife's brother, though far from proud of the connection; when the Wilde scandal erupted he changed his name to Holland to distance himself from his disgraced brother-in-law. Cravan, on the other hand, often boasted of his relation to Uncle Oscar, and even claimed a resurrected Wilde came to visit him in 1913, bestowing on his nephew the ambiguous blessing, "*You are a terrible boy.*" Cravan initially made his name not through literature but boxing. For a time he was light heavyweight champion of France – though only because his opponent didn't show up – and in 1916 in Barcelona he fought world heavyweight champion Jack Johnson, going down in the sixth round. This bout was more a money-making stunt than a genuine contest, for it seems Cravan was only an averagely skilled pugilist. As a literary combatant, however, he certainly never pulled his punches. From 1912–15 he published a magazine called *Maintenant* in which, under various different pen-names, he attacked virtually every artist and writer then resident in Paris, with an especially contemptuous emphasis on André Gide, whose Lafcadio, inventor of the *acte gratuit,* is modelled on the anarchic, amoral Cravan. Cravan's famed "lectures" owed something to Marinetti's insolent performances. A full house turned up at the *Noctambules* in Paris to watch Cravan commit suicide by drinking a carafe of absinth wearing only a jock-strap, though in the event the poet-boxer merely harangued the audience for their prurient interest in his death. In New York he engaged to talk on "The Independent Artists of France and America" at the Grand Central Palace. Plied with drinks beforehand by Duchamp, Cravan wobbled to the lectern, undressed, hurled his clothes at the audience, and then began roaring obscenities until arrested and thrown into jail.

For Loy Cravan was the "acme of communion // who made euphonious / our esoteric universe", as her plangent elegy, "Letters of the Unliving", phrases it, uniquely able to transform whatever he touched. In her memoir of their relationship she wrote: "Light – passed through the poet Cravan – became brilliance." Cravan, despite his aggressive instincts and impressive physique, was violently anti-militaristic; called up for action by the American military authorities in the summer of 1917, he decided to escape, disguised as a soldier, to Mexico where Loy later joined him. In January of 1918 they married. Their funds dwindling, Cravan arranged a fight with an American boxer called Jim Smith, hoping to repeat his lucrative contest with Jack Johnson. Unfortunately Smith dispatched his opponent in only the second round, and the angry crowd demanded a refund. As the military authorities began to close in on the Slackers, as draft dodgers were known, Cravan and Loy – who was by this time pregnant – drifted down to Salina Cruz on the west coast of Mexico, from where they hoped to make their way to Buenos Aires. They bought a small, leaky sailing boat with the idea of patching it up and trading it

in for a more sea-worthy vessel. In early November, only days before
the Armistice was signed, Cravan set sail in the repaired craft for the
nearby coastal village of Puerto Angel. The weather was fine and the
boat apparently in good shape. Loy waited for days on the beach, gaz-
ing out to sea, but Cravan never returned.

It seems likely he simply drowned, though neither boat nor body
was ever recovered. Over the following decades it was frequently ru-
moured that he had resurfaced under a new alias, and even that he
was responsible for a series of Oscar Wilde forgeries that bamboozled
Wilde experts in the early Twenties. For years Loy followed up every
possible lead, only gradually coming to accept that she would never
see her "Colossus" again.

Their daughter, named Fabi, was born in April of the following
year. Loy returned to Europe, but found it difficult to settle. Her
poem "The Widow's Jazz" most directly expresses the trauma of Cravan's disappearance, figuring her desire as recessed to "the distance
of the dead", numbly searching "the opaque silence / of unpeopled
space". But Loy was not the type, even in widowhood, to allow her
life to become a blank. In 1923 Robert McAlmon published *Lunar
Baedeker* (with the title misspelled Baedecker on both cover and title-
page) which included, along with a selection of her early work, a series
of poems written in 1921–22. Many of these new pieces dramatize
the struggle for expression against seemingly overwhelming odds. Loy
writes poems celebrating figures such as Edgar Allan Poe, Brancusi,
James Joyce, and Wyndham Lewis, and in "Apology of Genius" de-
fends the "criminal mystic immortelles" of the leprous artist against
the sweeping "censor's scythe". In the wonderful "*Der Blinde Junge*"
Loy describes a blind war veteran busking for small change on the
streets of Vienna:

> Void and extinct
> this planet of the soul
> strains from the craving throat

in static flight upslanting

A downy youth's snout
nozzling the sun
drowned in dumbfounded instinct

Listen!
illuminati of the coloured earth
How this expressionless "thing"
blows out damnation and concussive dark

Upon a mouth-organ

The poem delicately picks its way between the sardonic and the sentimental, renouncing all easy options, its ringing final line somehow
triumphant and bathetic at once.

Not all of Loy's poetry is as skilfully controlled and impassioned as
this. Her formidable powers of compression can leave one gasping
for air. In her poetic tribute Loy praised Gertrude Stein for having
"crushed / the tonnage of consciousness", and her own idiom can similarly seem the result of aeons of concerted pressure upon language. It's
not a style that can be made to suit every genre; *Anglo-Mongrels and
the Rose* in particular suffers from Loy's relentlessly elliptical methods.
Roger L. Conover is probably right to exclude it from his new selection of her work, which offers instead some fifty pages of detailed
notes outlining the publishing history and critical reception of each
of Loy's poems.

Anglo-Mongrels and the Rose appeared in 1925, by which time Loy
was a leading name in Modernist circles. She cared nothing, however,
for literary politics, for canons and hierarchies, indeed probably never
thought of herself as primarily a poet. In Paris in the Twenties she set
up in business designing lampshades constructed mainly from materials picked up in flea-markets. In the early Thirties she turned artists'

agent, helping her son-in-law Julien Levy develop his New York gallery into the leading space for Surrealist art. She wrote a *roman à clef* called *Insel* based on her friendship with the German painter Richard Oelze, a text which, though more or less finished, remained unpublished until 1991. Other fictional projects waxed and waned. In 1936 she moved from Paris to New York where she attempted, without much success, to market her designs and inventions. In the Forties she took a room in the Bowery district of New York, where she hung out with bums and drunks, scavenging litter from the streets with which she fabricated a number of assemblages depicting the lives of the destitute. Her few poems of this period, such as "Hot Cross Bum" or "On Third Avenue", are concerned with the "compensations of poverty", the delirious world of the "choicelessly corrupted", the "blowsy angels" of the New York streets. Eventually her daughters persuaded her to abandon her Bowery comrades, and settled her in Aspen, Colorado where she died in 1966.

Loy moved in so many different spheres, through so many phases, that it's difficult to be sure of the best way to define her achievement. In this superb biography, the first ever, Carolyn Burke does full justice to the mercurial nature of Loy's temperament, and offers judicious assessments of her work. Burke captures both the glamour of Loy's presence and the cutting edge of her wit without ever lapsing into the rapturous tones of Loy-worship that often mar discussions of her life and writing. It is to be hoped that these two books will at last secure Loy's entry in the baedekers of Modernism that have hitherto ignored her pure "radium of the word".

New Republic, 1997: Review of *The Lost Lunar Baedeker: Poems by Mina Loy,* selected and edited by Roger L. Conover (Farrar, Straus and Giroux, 1997) and Carolyn Burke's *Becoming Modern: The Life of Mina Loy* (Farrar, Straus and Giroux, 1996).

W.H. Auden's "The Sea and the Mirror"

"The Sea and the Mirror" is the most brilliant and unsettling of the four long poems Auden composed during his furiously industrious first decade in America. It was begun in October of 1942 in the wake of a period of extreme turbulence and distress; and although the sequence is modestly subtitled "A Commentary on Shakespeare's *The Tempest*", the poems – and prose – Auden puts into the mouths of Prospero, Miranda, Caliban and co. reflect with exquisite subtlety and intelligence recent – and long-standing – inner conflicts and guilts. "The Sea and the Mirror" is "my Ars Poetica", he wrote to the Shakespeare scholar Theodore Spencer shortly before completing the poem in the spring of 1944 (it was published later that year in *For the Time Being*), "in the same way I believe *The Tempest* to be Shakespeare's." Like Browning, Ernest Renan, and Rilke before him, Auden discerned in the kaleidoscopic perspectives and unresolved tensions of Shakespeare's last play a means of dramatizing his own deepest concerns. "I am attempting", he continues, "something which in a way is absurd, to show in a work of art, the limitations of art."

Auden's anti-romantic conviction of the "limitations" of art is central to his attempts to redefine himself as a poet in the period following his emigration to America in 1939. "How glad I am", he observed in an essay of 1947, "that the silliest remark ever made about poets, 'the unacknowledged legislators of the world', was made by a poet whose work I detest." Auden's poetry of the Thirties had been as entangled as the work of the despised Shelley in politics and imminent revolution and anxieties about the state of England, "this country of ours",

to quote a phrase from *The Orators* of 1932, "where nobody is well."
It must have delighted him to think, while writing "The Sea and the
Mirror", that Shelley had initially christened the boat that led to his
death by water in the Gulf of Genoa in July of 1822 *Don Juan*, but at
the last minute changed it to *Ariel*.

It was in his wonderfully entertaining "Letter to Lord Byron", composed as part of the book he co-wrote with Louis MacNeice, *Letters
from Iceland* (1937), that Auden most lucidly explained his vision of
literary history:

> Until the great Industrial Revolution
>   The artist had to earn his livelihood:
> However much he hated the intrusion
>   Of patron's taste or public's fickle mood,
>   He had to please or go without his food;
> He had to keep his technique to himself
> Or find no joint upon the larder shelf.

The dark satanic mills, however, destroyed the poet's dependence on
patronage, and

> A new class of creative artist set up
> On whom the pressure of demand was let up
> He sang and painted and drew dividends,
> But lost responsibilities and friends.

The passing of the "bad old hack tradition" initially licensed "fireworks, fun, and games of every kind", but in the twentieth century
the party has turned very sour:

>   many are in tears:
> Some have retired to bed and locked the door;
>   And some swing madly from the chandeliers;

> Some have passed out entirely in the rears;
> Some have been sick in corners; the sobering few
> Are trying hard to think of something new.

For Auden that "something new" involved reconfiguring the poet's relationship to society, and a renunciation of the verbal fireworks and fun – and threats – that shot him to fame and determined the tone of British poetry of the Thirties. "Financier", he warns in one of his most exhilarating early poems, "Consider",

> leaving your little room
> Where the money is made but not spent,
> You'll need your typist and your boy no more;
> The game is up for you and for the others ...
> It is later than you think ...

The spoof element in these dire predictions of impending conflict is fundamental to the poetry's charm and power, and reached its apotheosis in *The Orators*, which fused public school prankishness with the idioms and trappings of a political revolutionary movement to create a mythical world of camaraderie, hero-worship, subterfuge and betrayal. Practical jokes are the main catalysts of the very English revolution the Airman hopes to foment, for "they are", he notes in his Journal, "in every sense contradictory and public, e.g. my bogus lecture to the London Truss Club. Derek's seduction of Mrs. Solomon by pretending to have been blessed by the Pope". Other proto-Pythonesque revolutionary activities include introducing gin into the lemonade at a missionary whist-drive, removing plugs and paper from lavatories, and inciting girl-guides to mob vicars at the climax of their sermons.

As Auden's executor and critic-in-chief Edward Mendelson has pointed out, "The Sea and the Mirror" itself mirrors the form and structure of *The Orators*, just as his first American long poem, "New Year Letter" (1941) had echoed "Letter to Lord Byron", and his second, "For the Time Being: a Christmas Oratorio" offered a sombre counterpart to the tribal warfare, knockabout farce, and gnomic urgencies of *Paid on Both Sides* (1928), a charade partly based on the Christmas mummers' play. *The Orators* and "The Sea and the Mirror" are both written in a mixture of poetry and prose, consist of a prologue, three central parts – or chapters as he called them in "The Sea and the Mirror" – and an epilogue. Both deploy a range of voices that pull the reader in contrary directions, are written in a dazzling variety of verse forms, and embody complex, at times baffling, explorations of the impulse to transform one's self and others. Both are concerned with the quest for, and the use and abuse of, power – political, poetic, and shamanistic (one of the sources for "The Journal of an Airman" was John Layard's description of initiation rituals practiced by sorcerers in New Guinea). And finally, of all Auden's long poems, *The Orators* and "The Sea and the Mirror" seem to me the two that engage most provocatively and searchingly with the work that cast a mesmeric, Prospero-like spell over its rivals, and "flamed amazement" for all poets of Auden's generation – Eliot's *The Waste Land*.

The Orators' mixture of slapstick and prophetic incantation, social comedy and neurotic self-diagnosis, often teeters on the verge of Eliot pastiche:

> For those determined to suffer; for those who believe they can control the weather,
>> O Jack Straw from your Castle hear us.

> For those capable of levitation; for those who have days of collapse; for those whose impulses are negative,
>> Fair Maid of Kent, hear us.

Like the hero of *The Waste Land*, the Airman projects his psychosexual anxieties onto the culture at large: plagued by his kleptomania, a secret symptom, Auden implies, of his homosexuality and compulsion to masturbate, he dreams of meeting the initiates' Messianic leader

> alone on the narrow path, forcing a question, would show
> our unique knowledge. Would hide Him wounded in a
> cave, kneeling all night by His bed of bracken, bringing
> hourly an infusion of bitter herbs; wearing His cloak re-
> ceive the mistaken stab, deliver His message, fall at His
> feet, He gripping our moribund hands, smiling.

The masochistic urge towards self-sacrifice climaxes in what one assumes to be his aerial suicide, a prospect that cures both his need to
steal and his acute sense of difference; recognizing, in his topsy-turvy
way, that he has so internalized the enemy's thought-processes that he
can never escape their mind-set, he decides his continued resistance
is just what keeps the enemy in power. Eliot-like, he seeks a state of
"absolute humility". "Pulses and reflexes normal", he observes in his
final entry; "Hands in perfect order."

Auden later decided *The Orators* had been written by "someone talented but near the border of sanity, who might well, in a year or two,
become a Nazi." "It was an unconscious attempt", he continues, "to
exorcise certain tendencies in myself by allowing them to run riot
in phantasy." The absurdity of the queer revolution the book pro-
poses aligns it with the farcical subversion of English social codes
developed by Wilde in *The Importance of Being Earnest. The Orators*
is subtitled "An English Study", and Englishness was one of the "tendencies" Auden determined to extirpate, if he could, by moving to
America in 1939, and applying for U.S. citizenship the following year.
America, he wrote to his friend E.R. Dodds in January of 1940, is "a
terrifying place", but at least honest in its acceptance that the modern
condition is essentially one of isolation and deracination. While the
great modern experimenters, Eliot and Pound, often reveal themselves
in thrall to an almost feudal vision of lost agrarian bliss ("it is necessary", Eliot sternly commanded in a *Criterion* article of 1938, "that

the greater part of the population should be settled in the country"), Auden consciously determined to avoid all temptations to belong: "At least I know what I am trying to do," he wrote to Dodds, "which is to live deliberately without roots. I would put it like this. America may break one completely, but the best of which one is capable is more likely to be drawn out of one here than anywhere else."

Auden's early American poems, such as his elegies for Yeats and Freud, express a deep scepticism about the forces of nationalism. Yeats is chastised for his megalomaniac belief his poetry could influence the course of Irish history ("For poetry makes nothing happen"), and Freud celebrated for his "technique of unsettlement" that threatens the myths of racial uniqueness on which the "ancient cultures of conceit" are founded. Abstractions (the Good Place, the Just City) begin to replace the proper names (Rookhope, Cashwell, Greenhearth) that pepper Auden's early work, and which he somehow infused with an aura of the legendary. But it was precisely his ability to transform such names and landscapes into sites of enchantment that Auden sought to renounce. The brand of Kierkegaardian existentialism Auden evolved in the wake of his return to Anglicanism in 1940, required him to figure himself as "sailing alone, out over seventy thousand fathoms", to quote Prospero quoting Kierkegaard in Chapter 1 of "The Sea and the Mirror", as he prepares to release Ariel and abandon his magic, which he glosses as "the power to enchant / That comes from disillusion". Auden, as "The Sea and the Mirror" makes clear, believed that disillusionment had to be faced, for ethical reasons, on its own terms, unmediated by art's enchantments, and that art could only regain its integrity by returning to its proper, subordinate place in the hierarchy of meanings. Art's complete failure to deliver on its impossible promises, as Caliban argues in the final paragraph of his address to the audience, allows us by antithesis a mystic glimpse into what Caliban variously calls "the real Word", "the Wholly Other Life", "the restored relation", and such moments only follow a resolute acceptance of our perilous, defenceless, naked condition, "swaying out on the ultimate wind-whipped cornice that overhangs the unabiding void".

Clearly this state of humility echoes, or rather corrects, that at which the fatally conflicted Airman had aimed; and it was the result not just of his immersion in the writings of, as well as Kierkegaard, St. Augustine, Reinhold Niebuhr, and Charles Williams, but also of the despair into which he had been plunged by what he called "l'affaire C", his discovery, that is, two years into his "marriage" to Chester Kallman, that Mr. Right had already conducted a long affair in secret, and had never taken seriously the vows of fidelity Auden had pressed upon him. This revelation temporarily unhinged him. "I was forced to know in person", he later revealed, "what it is like to feel oneself the prey of demonic forces, in both the Greek and Christian sense, stripped of self-control and self-respect, behaving like a ham actor in a Strindberg play." This refers in particular to a night in July of 1941, when, after a prolonged and bitter row, Kallman woke to find Auden's "large, thick fingers" around his throat. The sestina Auden gives *The Tempest*'s would-be assassin, Sebastian, is full of complex self-recriminations and guilty relief that seems to reflect his recognition of his own potential for violence:

> it is day:
> Nothing has happened; we are all alive:
> I am Sebastian, wicked still, my proof
> Of mercy that I wake without a crown.

In a wonderfully eccentric and desperate letter written on Christmas Day of 1941, Auden found ingenious ways of linking each of the main figures of the Nativity to his sacramental love for Kallman, with whom he would never, in fact, resume sexual relations:

> Because, suffering on your account the torments of sexual jealousy, I have had a glimpse of the infinite vileness of sexual conceit;

141

As this morning, I think of Joseph, I think of you.

Because mothers have much to do with your queerness and
mine, because we have both lost ours, and because Mary is
a camp name;
As this morning I think of Mary, I think of you.

Because, on account of you, I have been, in intention, and
almost in act, a murderer;
As this morning I think of Herod, I think of you.

Auden's understanding of what went wrong in his relationship with
Kallman underlies many of the themes and arguments developed in
"The Sea and the Mirror". "It's OK to say that Ariel is Chester," he
wrote to Isherwood in April of 1944, "but Chester is also Caliban,
'das lebendigste' [what is most alive], i.e. Ariel is Caliban seen in the
mirror". The German phrase is borrowed from Hölderlin's "Sokrates
und Alkibiades", a poem to which Auden often referred, and quoted
in full in a lecture on Shakespeare's *Sonnets* given at the New School in
1947. "Holy Socrates", his friend demands, in Michael Hamburger's
translation,

> why always with deference
> Do you treat this young man? Don't you know greater things?
> Why so lovingly, raptly,
> As on gods do you gaze on him?'

Who the deepest has thought loves what is most alive,
Wide experience may well turn to what's best in youth,
And the wise in the end will
Often bow to the beautiful.

If Hölderlin's lyric expressed for Auden his most positive interpretation of the humiliations heaped on his head by his beloved, Shakespeare's *Sonnets* offered him less uplifting perspectives on the failure of his "marriage". "The story of the sonnets", he observed bitterly in his introduction to the Signet edition, "seems to me to be the story of an agonized struggle by Shakespeare to preserve the glory of the vision he had been granted in a relationship, lasting at least three years, with a person who seemed intent by his actions upon covering that vision with dirt." But Auden also read the sequence more self-critically, as embodying a disastrous fusion of the myths of Pygmalion and Frankenstein that aptly described his early relations with Chester, who was only eighteen when they met. In the late 1940s he remarked to Howard Griffin that in the *Sonnets*

> Shakespeare desperately tries to do that which is forbidden: to create a human being ... Evidently he has selected someone at a stage of possibility. He wants to make an image so the person will not be a dream but rather someone he knows as his own interest. He wishes the other to have free will yet his free will is to be the same as Shakespeare's. Of course great anxiety and bad behavior result when the poet's will is crossed as it is bound to be.

Kallman certainly crossed the poet's will – "What a shame, Wystan," he'd remark when pressed by his sugar daddy to leave a party early, "that God invented free will" – and the resulting anxiety suffuses much of Auden's poetry of the early Forties. The lyrics he composed just after what he called "The Crisis" are full of self-reproach and pleas for forgiveness. In a trilogy of sonnets called "The Lesson", for instance, he records three dreams about Chester which all "rebuke" him for his Pygmalion-like egotism, while in "Canzone" he broods guiltily on "the hot rampageous horses of [his] will." Auden's determination in "The Sea and the Mirror" to expose the "limitations of art" undoubtedly derived much of its emotional urgency from his agonized struggles in this period to accept the limitations the loss of his erotic relationship with Kallman imposed on his life; as late as 1947, five years after they'd stopped sleeping together, he perhaps only half-jokingly discussed with Alan Ansen the possibility of obtaining a spell from a witch doctor in Dahomey which would compel Chester to "love him faithfully and exclusively again".

The muted, world-weary, vulnerable cadences of Prospero's address to Ariel in Chapter 1 of "The Sea and the Mirror" initiate a new tone in Auden's poetry, that of prosy resignation:

> In all, things have turned out better
> Than I once expected or ever deserved;
> I am glad that I did not recover my dukedom till
> I do not want it; I am glad that Miranda
> No longer pays me any attention; I am glad I have freed you,
> So at last I can really believe I shall die.

In his various essays and lectures on *The Tempest* Auden is outspokenly critical of Shakespeare's mage. "One must admire Prospero because of his talents and his strengths," he declared in an essay of 1954, "one cannot possibly like him. He has the coldness of someone who has come to the conclusion that human nature is not worth much, that human relations are, at their best, pretty sorry affairs." This is hardly a just assessment of the character; it does, however, accurately reflect Auden's ever-gathering distrust of the Prospero-ish gifts with which he had himself been showered, and his dislike of the drive towards an authoritative, enchanting rhetoric so exuberantly enacted in his own early work. Whereas in *The Waste Land* Eliot's allusions to *The Tempest* work to unify the narratives of aesthetic and spiritual transfiguration ("Those are pearls that were his eyes. Look!"), Auden's Prospero can only "really believe [he] shall die" by abandoning art: "For under your influence", he tells Ariel, "death is inconceivable": "the way of truth", he discovers, is "a way of silence where affectionate chat / Is but a robbers' ambush and even good music / In shocking taste".

For all his antipathy to Prospero, as the letter to Isherwood aligning Chester with both Ariel and Caliban makes clear, Auden, although only thirty-five when he began work on the poem, suggests numerous analogies between his own situation and that of the post-play Prospero bound for Milan, where every third thought will be of his death. His rueful meditation builds to a plangently restrained relinquishing of Ariel ("How I shall miss you. Enjoy your element. Good-bye"), but is interspersed with lyrics that lament less temperately Chester's defection:

> *Inform my hot heart straight away*
> *Its treasure loves another,*
> *But turn to neutral topics then,*
> *Such as the pictures in this room,*
> *Religion or the weather;*
> *Pure scholarship in Where and When,*
> *How Often and With Whom,*
> *Is not for Passion that must play*
> *The Jolly Elder Brother.*

Cancelled passages from Auden's manuscripts included in the notes of this sumptuous new edition of the poem strengthen our sense of Prospero as Auden's prematurely assumed alter ego. His alienation from the rest of the cast was initially signalled, like the Airman's, by his early addiction to onanism ("the magical rites of spring in the locked bathroom"), and his deviation from the straight and narrow of the heterosexual norm implied in his assessment of the trials facing Ferdinand and Miranda in their forthcoming union: "I probably overestimate these difficulties", he reflects in a draft, "For natures less indirect than mine." This "indirectness" relates Prospero to all the "crooked" or "backward" lovers of Auden's early poetry, and his appropriation in his "Letter to Lord Byron" of Shakespeare's defiant use of the trope in Sonnet CXXI:

> "No, I am that I am, and those that level
>   At my abuses reckon up their own.
> I may be straight though they, themselves, are bevel."
>   So Shakespeare said, but Shakespeare must have known.
>   I daren't say that except when I'm alone,
> Must hear in silence till I turn my toes up,
> "It's such a pity Wystan never grows up."

The stanza wittily fences with the condemnations of such as F.R. Leavis of Auden's "immaturity", and suggests these attacks were in fact coded ways of denouncing his homosexuality – a preference shared, to some degree anyway, by Shakespeare, who "must have known". On the other hand, in his introduction to the *Sonnets*, Auden was himself somewhat sarcastic about attempts to figure "our Top Bard as a patron saint of the Homintern", and this ambivalence is perhaps reflected in the division between the stately ruminations on art and life of the main body of Prospero's speech, and the gay slang and obscure personal references that emerge in the lyrics. Auden later decided that the whole of the chapter should be considered part of the "published record of l'affaire C" (letter to Alan Ansen, August 27, 1947).

"It never occurs to [Prospero]", Auden observed in his 1954 essay on the play, "that he, too, might have erred and be in need of pardon." His own Prospero convicts himself of tempting Antonio to treason, and, more seriously, of corrupting Caliban, whom he describes as his "impervious disgrace". Again vanity, the urge to shape and control another's life in the manner of Pygmalion or Frankenstein, or the worshipper of the young man in Shakespeare's sonnets, is to blame. In his education of Caliban, Auden suggests, Prospero has succumbed to the temptation to believe his art is all-powerful, with disastrous results:

We did it, Ariel, between us; you found on me a wish
For absolute devotion; result – his wreck
That sprawls in the weeds and will not be repaired:
My dignity discouraged by a pupil's curse,
I shall go knowing and incompetent into my grave.

In terms of the overall moral scheme of "The Sea and the Mirror",
however, such failures, or rather the characters' recognition of them,
are redemptive. Mendelson goes so far as to say that the poem's main
argument is "that success isolates because, in requiring another person's failure, it is *criminal*." This theme he then relates to a miscarriage
Auden's mother suffered between the birth of his older brother, John,
and himself, a loss, Auden later confessed in a letter to a friend in
1944, for which "I cannot be sorry, because, if she hadn't, perhaps I
shouldn't exist." It is impossible to prove or disprove such a reading,
but certainly the caustic Antonio, the principle of pure negativity,
shadows his brother's various triumphs by insisting on all that cannot
be transformed and made to participate in the joyful dance of forgiveness and reconciliation:

> *Your all is partial, Prospero;*
> *My will is all my own:*
> *Your need to love shall never know*
> *Me: I am I, Antonio,*
> *By choice myself alone.*

Each of the poems allotted to the supporting cast in Chapter 2 of
"The Sea and the Mirror" is exposed at its conclusion to the cynical
Antonio's resolute refusal to abandon his solitude. On one level Auden
is making explicit one of the most astonishing aspects of Shakespeare's
drama, its openness to division, the way characters such as Malvolio
or Jaques or the Antonios of *The Merchant of Venice*, *Twelfth Night*,
and *The Tempest* – the first two of whom, intriguingly, resemble the

147

narrator of the sonnets in their irresistible attraction to a young man
– are allowed to remain outside the spell of the play's transformations.
But Auden is also aware that the "fireworks, fun, and games" of romanticism have rendered impossible this kind of freedom for a poetry
obsessed with subjectivity. His Antonio may enjoy celebrating his re-
calcitrance in gloriously sinister choric interludes, but acknowledges
at the conclusion of his own monologue, written in *terza rima*, that
he and Prospero are in a kind of symbiotic relationship:

> As I exist so you shall be denied,
> Forced to remain our melancholy mentor,
> The grown-up man, the adult in his pride,
>
> Never have time to curl up in the center
> Time turns on when completely reconciled,
> Never become and therefore never enter
> The green occluded pasture as a child.

Since, as Caliban explains at length in his address to the audience in
Chapter 3, the nostalgic longing to return to the "green kingdom"
of childhood is one the seeker for grace must resist at all costs, the
vigilance Antonio's wickedness makes necessary is generally good for
the conscience. In this respect, he plays as crucial a part as any in the
existential comedy, where only motley is worn.

The poems of Chapter 2 display the full range of Auden's virtuosity:
the metaphysical complexities of Ferdinand's sonnet, which Auden
described to Isherwood as "fucking in completely abstract words",
are played off against Miranda's naïve, rapturous villanelle, with its
alternating end lines:

> My Dear One is mine as mirrors are lonely,
> And the high green hill sits always by the sea.

Dualities, antitheses of this kind abound. The sea and the desert are contrasted in Alonso's moving meditation on the difficulties that will confront his son when he ascends the throne of Naples, and will have to balance on the tightrope of "the Way of Justice", "Where no prince is safe for one instant / Unless he trust his embarrassment". Stephano is torn between mind and belly, as he shuttles between bottle and loo, Trinculo between wit and feeling, while Gonzalo broods on the way the "booming eloquence" of his reason inhibited his impulse to trust the wondrous and irrational. It is "embarrassment", to use Alonso's term, the self-consciousness induced by Prospero's magic that forces the guilty to attempt a diagnosis, if not a cure, of the particular "great anxiety" which caused each one's "bad behaviour". Auden also, however, appeals at moments to the mysterious operations of grace, theatrically signified by music, that rescue the characters and plots in Shakespearean romance; like Prospero, Alonso is ready to welcome death, having witnessed a miracle he compares to that with which *A Winter's Tale* concludes:

> rejoicing in a new love,
> A new peace, having heard the solemn
> Music strike and seen the statue move
> To forgive our illusion.

The illusions the characters nurtured are more harshly examined still in Caliban's twenty-five-page address to the audience, written in a convoluted pastiche of the late Henry James. Perhaps mindful of the shade of Browning, whose "Caliban Upon Setebos" developed a thickly textured, organically guttural idiom for Shakespeare's "savage and deformed slave", Auden decided, after months of what he called "prospecting", to use the most elaborately artificial diction he could think of, so as to stress the gap between the unvarnished, inarticulate nature the pre-Prospero Caliban symbolizes, and the distortions inherent in all representations of the natural in the mirror of art. Caliban is variously glossed as the id, Eros, "the Prick" (this in letters to Isherwood and Spencer), as "unrectored chaos", as all art is in opposition to and cannot accommodate: "how *could* you", he has Caliban imagining a disgruntled audience complaining to Shakespeare after the play,

> be guilty of the unpardonable treachery of bringing along the one creature [i.e. Caliban], as you above all men must have known, whom she [i.e. the Muse] cannot and will not under any circumstances stand, the solitary exception she is not at any hour of the day or night at home to, the unique case that her attendant spirits have absolute instructions never, neither at the front door nor at the back, to admit?

More alarming still to the playgoers is the thought Shakespeare may have forgotten that poetry makes nothing happen, and have unleashed Ariel into the world of Caliban, the world we live in:

> For if the intrusion of the real has disconcerted and incommoded the poetic, that is a mere bagatelle compared to the damage which the poetic would inflict if it ever succeeded on intruding upon the real. We want no Ariel here, breaking down our picket fences in the name of fraternity, seducing our wives in the name of romance, and robbing us of our sacred pecuniary deposits in the name of justice. Where is Ariel? What have you done with Him? For we won't, we daren't leave until you give us a satisfactory answer.

Auden was inordinately proud of Caliban's monologue, and often claimed it was the best thing he'd ever written. Certainly it is one of his funniest performances, and gives full reign to the talent for mimicry so brilliantly exploited in *The Orators*. He also felt it was "more me than the sections written in my own style", and that this was precisely the "paradox" he was aiming for. In this case at least, Auden's urge to renounce resulted in an expansive exfoliation, rather than a constriction, of his natural gifts.

The brilliance of the prose, which is impossible to illustrate by quotation since the sentences go on for so long and the aesthetic arguments developed are so complex, almost disguises the sleight-of-hand whereby Caliban claims to resolve the theological issues at the heart of "The Sea and the Mirror". In the end he makes use of a strategy not dissimilar from Prospero's address to the audience in the epilogue to *The Tempest*:

> Gentle breath of yours my sails
> Must fill, or else my project fails,
> Which was to please. Now I want
> Spirits to enforce, art to enchant;
> And my ending is despair
> Unless I be relieved by prayer,
> Which pierces so, that it assaults
> Mercy itself, and frees all faults.

As Prospero's appeal for grace depends on insisting, through theatrical metaphor, on his helplessness, so Caliban finds in the image of "the greatest grandest opera rendered by a very provincial touring company indeed" a means of figuring the gap between this world and the hereafter:

> Here we really stand, down stage with red faces and no applause; no effect, however simple, no piece of business, however unimportant, came off; there was not a single aspect of our whole production, not even the huge stuffed bird of happiness, for which a kind word could, however patronisingly, be said.

It is at this moment of utter disillusion and disenchantment, that we may hear "the real Word which is our only *raison d'être*". Art's abject failure to imitate life convincingly can be understood as miming the gap between this world and

> that Wholly Other Life from which we are separated by an essential emphatic gulf of which our contrived fissures of mirror and proscenium arch – we understand them at last – are feebly figurative signs, so that all our meanings are reversed and it is precisely in its negative image of Judgement that we can envisage Mercy; it is just here, among the ruins and the bones, that we may rejoice in the perfected Work which is not ours.

The overarching, unspoken context of "The Sea and the Mirror" was the Second World War. Auden had been pilloried in the British press for fleeing England in her hour of need, and had been classified 4F (unfit for service) on account of his homosexuality by the U.S. draft board. An early version of Caliban's speech, at this point in verse, opens with the warning that "an unidentified plane is reported / Approaching the city", and instructs the audience to sit in the dark and wait for developments. The poem's preoccupation with death and guilt was no doubt partly motivated also by the death of his mother in the summer of 1941, shortly after The Crisis. As in *The Waste Land*, the invocation of the peace which passeth understanding – "Shantih shantih shantih" – or in Caliban's phrase, "the full bloom of the unbothered state", probably ends up convincing only those who happen to share the poets' religious views, though in both cases unbelievers can be affected by the emotional turmoil from which only religion offers an escape. "The Sea and the Mirror" concludes with a postscript in the form of an aria – perhaps in tribute to the opera-loving Kallman – in which Auden posits a tentative reconciliation of body and spirit, united by their shared fascination for "drab mortality". While Eliot moved through the sacramental vision of "What the Thunder Said" to a poetry – and a personal life – largely determined by his spiritual quest, Auden turned away from rigorous pursuit of the *via negativa* outlined in the closing paragraphs of Caliban's speech. In a sense the postscript renounces renunciation, or to borrow Eliot's terms, "the intolerable shirt of flame", the longing to be "redeemed from fire by fire". Auden, by contrast, accepts, whatever "humiliation" awaits him, that Ariel and Caliban can never separate:

> Never hope to say farewell,
> For our lethargy is such
> Heaven's kindness cannot touch
> Nor earth's frankly brutal drum;
> This was long ago decided ...

Decided by whom? The only answer is another question, that posed in the Preface: "O what authority gives / Existence its surprise?" And it is surprise that must compensate the reader for the lack, in Auden's career, of the kind of coherence that links, say, early to middle to late Eliot. "The Sea and the Mirror" represents his most determined and considered attempt to "grow up", but it moves most by its failure to do so: in the words of Ariel to Caliban, "only / As I am can I / Love you as you are."

New York Review of Books, June 2004: Review of W.H. Auden's *The Sea and the Mirror*, edited by Arthur Kirsch (Princeton University Press, 2003).

The Prince of Morticians:
Thomas Lovell Beddoes

Thomas Lovell Beddoes was one of the most peculiar, haunting, and prodigiously gifted English poets of the nineteenth century. He published only two books in his lifetime: *The Improvisatore* (1821), a collection of Gothic tales in verse, and *The Brides' Tragedy* (1822), a pseudo-Jacobean drama that was widely praised by reviewers, and even prompted the odd favourable comparison with Shakespeare and Marlowe. Yet he set little store by these juvenilia – indeed he was so ashamed of *The Improvisatore* that he took to buying up all copies he could find and destroying them; if he noticed the volume on a friend's bookshelf, he would surreptitiously remove its pages with a razor, and then return the empty binding.

Beddoes's dissatisfaction with his own work is one of the most striking features of his self-aborting literary career. Between 1823–25 he embarked on four separate verse dramas – *The Last Man, Love's Arrow Poisoned, Torrismond*, and *The Second Brother*. Many of the scenes and fragments that survive from these are quite superb; consider, for instance this preternaturally vivid passage from *The Last Man* describing an adult and baby crocodile:

> Hard by the lilied Nile I saw
> A duskish river-dragon stretched along,
> The brown habergeon of his limbs enamelled
> With sanguine almandines and rainy pearl:
> And on his back there lay a young one sleeping,
> No bigger than a mouse; with eyes like beads,

And a small fragment of its speckled egg
Remaining on its harmless, pulpy snout;
A thing to laugh at, as it gaped to catch
The baulking merry flies. In the iron jaws
Of the great devil-beast, like a pale soul
Fluttering in rocky hell, lightsomely flew
A snowy trochilus, with roseate beak
Tearing the hairy leeches from his throat.

In the summer of 1825, however, on the eve of his departure from England to study medicine at the University of Göttingen in Germany, Beddoes wrote to his friend Thomas Forbes Kelsall with news of yet another projected verse drama, "a very Gothic-styled tragedy, for which I have a jewel of a name – DEATH'S JESTBOOK". In it he planned to approach the problem that motivated both his medical researches, which centred on anatomy, and his imagination: for Beddoes the "only truth worth demonstrating" was the exact nature of death.

This obsession may have had its origins in his early years. Beddoes's father, the polymathic Dr Thomas Beddoes, was a political radical, a poet, and a scientist: expelled from his readership at Oxford because of his republican sympathies during the French Revolution, he settled in Bristol where he became friends with Coleridge and Southey, composed an unreadable verse epic, *Alexander's Expedition down the Hydaspes and the Indus to the Indian Ocean*, and co-founded the Pneumatic Institution with James Watt and Josiah Wedgwood. Dr Beddoes believed that children should be inducted into the mysteries of birth and death as early as possible. Accordingly, the Beddoes offspring were made to witness "the labour pangs of a domestic quadruped", and to participate in the dissection of pregnant frogs and hens. Thomas Lovell was only five and a half when his father died in 1808, but his life, like the Doctor's, was to be divided between medicine, radical politics, and poetry.

Beddoes was firmly convinced that "the dramatist & physician are closely, almost inseparably allied"; dissecting and writing were both ways of probing the secrets of death, and possibly of discovering, in a quest that resembled that of another Romantic "modern Prometheus", Mary Shelley's Victor Frankenstein, the origins of life also:

> And even as there is a round dry grain
> In a plant's skeleton, which being buried
> Can raise the herb's green body up again;
> So is there such in man, a seed-shaped bone,
> Aldabaron, called by the Hebrews Luz,
> Which, being laid into the ground, will bear
> After three thousand years the grass of flesh,
> The bloody, soul-possessed weed called man.

This speech is given in *Death's Jest-Book* to Ziba, a necromantic Moor who is about to raise a ghost from the grave – as it turns out, the wrong one! – but is supported by a long note by Beddoes himself in which he quotes Talmudic texts relating to this mystical bone, "the only one which withstands dissolution after death, out of which the body will be developed at the resurrection".

Beddoes was fascinated by the hinterland between here and after, by ways of representing the transition between life and death – and vice versa. In a passage of couplets composed for this scene, but eventually cut, he sardonically imagines a body poised for resurrection:

> Thread the nerves through the right holes,
> Get out of my bones, you wormy souls,
> Shut up my stomach, the ribs are full:
> Muscles be steady and ready to pull.
> Heart and artery merrily shake
> And eyelid go up, for we're going to wake.

But the theme also inspired some of his most magically lyrical and subtle effects, as in the fragment from *The Last Man* that pictures a corpse "Turning to daisies gently in the grave", or the fantasy of recovered love momentarily indulged in Beddoes's best-known poem, "Dream Pedlary":

> If there are ghosts to raise,
>   What shall I call,
> Out of hell's murky haze,
>   Heaven's blue hall?
> Raise my loved longlost boy
> To lead me to his joy.
>   There are no ghosts to raise;
>   Out of death lead no ways;
>   Vain is the call.

"Dream Pedlary" was composed in 1830 in the wake of Beddoes's first attempt at suicide. In 1827 he had met an impoverished Jew called Bernard Reich, from whom, or so he claims in his note, he first learned of the Hebrew belief in the bone Luz. Beddoes and Reich shared lodgings in Göttingen in 1827 and '28, and moved together to Würzburg in the autumn of 1829. Reich then abruptly vanishes from the record: he may, as Beddoes's first biographer, H.W. Donner has speculated, have died, but the conjecture is based more on the desire to identify the "loved longlost boy" of "Dream Pedlary" than on hard evidence. It does seem certain, however, that the disappearance or loss of Reich compounded a crisis in Beddoes's literary career, a crisis from which, in a sense, he never recovered.

Beddoes dispatched what has come to be known as the 1829 version of *Death's Jest-Book* in February of that year to three friends in England; the heroically loyal Thomas Forbes Kelsall, a solicitor based in Southampton, Bryan Waller Procter (who himself wrote faux-Jacobean plays under the pseudonym Barry Cornwall), and the novelist and poet J.G.H. Bourne. While the ever-supportive Kelsall was all for immediate publication, Procter and Bourne strongly counselled Beddoes to embark on root-and-branch revision. "Am I right in supposing", Beddoes wrote in response to Procter (whose original letter does not survive), "that you would denounce, and order to be rewritten, all the prose scenes and passages? – almost all the 1st and 2nd , great part of the 3rd act, much of the principal scenes of the 4th, and the 5th to be strengthened and its opportunities better worked on? But you see this is no trifle, though I believe it ought to be done." Procter's and Bourne's advice was effectively to imprison Beddoes in the ghoulish, labyrinthine world of *Death's Jest-Book* for the rest of his life. He ended up spending the next two decades emending and expanding his masterpiece, rewriting speeches, adding lyrics, tinkering with names, and complicating still further the plot of what he aptly called, in 1844, his "unhappy, strange conglomerate". "What good", expostulated Robert Browning, one of Beddoes's greatest admirers, in a letter to Kelsall of 1868, "was got by suppressing the poem, or what harm could have followed the publication even in the worldly way of looking at things? Suppose it had been laughed, blackguarded in Blackwood, fallen flat from the press? The worse for the world for the quarter of an hour: Beddoes would not have much cared, but probably made a clean breast and begun on something else. It is infinitely regrettable."

Beddoes himself freely acknowledged the defects in his play – indeed seems always to have been witheringly critical of his own abilities. He confesses that the "power of drawing character & humour – two things absolutely indispensable for a good dramatist – are the two first articles in my deficiencies." It's true that all the characters in *Death's Jest-Book*, and in all of Beddoes's other verse dramas, speak the same gorgeous literary fustian. What kind of poet, Ezra Pound wondered in an essay of 1913, might Beddoes have been had he "used a real speech instead of a language which may have been used on the early Victorian stage, but certainly had no existence in the life of his era?" Yet

Pound, like Browning, found himself enthralled by the extraordinary delicacy, verve, sweep and intelligence with which Beddoes energizes his literary imaginings. Beddoes's œuvre – and in this again it resembles Frankenstein's monster – seems made up of dislocated fragments dug up from the past, uneasily stitched together, then suddenly galvanized into an unnerving, startling life. "What is the lobster's tune when he is boiled?" demands Death's principal jester, Isbrand, by way of introduction to a song which, he explains, he "made / One night a-strewing poison for the rats / In the kitchen corner":

> Squats on a toad-stool under a tree
>> A bodiless childfull of life in the gloom,
> Crying with frog voice, "What shall I be?
> Poor unborn ghost, for my mother killed me
>> Scarcely alive in her wicked womb.
> What shall I be? shall I creep to the egg
> That's cracking asunder yonder by Nile,
>>> And with eighteen toes,
>>> And a snuff-taking nose,
>> Make an Egyptian crocodile?"

Something of the homelessness of this "childfull of life in the gloom" permeates Beddoes's singular poetic sensibility, as it sifts through archaic literary idioms, fitfully animating the properties it borrows from the traditions of the grotesque, the tragic, and the sublime. As Pound declared in Canto LXXX, Beddoes is truly "the prince of morticians".

Beddoes's characters are all, as Lytton Strachey remarked in a wonderful essay of 1907, "hypochondriac philosophers, puzzling over eternity and dissecting the attributes of death." The plot of *Death's Jest-Book*, even in its original simpler version of 1829, is hard to summarize concisely. Set in Ancona, Egypt, and Grüssau in the late 13th (1829) or 14th (later text) century, it involves betrayal, revenge, love-rivalry, conspiracy, revolution, fratricide and sorcery. The play opens with an expedition led by the noble Wolfram to rescue the Duke of Münsterberg, Melveric, who has been taken captive by "wild pagans" on a pilgrimage to the Holy Land. Although Wolfram knows Melveric murdered his father, he has not only forgiven him this, but the pair have entered into a pact of blood-brothership. Wolfram's real brother, Isbrand, at this point the court-jester, is not so "womanish", and vows to revenge his father and usurp the dukedom. In Egypt, meanwhile, Melveric has fallen in love with one Sybilla, who is herself in love with Wolfram, with whom she had once shared a cell during an earlier captivity. Wolfram rescues both, but is then heartlessly murdered by the ungrateful Duke. Wolfram's body is shipped home for burial, but is smuggled by Isbrand into the vault containing the remains of Melveric's ex-wife, so when Ziba performs his spell, it is the ghost of his murdered friend rather than that of his saintly spouse that emerges from the tomb.

An equally elaborate line of action concerns the Duke's two sons, Adalmar and Athulf, who are both in love with the same woman, Amala. Although betrothed to the warrior-like Adalmar, she secretly loves the satirical and licentious Athulf. On the night before the wedding, Athulf drinks what he thinks to be a fatal vial of poison, confesses his love, which, thinking he is about to die, she reciprocates; but the poison, provided by the all-purpose Ziba, turns out to be merely an opiate. On discovery of this, Athulf proclaiming "Now that I live, I *will* live ... Away to Abel's grave!" murders Adalmar, only to be overwhelmed immediately by a terrible remorse, imagining himself, in a typically Beddoesian flight of fancy, transformed into

> A wild old wicked mountain in the sea:
> And the abhorred conscience of this murder,
> Shall be created and become a Lion
> All alone in the darkness of my spirit,
> And lair him in my caves

And when I lie tremendous in the billows,
Murderers, and men half ghosts, stricken with madness,
Will come to live upon my rugged sides,
Die, and be buried in it.

That same night Isbrand's conspiracy, which has been infiltrated by
the Duke himself disguised as a pilgrim, comes to a head and sparks
off the general mayhem with which the play climaxes. Beddoes's commitment to radical politics emerges in the curious character of Mario,
an allegorical embodiment of the spirit of revolution who – although
blind – manages to stab Isbrand ("Down, thou usurper, to the earth
and grovel!") at the moment of his seeming triumph. The play's concluding image is of the Duke being dragged alive into the world of
the dead by Wolfram, his mild-mannered ghostly nemesis. Both versions also feature a set of prose-speaking grotesques with names like
Titmouse or Homunculus Mandrake who offer somewhat laboured
Jonsonian light relief, and are studded – particularly the later one
– with exquisite songs and macabre lyrics that delay still further the
inching progress of the convoluted action.

"Just now", Beddoes observed in a letter of 1825, "the drama is a
haunted ruin." It could be awakened only by "a bold trampling fellow – no creeper into wormholes – no reviser even – however good.
These reanimations are vampire-cold." But far from reinvigorating
the contemporary stage – which was dominated by the vogue for the
pseudo-Jacobean – as he seems to have planned, Beddoes devoted his
extraordinary talents to what is essentially an agonizingly prolonged
dissolution of the genre of verse drama, a kind of unending kiss of
death, an ultimate and literal enactment of the crisis he had diagnosed. Like his own ghostly "Phantom-Wooer", Beddoes seems like a
spectre enticing his chosen medium into oblivion:

A ghost, that loved a lady fair,
Ever in the starry air

161

> Of midnight at her pillow stood;
> And, with a sweetness skies above
> The luring words of human love,
> Her soul the phantom wooed.
> Sweet and sweet is their poisoned note,
> The little snakes of silver throat,
> In mossy skulls that nest and lie,
> Ever singing "die, oh, die."

Death's Jest-Book became itself the "haunted ruin" to end all haunted ruins, one Beddoes could neither complete nor abandon. It is both unperformable, and, as he himself pointed out, "perfectly adapted to remain unread". Yet, from another perspective, *Death's Jest-Book* is a startlingly prescient work, one that anticipates not only the dramatic monologue, as developed by Tennyson and Browning – a point first made by Christopher Ricks in an excellent essay on Beddoes published in 1984 – but the black humorous worlds of such as Samuel Beckett or Ionesco. And in its conflicted, doomed, self-defeating form, at once fragmentary and endlessly expansive, it now seems the perfect expression of Beddoes's vision of "the absurdity and unsatisfactory nature of human life".

Beddoes's own life ended particularly unsatisfactorily. Expelled from Würzburg for his incendiary political views and speeches, he settled for a while in Zurich, then drifted on to Berlin then Baden then Frankfurt, where he met Konrad Degen, an aspiring actor, but professional baker, who was to be his companion for the last years of his life. Beddoes also took to making occasional trips to England, or Cantland, as he called it. During one of these in 1846, in protest at the poor state of the English theatre, he attempted to burn down Drury Lane by lighting a £5 note and holding it underneath a chair. He was never an entirely welcome guest at the family seat at Cheney Longville, for he refused to meet fellow guests or talk to his hosts; once he arrived drunk astride a donkey, and spent the entire six month visit that followed alone in his room, smoking and drinking.

Beddoes's lawyer, Revell Phillips, was convinced his second suicide attempt in 1848 was due to a "love disappointment". While staying at the Cigogne Hotel in Basle he cut open an artery in his left leg. He was admitted to the Basle Hospital, where he kept tearing off the bandages in the hope he might bleed to death. Eventually the leg had to be amputated. Beddoes remained in the hospital until on January 26th of 1849, he was found dead with a suicide note addressed to his lawyer on his chest. "My dear Phillips," it began, "I am food for what I am good for – worms." He instructs his only consistent admirer, Thomas Forbes Kelsall to go through his manuscripts and "print or not as he thinks fit." "I ought to have been", Beddoes continues, "among other things a good poet. Life was too great a bore on one peg [a reference to the amputation] and that a bad one. Buy for Dr Ecklin [Beddoes's doctor at the hospital] above mentioned [one of] Reade's best stomach pumps." Beddoes, it later transpired, had taken poison, although it has never been established exactly how he obtained it. The stomach pump he bequeathed his physician, therefore, was Beddoes's final jest with death; since Dr Ecklin would only receive it on the poet's decease, it could never be used to clear his own system of the poison he had deliberately taken. One can't help imagining him murmuring, as he approached the threshold he had addressed in so many soaring monologues and mournful dirges, the chorus of his final lyric:

> Sweet and sweet is their poisoned note,
> The little snakes of silver throat,
> In mossy skulls that nest and lie,
> Ever singing "die, oh, die."

Poetry Review, 2004: Review of Thomas Lovell Beddoes's *Death's Jest-Book* (The 1829 Text), edited with an introduction by Michael Bradshaw (Fyfield Books, 2003), and *Death's Jest-Book* (a new edition of the later text established by H.W. Donner), edited and introduced by Alan Halsey (West House Books, 2003).

James Schuyler and Englishness

"Wigging in, wigging out", begins "Trip", the first of a series of poems James Schuyler composed in 1975 during a two-month hospitalisation in Payne Whitney, the psychiatric unit of New York Hospital; "when I stop to think / the wires in my head / cross: kaboom." The poem's 21 short lines summarise Schuyler's troubled psychiatric history with unusual directness:

> How
> many trips
> by ambulance (five,
> count them five),
> claustrated, pill addiction,
> in and out of mental
> hospitals,
> the suicidalness (once
> I almost made it)
> but – I go on?
> Tell you all of it?
> I can't. When I think
> of that, that at
> only fifty-one, I
> Jim the Jerk, am
> still alive and breathing
> deeply, that I think
> is a miracle.

Schuyler in fact stayed "alive and breathing" a further 16 years, during which he wrote much of his best poetry, an enchanting, hilarious novel called *What's For Dinner?* (1978), and achieved something like cult status among America's poetic cognoscenti. "I like his poetry so much", wrote Elizabeth Bishop in a late letter, "& I have never told him so, nor seen him, & know next to nothing about him." "Your work makes up an 'underground movement' all by itself!" declared Ted Berrigan. When Schuyler finally gave a poetry reading in 1988, having always refused before on account of his extreme shyness, the queue for tickets stretched several deep around the block.

Schuyler was born in Chicago in 1923, but grew up mainly in Washington D.C. and East Aurora, a small town near Buffalo in upstate New York. He later compared his home-life with his mother and stepfather to "a novel by Dostoyevsky". He attended a small college in West Virginia called Bethany, where he fared dismally and left without a degree, mainly because he spent nearly all his time playing bridge. In 1943 he joined the Navy, and saw action while on convoy duty in the North Atlantic; the following year, however, he went AWOL in New York for several weeks, and at the hearing that followed his arrest his homosexuality was revealed. He was branded "undesirable", and discharged from further naval duties.

Schuyler didn't begin writing poetry until the early Fifties. He travelled to Europe in 1947 with the vague idea of developing into a *New Yorker*-style short story writer. He spent two years there, mainly in Italy, with his partner of the time, Bill Aalto, a specialist in guerrilla warfare who had fought on the side of the Republic in the Spanish Civil War. Schuyler and Aalto visited Auden and Chester Kallman on Ischia, and for a while Schuyler worked as Auden's secretary, typing up the manuscript of *Nones*: "Well, if this is poetry," he later recalled thinking as he pecked away, "I'm certainly never going to write any myself." Their Ischian idyll ended when the volatile Aalto – whose right hand had been blown off by a hand-grenade during a training session for recruits – attempted to kill Schuyler with a carving knife.

165

He returned to New York in August of 1949. In the course of the next few years he met Frank O'Hara, John Ashbery, Barbara Guest, and Kenneth Koch. He also suffered his first major manic attack, which took the form of a religious ecstasy: he was convinced he'd had a long conversation with the Virgin Mary, who informed him that Judgement Day was nigh. He was sent to Bloomingdale mental hospital in White Plains, and it was during his three-month stay there that his earliest poems were written. Further breakdowns and hospitalisations followed in 1956, in 1961, in 1971 (on this occasion he believed he was Jesus Christ and spent hours carefully washing dollar bills in the bathtub, then pegging them on a clothes line to dry), in 1973, 1975, 1976, 1977, 1978, 1979, and finally 1985. He rarely had any money, and lived mainly with friends such as Fairfield Porter – whose wife Anne once joked that Schuyler came for a visit and ended up staying eleven years – Kenward Elmslie and Darragh Park. In the late Seventies he shuttled between psychiatric units, nursing homes, flea-pit hotels and rooming-houses – in one of which he nearly died in a fire he caused himself by falling asleep holding a lighted cigarette. Finally, in 1979, a grant from the Frank O'Hara Foundation enabled him to settle in the Chelsea Hotel on West 23rd Street, and be looked after by a series of paid assistants.

Schuyler's work is nearly always considered in the context of "The New York School", the label dreamed up by John Bernard Myers, who was the director of the Tibor de Nagy Gallery and published the early work of Ashbery, Koch, and O'Hara in a series of Tibor de Nagy poetry pamphlets in the 50s. Schuyler's early poems would have appeared in this series too, but it seems he suddenly lost faith in his poethood, and then – this was in the run-up to his breakdown of 1961 – took to blaming Frank O'Hara for undermining his self-esteem. O'Hara was, in many ways, everything Schuyler wasn't: brash, prolific, confident, talkative, robust, always the centre of attention, and any number of people's best friend: "and it was given to me," O'Hara writes in a 1954 poem dedicated to Schuyler, "as the soul is given the hands / to hold the ribbons of life!" The more passive Schuyler rarely gives the impression of having a firm grip on the ribbons, let alone the reins, of life, and the dilemmas his poetry ponders tend to be quotidian and specific: "There is a hornet in the room," begins his superb elegy for O'Hara, "Buried at Springs",

> and one of us will have to go
> out the window into the late
> August midafternoon sun. I
> won. There is a certain challenge
> in being humane to hornets
> but not much.

Characteristically the poem alludes only obliquely to his friend's violent death in a gruesome accident on Fire Island in 1966: "a faintly clammy day," it concludes,

> like wet silk
> stained by one dead branch
> the harsh russet of dried blood.

While O'Hara loved singing the praises of "life-giving vulgarity", Schuyler was all reticence and tact. It has even been suggested by David Lehman in his study of the group, *The Last Avant-Garde: The Making of the New York School of Poets* (1998), that O'Hara's death "acted as a sort of imaginative liberation for Schuyler"; it allowed him, Lehman argues, to assume "O'Hara's project and adapt it to his own sensibility". His first collection, *Freely Espousing*, was published in 1969, long after Koch, Ashbery and O'Hara had become, if not household names, reasonably well-known in American poetry circles.

Certainly O'Hara's and Schuyler's representations of the urban could hardly be more different. In poem after poem O'Hara charts his love of Manhattan, and his fractured, pulsing, open forms seem ways of miming the city's random juxtapositions and erotic and aesthetic energies, its plenitude of choice and almost overwhelming sense of possibility. Even nature is better in the city – "One need never leave the confines of New York to get all the greenery one wishes", he informs us in the prose poem "Meditations in an Emergency", "I can't even enjoy a blade of grass unless I know there's a subway handy, or a record store or some other sign that people do not totally *regret* life." Schuyler, on the other hand, often figures himself yearning for the joys of rural calm, as in the short diary poem, "The Morning", written soon after he moved into the Chelsea Hotel:

> I
> almost accept the fact
> that I am not in
> the country, where I
> long to be, but in
> this place of glass
> and stone – and metal,
> let's not forget
> metal – where traffic sounds and the day
> is well begun. So
> be it, morning.

Both O'Hara and Schuyler – much more than Koch, Ashbery or Guest – liked to fill their poems with references to friends, to social events, to everyday activities such as making toast or shopping or eating lunch, and to their favourite painters, musicians and writers. O'Hara's literary allusions tend to be to avant-garde French and Russian poets, such as René Char, Pierre Reverdy ("My heart is in my / pocket, it is Poems by Pierre Reverdy"), Paul Éluard, Mayakovsky, Marcelin Pleynet, Apollinaire and so on; Schuyler, meanwhile, always seems to be immersed in Trollope ("we settle down / to read; he, a Ross / MacDonald, me *Phineas / Redux*") or Virginia Woolf, or in

Herrick or Traherne or Vaughan or Tennyson or Lady Mary Wortley
Montague or Gilbert White or Vita Sackville-West or the Sitwells.
"I'm reading", he writes in "A Few Days" (1985),

> Osbert Sitwell's autobiography stitched in brocade. I
> read a page, then rush back to my poem. I would once have
>   thought that Sitwell
> was "influencing" me. I'm too me for that. Poor trembling
>   Osbert, suffering from
> Parkinson's disease. I met him at a party Wystan gave for them.
>   John was
> dashing tears from his eyes: "What's wrong?" "I just met Edith
>   Sitwell." Tender
> heart. Edith looked less like her photograph. She was creased
>   and had that
> famous nose.

These references testify to a deep and intriguing Anglophilia. Schuyler
never in fact visited England, but in the 50s he worked for several
years at an English specialist bookstore, the Periscope-Holliday on
East 54th street, and in later life grew into a devotee of magazines such
as *The Countryman, The Tatler, The Field* and *Private Eye*, which he
used to buy from an import magazine shop on Broadway. One poem
of his, "The Fireproof Floors of Witley Court (English Songs and
Dances)" is based on extracts from back issues of *Country Life* ("Fry's
Cocoa! The word / means food of the gods ... Swan and Edgar / Good
linen / Swan and Edgar / Good linen") while "Under the Hanger",
which is three pages long, consists entirely of phrases lifted from the
journals of Gilbert White:

> Wood lark whistles. Hogs carry straw.
> Sky lark sings.
> Young cucumber swells.

Frogs croak: spawn abounds.
Cold & black. Harsh, hazy day.
Backward apples begin to blow.
Frost, sun, fog, rain, snow. Bunting twitters.
No dew, rain, rain, rain.
Swans flounce & dive.
Chilly & dark.
Dark & spitting. Indian flowers in Dec'r!
Ground very wet. The nightingale sings ...

Although he never owned a garden, in the late Sixties Schuyler opened an account with Landsman's in Herefordshire, a "Specialist Postal Bookshop for Farmers and Gardeners", from whom he used to acquire manuals that enabled him to keep up with the latest in English horticultural fashions. One of his most delicate late poems describes an English rose called "Princess Di"; this poem, although composed over a decade before the fatal crash in the Parisian underpass, with hindsight seems eerily prophetic – indeed might even be claimed to be the first ever, and perhaps the finest, elegy for Diana. This rose, given him by his secretary while he convalesces in hospital, resembles a Georg Arends hybrid:

> silvery, pink
> larger, with sharply
> pointed petals, the only
> rose to do so (I thought,
> I imagined) what joy
> to see it recur in Princess
> Di named for we all know
> who and the Chinese lady
> heard what I said when
> she asked and she said,
> "Princess Diana the Princess

Diana" and as the days
passed and you came
to escort me home and
the rose I had watched
grown fat and soft
expired as I left
and I thought, "Beautiful
Princess, farewell!"

And while on the subject of royalty, what other American poet of the post-war era has managed to work in references to Princess Anne – glimpsed performing in the Montreal Olympics – the Queen, Prince Philip, and the Prince of Wales, who are all mentioned in "The Morning of the Poem"?

Schuyler was particularly fond of English diarists, and his own *Diary*, which was published by Black Sparrow in 1997, is full of references to such as Kilvert, (whose magnum opus Schuyler read "many many times"), Dorothy Wordsworth, the Bloomsbury diarist Frances Partridge, and the eighteenth–century parson James Woodforde, whose five-volume journal records the minutiae of daily life in Western Longeville, Norfolk. Schuyler also loved the work of memoirists such as Constance Spry, the pre-eminent London society florist of her day and author of botanical tomes such as *Come into the Garden, Cook* (1942) and *Favourite Flowers* (1959), Harry Daley, a policeman from Lowestoft who had an affair with E.M. Forster and published his reminiscences in *This Small Cloud* (1986), and Arthur Randell, author of *Fenway Railwaymen* (1968), of which, Schuyler observes, "it might be possible to say it contains not one memorable word, and therefore has a pleasant clarity, like a clear glass of water." Other favourite writers mentioned include Malcolm Elwin (author of *Victorian Wallflowers* (1934)), Iris Origo, Sydney Smith, Andrew Young, William Cobbett, William Robinson, Patrick Leigh-Fermor, Richard Jeffries, and the nineteenth-century English historian of the law, F.W. Maitland, from whose "Leet and Tourn" (1888), Schuyler quotes a sentence which struck him as particularly "beautiful": "To the student of manorial rolls by far the most interesting franchise is the 'court leet or view of frank-pledge', because it is very common, because it has great importance in the history of society, because its origin is extremely obscure; so obscure that we may be rash in speaking about it; still a little may be ventured."

A little may be ventured, I hope not too rashly, on the subject of Schuyler's delightfully camp enjoyment of a certain kind of Englishness, and its importance to his development as a writer. He was not, it must be said, much interested in 20th century English poetry, and shared with the Beats and the Objectivists and the Black Mountaineers as well as with his fellow New York School poets an energizing contempt for the conservative East Coast poetic establishment, "the campus dry-heads", as he once characterised them, "who wishfully descend tum-ti-tumming from Yeats out of Graves with a big kiss for Mother England". His earliest writings, collected in *The Home Book 1951–1970*, reveal a slightly uneasy determination to experiment with the kind of goofy Surrealist-inspired disjunctions characteristic of the early work of Koch, O'Hara and Ashbery. Schuyler's first publication, however, was the short fiction *Alfred and Guinevere* (1958, reissued 2001), an elusive, haunting fusion of the clichés of small-town American novels, movies and children's stories with the English comedy of manners as written by such as E.F. Benson, Henry Green, Ronald Firbank, Ivy Compton-Burnett, and George and Weedon Grossmith. *Alfred and Guinevere* is almost entirely in dialogue, and mainly very simple dialogue, since its principal characters, the siblings Alfred and Guinevere, are around 8 and 10 years old respectively. But beneath the whimsical repartee and kiddie joshing and one-upmanship circulate complex emotional currents the novel refuses ever to define or drag to the surface. In this it greatly resembles Jane Bowles's *Two Serious Ladies*, published 15 years earlier, which also uses manners and dialogue to develop an elliptical narrative that continually undermines our expectations and unsettles our perspective on events and characters. Bowles and Schuyler both, I think, found in the English society novel a means of side-stepping what might be called its antithesis, the Great American Novel, which must somehow include and interpret as much of the American past, present and future as possible, and ideally should create a new fictional form for itself to boot. Schuyler, who worshipped Bowles, recorded with delight in his diary her Firbankian response to a publisher explaining why she didn't want her novel reissued: "it has its own little following, like a Lily Daché hat." Manners and fashion here serve to mock the very idea there could be anything superior to a minor or cult classic.

"So modest," Schuyler writes of Darwin, whose autobiography he has just started, in "Empathy and New Year" (the New Year in question was 1968), "so innocent, so pleased at / the surprise that *he* / should turn out to be *him*." Modesty is a crucial aspect of Schuyler's poetics, and so is the pleased and surprised discovery of one's individuality – the sense one can be too "me" to be influenced by others. This notion of developing into a particular, determined identity runs interestingly – and modestly – against the grain of the standard American ideal of the self as fluid, beyond definition, and somehow infinite. "Encompass worlds but never try to encompass me", admonishes Whitman in "Song of Myself". O'Hara also frequently explores a Whitmanesque vision of the poet instantly metamorphosing into whatever he imagines or identifies with, as in the litany of selves that succeed each other in "In Memory of My Feelings": "I am a Chinaman climbing a mountain / I am a child smelling his father's underwear I am an Indian / sleeping on a scalp ..." O'Hara is of course on one level mocking the whole nationalist ideology of self-reliance – "What land is this, so free?" he asks caustically a few lines later – but the poem's collage of discourses and compendium of images also situate it squarely in the tradition of the American song of one's self. Schuyler clearly needed to evade the implications of the carpetbag form of the American long poem as it developed from Whitman to Pound to

Williams to O'Hara. What he found in the journals of such as Kilvert and Woodforde and Gilbert White was not only a form of pastoral, but a way of writing that concentrated on the everyday, and in which things were described for their own sakes. They in turn suggested how his own poetry might avoid dealing with what John Ashbery calls in "Daffy Duck in Hollywood" "the big / Vaguer stuff" – metaphysics and symbolism and issues of self-figuration – and instead accommodate the random trivialities of experience without either loading them with significance, or making them seem mere illustrations of chaos and contingency. Indeed the English diarists offered a template both for long poems such as "Hymn to Life", "The Morning of the Poem", and "A Few Days", and for the seemingly artless day to day bulletins offered by short poems such as "The Morning".

A number of these short pieces are simply titled by their dates: "8 / 12 / 70", "June 30, 1974", "Dec. 28, 1974", "October 5, 1981", and many start out, like diary entries, recording a change in the weather:

> After two rainy days, a sunny one
> of cloud curds breaking up in blue ...
>
> ("Evenings in Vermont")

> Awoke to rain
> and mist, down
> there in Gospel
> Hollow: a cloud
> that frayed and
> flowed uphill
> as the drizzling day
> wore on ...
>
> ("Awoke")

> Then it snowed. I
> saw it when I let

174

>   the dog out into
>   the dark yard, fat
>   damp flakes, ag-
>   glomerations of
>   many flakes ...
>
>   ("Afterward")

Schuyler's observations, like those lifted from Gilbert White's journals in "Under the Hanger", tend to be low-key, accurate, and mundane, "threaded", as he puts it in "Hymn to Life", "with dailiness":

>   Another day, the sun
> Comes out from behind unbuttoned cloud underclothes – gray
>   with use –
> And bud scales litter the sidewalks. A new shop is being built,
> An old one refurbished.

Much of his poetry is written in either very short or very long lines: either extreme functions somewhat as the continuous use of dialogue in *Alfred and Guinevere* – one feels afloat in a medium wholly absorbed in the specifics of what it's presenting but which refuses to offer a "tum-ti-tumming" framework which makes explicit why either he or we should be interested in the opening of a new shop or a change in the weather. The effect is very different from that of the *culte de moi* enacted in O'Hara's "I do this, I do that" poems, which radiate both an insouciant coterie glamour, and an urgent, thrilling excitement at being in the thick of the action:

> It is 12.20 in New York and I am wondering
> if I will finish this in time to meet Norman for lunch
> ah lunch! I think I am going crazy
> what with my terrible hangover and the weekend coming up
> at excitement-prone Kenneth Koch's ...

Schuyler's descriptions of life in the city never make us feel his friends are more gifted than anyone else's or that Manhattan is the centre of the universe – indeed he often seems to wish he were somewhere else: "Lincoln, the Lincolnshire wolds, the Peak District, Ely, the gardens at Chatsworth," he ruminates in "The Morning of the Poem" on receiving a letter from friends holidaying in England, "I wish I had been with you." More fervently still he wishes he'd been at Rodmell in March of 1941

> to parlay with Virginia Woolf
> when she was about to take
> that fatal walk: "I know you're
> sick, but you'll be well
> again: trust me: I've been there."

Neither Woolf nor Schuyler fashioned from their "suicidalness" an expressionist drama of anguish, confession, or revenge. Even at his most fragile, in, say, "The Payne Whitney Poems", Schuyler seems as interested in the weather as in his own condition, while his long poems continually reflect upon – and ground themselves in – the cycles of seasonal change. In the best of Schuyler's work the forces of time, language, and nature come to seem as helplessly and inextricably intertwined as in the image with which he concludes his salute to the "poor lovely lady" whose writings – in particular her diaries – he adored:

> Angular Virginia Woolf, for whom
> words came streaming
> like clouded yellows over the downs.

Poetry Review, 2002

The Bitterness of Weldon Kees

On July 18th 1955, the Californian Highway Patrol reported two abandoned cars in the sightseers' parking lot at the north end of the Golden Gate Bridge. One belonged to a fifty-nine year old salesman called Joseph R. Eppler, who left a suicide note acknowledging the failure of his business and requesting forgiveness; the other car belonged to Weldon Kees, a – a what? All that was found in his 1954 Plymouth was a lab coat from the Langley Porter Psychiatric Clinic, where he had worked part-time for a number of years, collaborating with the psychologist Jurgen Ruesch on a book published the following year entitled *Nonverbal Communication*. All the photographs in this book are by Kees. He was also a maker of science documentaries and avantgarde short films (one of which was about the Golden Gate Bridge), a jazz pianist and song-writer, a well-regarded Abstract Expressionist painter and collagist, a reviewer of books, exhibitions and films for *Time*, *The New Republic*, *The Nation* and *Partisan Review*, a radio presenter, an impresario who organized artistic conferences in Provincetown and musical and theatrical events in San Francisco, a novelist, a scriptwriter, a playwright, a briefly but highly acclaimed short story writer, and the author of three slim volumes of poetry he had enormous difficulty getting published, but on which his reputation now rests.

Kees's body was never found, and if he's still alive, he'll have just turned 90. In the weeks before his disappearance he'd talked of moving incognito to Mexico, as Ambrose Bierce had done in 1914, but he'd also – or so he told a friend the night before he vanished – attempted

177

to jump off the Golden Gate Bridge the previous week. Among his papers was found a file of suicide notes copied from the Langley Porter archives. All his friends knew he had become deeply depressed – "slack & lethargic & miserable", in the words of Pauline Kael. His wife of sixteen years, Ann, had suffered a nervous breakdown the year before, been institutionalised, and the couple had divorced. Kees had had a few unsatisfactory affairs, but now lived alone. He had had to borrow yet more money from his parents to get his third, and best, collection of poems into print. He suffered from insomnia, was permanently on Dexedrine, and his behaviour had become erratic. Despite the absence of a note, and "sightings" of Kees in the Sixties in Sydney Harbour, in a cantina in Mexico, in a jazz club in New Orleans, his biographer James Reidel is in no doubt that he leapt from the bridge that day, having finally given up waiting for an answer to the "Small Prayer" with which his third volume concludes:

> Change, move, dead clock, that this fresh day
> May break with dazzling light to these sick eyes.
> Burn, glare, old sun, so long unseen,
> That time may find its sound again, and cleanse
> What ever it is that a wound remembers
> After the healing ends.

Kees's writings – and his life as presented by Reidel in this well-researched biography, which is the first – offer few explicit clues to the origins of his "wound". He was born and grew up in Beatrice, Nebraska, the only son of a prosperous manufacturer of hardware and farm implements, and a school teaching mother who always encouraged her precocious son's artistic enthusiasms. In his laconic, Hemingwayesque short stories, Kees clinically captured the limited horizons and "subnormal calm" of small-town life in the Mid West; his poetry, on the other hand, tends to translate childhood into something gothic and horrifying, shadowed rather than redeemed by the child's unawareness of the world that awaits. In the sestina "After the Trial", the end-words *sentence, guilt, rooms, parents,* and *forever,* vanquish over and again the child's culpable *innocence*:

> Hearing the judges' well-considered sentence,
> The prisoner saw long plateaus of guilt,
> And thought of all the dismal furnished rooms
> The past assembled, the eyes of parents
> Staring through walls as though forever
> To condemn and wound his innocence.

More unsettling still is the short poem "1926", which ensnares, as with a single perfect throw of a lasso, the urge to indulge in the nostalgic comforts of American pastoral:

> The porchlight coming on again,
> Early November, the dead leaves
> Raked in piles, the wicker swing
> Creaking. Across the lots
> A phonograph is playing *Ja-Da.*
>
> An orange moon. I see the lives
> Of neighbors, mapped and marred
> Like all the wars ahead, and R.
> Insane, B. with his throat cut,
> Fifteen years from now, in Omaha.
>
> I did not know them then.
> My airedale scratches at the door.
> And I am back from seeing Milton Sills
> And Doris Kenyon. Twelve years old.
> The porchlight coming on again.

The poem's skilfully layered form makes past and present, innocence and knowledge, imply each other, as if the only variable were the extent of the poet's awareness of the invincible forces that would leave R. insane and drive B. to suicide and the world to war, and would map and mar, along with so much else, his own life, even transforming, as the poem rounds on itself, what promised to be the recovery of a moment of childhood happiness (Milton Sills and Doris Kenyon were silent movie stars) into yet another ironically framed glimpse into emptiness and guilt.

While "others", Kenneth Rexroth observed of his friend in a letter of January 10th 1956, "have called themselves Apocalyptics, Kees lived in a permanent and hopeless apocalypse." In a poem from around the same period as "1926" called "The Furies" he attempts a physical description of the "retinue of shadows" with whom he lives, and whom "no door excludes": one is "a harelipped and hunchbacked dwarf", another is covered with matted hair, while another's crutches "shriek on the sidewalk / As a fingernail on a slate / Tears open some splintered door / Of childhood." He dreams of their death, but also concedes in the poem's chilling last line that they are what keep him from suicide: until they are at last satisfied, his voracious Eumenides are also the "protectors of [his] life".

Always immaculately groomed and dressed, the dandyish, reserved, ever-courteous Kees never "acted out" in the manner of Lowell or Berryman. Many of his generation of poets, however unstable, landed jobs in American universities' burgeoning Creative Writing departments, which were willing to tolerate their breakdowns and antics for the sake of the prestige they conferred. Kees, who was staggeringly well-read, could probably have wangled a post if he'd wanted one, but his college years in Nebraska left an insuperable distaste for academe: his only surviving novel, *Fall Quarter* (posthumously published in 1990), is set in an English department on a campus somewhere between Chicago and Kansas City, and can perhaps best be characterised as a dust-bowl cross between *Decline and Fall* and *Lucky Jim*, which it antedates by 13 years. After much initial encouragement from Knopf, Kees had the misfortune to have his increasingly wacky narrative of college screwballs and misfits read the day after Pearl Harbour by the firm's chief fiction editor, who concluded an America at war was unlikely to be interested in jazz-age shenanigans in a mid-western university town. Over twenty of his short stories, however, appeared in various prominent magazines in the Thirties and early Forties, and several in the influential *New Directions* and *Best Stories* annuals. They were mainly written during his six-year stint as a librarian in Denver, which came to an end in 1943, the year his first collection of poems, *The Last Man* was published (the title is borrowed from one of Kees's favourite writers, the equally saturnine Thomas Lovell Beddoes), and the year he moved to New York.

The majority of Kees's best-known poems are urban. In his four, or, if one includes the late "That Figure with the Moulting Beard" as I think one should, five Robinson poems, Kees created a desolate, haunting doppelgänger who, though a denizen of the metropolis, is as isolated as his ship-wrecked namesake. Initially defined by his absence and blankness, figured as a cipher dryly fulfilling the routines of city life ("Robinson walking in the Park, admiring the elephant. / Robinson buying the *Tribune*, Robinson buying the *Times*"), he suddenly emerges as the poet's nemesis, fixing him in "Relating to Robinson" with "dilated, terrifying eyes / That stopped my blood", awaiting him in "That Figure with the Moulting Beard" fully armed:

> But of the lead pipe in his pocket and the knife,
> The torch, the poison, and the nails, no doubt at all.

To read them in sequence is to witness comically existential urban angst, of the kind that greatly appealed to *New Yorker* readers, where the first three appeared, curdle into a different kind of city terror, which has the poet "running in sweat / To reach the docks", or being pursued by a man with a moulting beard down 63rd Street.

Kees worked for a while at *Time*, where his boss was Alger Hiss's accuser, Whittaker Chambers, and then at Paramount where he wrote scripts for newsreels; these were mainly about the war, and Kees and his editor would sit through hours of raw footage of, say, the battle for Iwo Jima, working out how much carnage the public could take. He must have felt like he was living out his own earliest poem, "Subtitle", written in 1936, in which a menacing, anonymous voice declares: "We present for you this evening / A movie of death". He managed to avoid action himself by getting a 4F classification; had he been drafted he might well have joined such as Robert Lowell and Kenneth Rexroth as a conscientious objector. His "June 1940", with epigraphs from Wilfred Owen, is a scathing attack on war-hysteria: "An idiot wind is blowing", it concludes; "the conscience dies."

One gets the sense, though, that the cataclysmic events through which Kees lived – the Depression, the war, the atom bomb, the Soviet purges, McCarthyism – did not so much shape his vision, as confirm it. "Subtitle", with which his *Collected Poems* opens, really says it all. There is no human dialogue in the "movie of death" it presents, rather a soundtrack of "squealings of pigs, slow sound of guns," and "No finis to the film unless / The ending is your own." The screen reveals, as his poetry does, a predetermined narrative of suffering – "Your heritage, the logic of your destiny."

During his time living in New York, Kees met, and was liked and had his work admired by, many of the leading writers and critics of the time: Edmund Wilson, Mary McCarthy, Dwight MacDonald, Philip Rahv, Elizabeth Bishop – with whom he visited Ezra Pound in St. Elizabeths – James Agee, Conrad Aiken, Malcolm Cowley, William Carlos Williams, Allen Tate, John Cheever ... But Kees never embedded himself in the literary establishment as he might have done, and, for all his prodigious and diverse activities, radiated something Bartlebyish: "Why don't you want to be a *success*?" Truman Capote rather astutely demanded of him at a party in March of 1948; "I can tell from the way you act you don't want to be a success ... Why, you're a much better poet than that old Robert Lowell."

By this time Kees was more often to be found with New York's painters and art-critics; he saw at once that Abstract Expressionism was the next necessary step beyond Picasso and Matisse, as he declared in a series of combative articles published in *Partisan Review* and *The Nation*. He began painting abstract canvases himself in 1944, and had a number of well-reviewed shows at the Peridot Gallery, where such as Philip Guston exhibited. Kees was prominent enough on the scene to be among the eighteen painters who, in 1950, signed a letter of protest to the Metropolitan Museum complaining about their exclusion from a giant exhibition of contemporary art. The other signatories included many of Abstract Expressionism's big beasts – Jackson Pollock, Robert Motherwell, Mark Rothko, Barnett Newman, Adolph Gottlieb, Hans Hofmann, Clyfford Still. In the huge controversy that followed they became known as the Irascible Eighteen, and, to illustrate a spread on their views and art, were gathered together by *Life* for a group por-trait. Kees, it goes without saying, was not present at this legendary shoot, having moved to San Francisco some weeks earlier.

His only trade-press collection, *The Fall of the Magicians*, was pub-lished in 1947, and dedicated to his wife Ann. For all his sleuthing, Reidel unearths little that throws light on the dynamics of their relationship, though it's clear they shared an aversion to the idea of parenthood. A steady drinker from the start, after moving west Ann developed into a full-blown alcoholic and classic Cold War paranoiac, convinced their phone was being tapped by the F.B.I. (If it had been, Kees would have had nothing to worry about: he despised Stalin, and never for a moment believed in the promises of Communism.) Still, his almost instant decision to divorce her after her breakdown seems both brutal and – if it was an attempt to safeguard his own equilib-rium – misguided. The frenetic, speed-fuelled activities of his last year were clearly strategies for countering the kind of despair articulated, or rather one should say, unleashed, in late poems such as "If This

Room Is Our World":

> If this room is our world, then let
> This world be damned. Open this roof
> For one last monstrous flood
> To sweep away this floor, these chairs,
> This bed that takes me to no sleep.

In the poem's last lines the blood of dead heroes and apocalyptically swollen seas are imagined combining to create a "devouring flood / That I await, that I must perish by."

Kees, it should be said, believed in art, his own and that of others, and was no high-minded Eliotic prophet of doom: his letters and reviews reveal an impassioned and intelligent respect for many aspects of popular culture, in particular Hollywood movies and New Orleans jazz. "Elizabethans", he points out in an early poem directed at Eliot, "had / Sweeneys and Mrs Porters too." He dreamed up several promising film-scripts – one of which concerns the search for a poet who disappears – and sent round demo tapes of his jazz songs to various record companies, but probably knew he was in the end too fastidious to accept the compromises success in such worlds entailed. More baffling for him, and for any who have fallen under the spell of his poetry, was the rejection by a series of publishers of his final volume, austerely entitled *Poems 1947–1954*. It was eventually brought out by what was effectively a vanity press, underwritten by funds Kees had to beg from his, by now, bitterly disappointed parents. Almost every piece in this book seems to me successful, and many leave indelible traces on the mind. As Rexroth pointed out in a review of 1955, they manage to be at once "almost unobtrusive" and "deeply moving – often terrifying". More recently Simon Armitage has compared them to "riddles, curses, inscriptions or charms", and certainly there is something both disorientating and mesmerising in their deadpan exposure of beliefs and illusions. Like Robinson's, their voice comes to us as an echo in the dark – implacable, unerring, addictive:

> I thought I saw the whirlpool opening.
> Kicked all night at a bolted door.
> You must have followed me from Astor Place.
> An empty paper floats down at the last.

Times Literary Supplement, 2004: Review of James Reidel's *Vanished Act: The Life and Art of Weldon Kees* (University of Nebraska Press, 2003) and *The Collected Poems of Weldon Kees*, edited by Donald Justice, with an introduction by David Wojahn (Bison Books, 2003).

Georges Perec

These are the first of Georges Perec's wonderful and extraordinary writings to be translated into English. Perec has been a household name in France since the runaway success of his first and most popular novel, *Les Choses* (1965), which still sells twenty thousand copies a year. *Les Choses* describes, with a sociological exactitude justified in the novel's concluding quotation from Marx, the motivations and disappointments of an utterly ordinary middle-class couple in a consumerist culture. Sylvie and Jérôme are both public opinion analysts, as indeed was Perec at the time: they emerge as a kind of generically rootless Parisian couple of the Sixties, whose experiences and emotions are such that no one of that generation could help but identify with them. The book ties in neatly with, indeed was partly inspired by, Barthes's theories on the language of publicity, which were appearing around the same time; its precision and syntactical ingenuity aspire to Flaubert, a major figure in Perec's pantheon of favourite authors.

Until recently in England Perec was simply known as the crazy writer who first wrote a book without any e's in it, *La Disparition* (1969), and then one with e's but no other vowels, *Les Revenentes* (1971). Both books certainly establish benchmarks in the virtuosity with which they sustain themselves within the most severe of constraints. Perec joined the Oulipo (Ouvroir de Littérature Potentielle – a group dedicated to exploring the relationship between mathematical structures and writing) in 1967 as its youngest member, but rapidly established himself as one of its most inventive. He excelled in composing bilingual poems, palindromes, *exercices d'homosyntaxisme* (in which a text must be written to a formula that predetermines the number of its words and the order of its verbs, substantives and adjectives), and in heterogrammatic poetry. "Ulcérations" is a good instance of the latter, a poem written using only the letters of its title, which also happen to be the 11 most frequently used letters in the alphabet. "Alphabets" is an even more prodigious feat; each of its 16 sections of 11 poems is written using only the ten most frequent letters – that is, a, e, i, l ,n, o, r, s, t, u – plus one variable letter. In the first 11 poems the variable letter is b, the next c, and so on through to z. In other poems the vowels used are not allowed to deviate from the strict order of a, e, i, o, u – *A demi-mot un art chétif nous parle*, and so on. In an interview with *L'Arc* magazine Perec revealed he treated such exercises as a wordsmith's equivalent of a pianist's scales, and found in their intense difficulty nothing compared to the horrors attendant upon any attempt to write poetry freely.

Practically all of Perec's texts are constructed, with varying degrees of extremity, in this kind of pre-programmed way. *Un Homme qui dort* is written entirely in the second person. *Je me souviens* is fabricated out of sentences all beginning Je me souviens, followed by some randomly chosen remembrance. *La Boutique obscure* relates 124 dreams Perec had over a period of years. (In a particularly harrowing one he dreams he finds first one e, and then two, then 20, then 1000 in the text of *La Disparition*.) *Life: A User's Manual* describes the contents and inhabitants of a Parisian apartment block at 11 Rue Simon-Crubellier. The block is ten storeys high and ten units wide, and the order in which the apartments are treated is determined by the route a knight at chess would have to take to cover all the squares on a ten x ten chessboard without alighting on the same square twice. Perec decided on the 42 constituent elements of each chapter, including references in each to three of the 30 authors systematically alluded to throughout the book, via a particularly complex mathematical algorithm. It's in *Life* in particular that Perec most exhaustively exploits the eccentric compositional techniques invented by another of his great heroes, Raymond Roussel.

Perec's obsession with autistic, self-propagating literary forms of this kind, which implicitly reject all preconceptions of depth and significance, is wholly compatible with Postmodernism's ideal of literature as a self-reflexive surface, a field of clues that reveal nothing beyond their internal chance coherences. *La Boutique obscure* ends with a quote from his close friend Harry Mathews's *Tlooth:* "for the labyrinth leads nowhere but out of itself." *La Disparition* more bleakly talks of an enigma that will destroy us whether it is solved or not. But Perec's own adherence to this idea of literature as a self-sustaining puzzle, a teasing game between writer and reader, developed also, as he most clearly explains in the autobiographical chapters of *W,* in response to the circumstances of his own childhood.

Both sides of Perec's family were Polish Jews who emigrated to Paris during the Twenties. His father's name was Icek Judko Peretz; but in France he became known as André Perec. (Peretz in Hungarian means "pretzel"; in a typical cross-reference Gaspard Winckler, in the other half of *W's* narrative, reveals that he never eats pretzels.) While his father's family was originally quite prosperous, his mother grew up in the Warsaw ghetto; from there they moved to Paris during her teens. Perec's parents married in 1934, and he was their only child, born in 1936. His father enlisted when war broke out and was killed by a stray shell the day after the armistice, bleeding to death in a church converted into a hospital. Perec was evacuated by the Red Cross as a war orphan in 1942. His mother remained in Paris. She made one failed attempt to reach the free zone. In January of 1943 she was picked up in a raid with her sister and deported to Auschwitz. Perec comments: "She saw the country of her birth again before she died. She died without understanding."

Perec's evocation of his childhood in *W* – through chance memories, closely argued hypotheses and wishful speculation – is achieved with exhilarating clarity. The few surviving photographs are minutely analysed for clues, remembered details sifted for evidence, contradictions carefully weighed. Perec, deprived not only of his parents but of all traces of his Jewish inheritance, confronts the bewildering absences of his childhood identity. (Derrida wrote: *Juif serait l'autre nom de cette impossibilité d'être soi.*) In this context writing itself, any kind of writing, becomes the psyche's ultimate defence against nothingness, though Perec is as clear-sighted as Beckett about its final ineffectiveness:

> I do not know whether I have anything to say, I know that I am saying nothing; I do not know if what I might have to say is unsaid because it is unsayable (the unsayable is not buried inside writing, it is what prompted it in the first place); I know that what I say is blank, is neutral, is a sign, once and for all, of a once-and-for-all annihilation ... I write because we lived together, because I was one amongst them, a shadow amongst their shadows, a body close to their bodies. I write because they left in me their indelible mark, whose trace is writing. Their memory is dead in writing; writing is the memory of their death and the assertion of my life.

The autobiographical chapters alternate with a fictional story Perec originally invented when he was 13, centred on "W", an island off the coast of Tierra del Fuego which is wholly in thrall to the Olympic ideal. In Part One Gaspard Winckler – a name Perec used for himself in his first unpublished autobiographical novel, and which turns up in *Life* as well – receives a mysterious summons from a certain Otto Apfelstahl, MD. They meet in a hotel. Gaspard Winckler is not Gaspard Winckler's real name, it turns out, but one accorded him with appropriate papers by a relief agency when he deserted from the Army. The original Gaspard Winckler is the deaf and dumb son of a fabulously wealthy opera singer. In an attempt to cure him she takes him on a round-the-world cruise on a yacht. Their ship is sunk in a hurricane off Tierra del Fuego. Only Gaspard Winckler's body is never found ...

The story breaks off abruptly here, and in Part Two an omniscient narrator tells us about the sports-dominated life of the inhabitants of W. The four Olympic villages on W compete against each other almost continually, under a system of penalties as well as rewards: while the day's winners are toasted and feasted, the losers are deprived of food, and forfeits often imposed on them. A losing athlete may have to run around the track with his shoes on back to front, or between rows of officials who beat him with sticks and cudgels. As in Borges's lottery in Babylon, the ultimate penalty is death. The athletes' diets are deliberately deficient in sugar and vitamins. In addition, the rules of the sports are often changed arbitrarily. It may be decided that the athlete who crosses the line last is the winner, or an official may suddenly shout "Stop", and the athlete who keeps still the longest is then declared the victor. The athletes' names also depend on their performance on track or field, as the winners and runners-up of each event inherit the names of the original winners of the event, for as long as they hold their title. The current holder of the 100 metres Olympiad title would be simply known as the Jones, of the 400 the Gustafson, of the high jump the Andrews, and so on: names are added or lost as the athlete wins or loses. The most horrendous event on W takes place at the Atlantiads. Women are severely culled on W, only one in five being allowed to survive. On reaching child-bearing age, they are taken in batches of around fifty to the stadium, their clothes are removed, and they are released onto the track, where they start to run. When they are half a lap ahead, 176 of W's best athletes, also naked except for keenly spiked running shoes, are released in pursuit of them; the women are of course soon caught and raped by the fifty fittest and most cunning sportsmen.

The double narratives of *W* surreptitiously allude to each other; their juxtaposition is at once startling and seemingly inevitable. In their "fragile overlapping", to use Perec's words, they complete each other. As the Olympic community becomes more and more like a concentration camp, the gaps and links between Perec's imagination and his experience become ever clearer. In a further twist to the tale, Perec concludes the book by remarking that several of the islands off Tierra del Fuego are, at the time of writing (1974), deportation camps run by Pinochet's fascists. The fiction, which must nave originated in the young Perec's imagination as a form of consoling escapism, not only reflects political reality but also anticipates it.

W's split between the opposite worlds of carefully documented reality and total imaginative freedom is typical of much of Perec's writing. He took the Nouveau Roman's concern with everyday living to new heights, martyring himself with minute enumerations of the *infra-ordinaire,* as he called it. His "Attempt at an Inventory of the Liquid and Solid Foodstuffs Ingurgitated by Me in the Course of the Year Nineteen Hundred and Seventy-Four", for instance, is exactly what its title suggests, a record of everything he ate in a particular calendar year. Perec had a prodigious memory – indeed, like Joyce, he saw literary composition as largely a question of memory and problem-solving, and in the epilogue to *La Disparition* he rubbishes the idea of inspiration. Perec liked the idea of cataloguing in neutral, objective terms the physical facts of external reality. For a half-achieved project called *Les Lieux* he chose 12 places of personal significance to him in Paris and set out to visit and describe each one once a year in a different month over 12 years. These careful documentary pieces would be played off against 12 evocations of each place generated solely by memory. At other times Perec finds a form to blend the two opposites. *Un Cabinet d'amateur* describes a series of paintings in meticulously precise detail, as if for an auction catalogue. It's with a shock that you learn at the end of the book that none of the pictures actually exist. Absolute fixity and absolute freedom are fused in the illusion.

In a short introduction to *W* Perec explains how the book's meaning begins in the hiatus between the Gaspard Winckler story and the depiction of W. "In this break, in this split suspending the story on an unidentifiable expectation, can be found the point of departure for the whole of this book: the *points de suspension* on which the broken

191

threads of childhood and the web of writing are caught." The image of suspension is important in the book. Twice – once when saying goodbye to his mother for the last time at the train station, and once during his stay at Villard-de-Lans – Perec remembers himself clearly with an arm in a sling. In fact, he later works out, neither memory is true: these fractures occurred only within his imagination. They must have served psychically both to give an external expression to his inner suffering, and to suggest that that suffering, after a period of suspension, would eventually heal. Most of Perec's fiction hangs in a similar void, deliberately indifferent to the sensible aims with which we try to justify our lives. *Un Homme qui dort* is about a student who one day gives up, for no particular reason. He lies on his bed, staring at the cracks in the ceiling, refuses to answer the door, and wanders haphazardly around Paris at night. The story alludes frequently to Sartre, but is more an undoing of Existentialism – as *Les Choses* also was of the Nouveau Roman – than an addition to its literature. Perec's dead-pan style leads absolutely nowhere. The story is picked up again in Chapter 52 of *Life*. Here the student is called Grégoire Simpson, after the insect man in Kafka. In the end he simply disappears, but the chapter concludes movingly with an incident from Simpson's childhood in which the young boy dresses up in traditional costume to join in a mid-Lent procession, "as proud as Punch and as grave as a judge". Later he rushes about excitedly, pausing only "to stuff himself with juniper-roast ham and to slake his thirst with great gulps of Ripaille, that white wine as light as glacier water, as dry as gunflint". The more flexible medium of *Life* can both include and transcend Perec's earlier style.

The emptiness of *Un Homme qui dort* becomes positive emasculation in *La Disparition*. The absent e broods like a vengeful god over the text. As e is the fifth letter of the alphabet, the fifth of the novel's 26 chapters is missing, as is the second of its six books, e being the second of the vowels. The fifth of the 26 boxes containing Anton Voyl's manuscripts is also missing; Anton Voyl's name itself seems heartlessly truncated. Indeed, contact with e in the book means death. In a famous scene a bartender drops dead when asked to make a Porto-flip because it requires *oeufs,* and they have an e in them. The absence of by far the most popular letter in the French alphabet is a self-imposed handicap similar to the young Perec's imaginary slings, and indicative of a similarly fundamental lack. *La Disparition* adopts the plot of the detective novel with a few epistemological knobs on; the characters who solve its enigma automatically die, or rather disappear. A finished crossword or jigsaw puzzle might be seen as an analogue to these fictional vanishings. More sinisterly, they suggest the limitless powers of modern techniques of annihilation, capable of extinguishing all traces of a disappeared person.

Perec's games parody our instinctive willingness to believe in language's absolute authority, and release language into a neutral space where words fulfil their own random, intrinsic connections. One of the most appealing features of Perec's writing is its lack of self-righteousness, its whole-hearted enjoyment of its own fictive procedures. *Life: A User's Manual* is very much the consummation of his achievement, bringing together stories and characters from much of his previous writing, and continually alluding to those writers who define the fictional space in which Perec's texts also aspire to move. In a short piece in *L'Arc* on his borrowings from Flaubert, he explained that he saw these references as being like indications of land-measuring or the nodes of a network, establishing the contexts and parameters of his own literary sensibility: but they can be seen as even more than this. In the disembodied world of his childhood, as described in *W,* he finds in reading almost a substitute for his lost parents:

> I reread the books I love and I love the books I reread, and each time it is the same enjoyment, whether I reread twenty pages, three chapters, or the whole book: an enjoyment of complicity, of collusion, or more especially, and in addition, of having in the end found kin again.

Intertextuality is built into the very structure of *Life,* but in highly un-Modernist fashion. The references argue for no unified cultural tradition, and noticing them adds nothing to the text's meaning: they simply furnish Perec with elements of material requiring to be worked into each chapter.

Life: A User's Manual follows the poetry of Roussel in approaching its location – the apartment block – from the vantage-point of an instant frozen in time. Perec first got the idea for the book from a painting of Saul Steinberg's called *The Art of Living,* which shows an apartment block with part of its facade removed, revealing the interiors of twenty or so rooms. (Within the novel the painter Valène is embarked on, but will never complete, a similar project.) Each of the book's 99 chapters describes a room, or section of the stairs, or lift, itemising its contents, and filling in the often wildly improbable backgrounds of its present and previous inhabitants. The most important of the book's multifarious narratives concerns Percival Bartlebooth, an eccentric Harrow-educated millionaire.

Strung between the extreme asceticism of Melville's Bartleby and the prodigal generosity of Valery Larbaud's A. O. Barnabooth, Bartlebooth organises his life into a single massively self-contradictory project. Though absolutely talentless, he spends ten years having himself taught to paint water-colours by Valène. The next twenty years, accompanied by his servant Smautf, he spends tracking around the globe, indifferent to political upheavals, painting water-colours in 500 arbitrarily chosen ports. These are dispatched every fortnight or so back to 11 Rue Simon-Crubellier, where Gaspard Winckler glues them onto plywood and then cuts them into ever more difficult jigsaw puzzles of 750 pieces each. On his return Bartlebooth completes the puzzles in chronological order. When solved, the joins of the puzzles are recomposed by a special machine, separated from their backing and glaze, and returned to the spot where they were originally painted, to be dipped in the sea until the colours dissolve and the paper is its original white again. Bartlebooth's self-cancelling scheme is a typically Perecian one: "his aim was for nothing, nothing at all, to subsist, for nothing but the void to emerge from it, for only the immaculate whiteness of a blank to remain, only the gratuitous perfection of a project entirely devoid of utility."

The image of the puzzle dominates *Life: A User's Manual.* Each of every chapter's 42 constitutive elements are fitted together like parts of a puzzle, and the chapters themselves fit together like pieces in the overall jigsaw of the book. The fictions with which Perec links his given elements reveal him at his most inventive and playful. The book teems with startling characters and fictions, and seems as endless in its narrative resources as even the greatest of Victorian three-deckers. There is the ethnologist Marcel Appenzzell who pursues for five years and 11 months an unknown tribe of Sumatrans without getting them once to acknowledge his existence; there is the domino-playing hamster Polonius; there is Cinoc, the word-killer, who is hired by Larousse to diagnose obsolete words and eliminate them from the dictionary but who, on leaving his job, sets about compiling a dictionary of all the forgotten words that still appeal to him; there is James Sherwood, collector of *unica* (one-of-a-kinds), who pays a million dollars in counterfeit currency for the vase in which Joseph of Arimathaea supposedly gathered the blood of the dying Jesus; there is Monsieur Jérôme who left Paris in the diplomatic service as cultural attaché in Lahore and returned home penniless years later, but will never talk of his Eastern experiences; there is Hutting the artist, famous for his "haze period", which places him on a par with his famous quasi-namesake Huffing, the New York pioneer of *Arte brutta* who first appears in Harry Mathews's *The Conversions.*

Perec, like Bartlebooth, was haunted by ideas of incompletion, despite his manic productiveness. In an interview a couple of years before his death of lung cancer in 1982, he pictured his achievement as *l'image d'un livre inachevé, d'une "œuvre" inachevée à l'intérieur d'une littérature jamais achevée.* Though each of his books is an element in an overall ensemble, the only thing about that ensemble he can ever know is that he will never finish it. Bartlebooth's project is similarly doomed. Time is frozen in *Life: A User's Manual* at a little before eight on the evening of the 23rd of June, 1975. Bartlebooth has just died in the middle of his 439th puzzle. His efforts to complete his arbitrarily self-imposed scheme have been complicated both by the fiendish cunning of Gaspard Winckler and by the loss of his eyesight. The 439th puzzle is almost finished except for a space in the perfect shape of an X: but the piece the dead Bartlebooth holds is shaped like a W.

In *W* also the young Perec sees in an X the story of his childhood: by extending its branches you get a swastika, by unjoining and rotating it you get an SS sign. Two X's joined horizontally can be easily made into the Star of David. Bartlebooth's defeat at the hands of the already dead Winckler is both poignant and uplifting; all the systems of life, from Nazism to the Olympics, must leak at the seams, and only through the encroachments of chaos does existence transcend the absolutes it craves and become livable.

London Review of Books, 1989: Review of Georges Perec's *W or the Memory of Childhood*, translated by David Bellos (Collins Harvill, 1988) and *Life: A User's Manual*, translated by David Bellos (Collins Harvill, 1988).

Mont d'Espoir or *Mount Despair:*
Early Bishop, Early Ashbery, and the French

I

"I'd time enough to play with names", observes Bishop's Crusoe of his years on his "still / un-rediscovered, un-renamable" island. Back in England – "another island, / that doesn't seem like one, but who decides?" – the gap between names and things, *d'espoir* and despair, uses and meanings, island and mainland, dwindles to nothing:

> I'm old.
> I'm bored too, drinking my real tea,
> surrounded by uninteresting lumber.
> The knife there on the shelf –
> it reeked of meaning, like a crucifix.
> It lived. How many years did I
> beg it, implore it, not to break?
> I knew each nick and scratch by heart,
> the bluish blade, the broken tip,
> the lines of wood-grain on the handle ...
> Now it won't look at me at all.
> The living soul has dribbled away.
> My eyes rest on it and pass on.

The "island-dweller" of John Ashbery's "The Skaters" suffers a similar awakening from his boy's own fantasy of life as a cast-away. Like Crusoe he climbs to the island's highest point "to scan the distances", watches waterspouts that are "beautiful, but terrifying" – an echo, surely, of Bishop's "awful but cheerful" – and forgets much of what he thought he knew. Fortunately he has a weathered child's alphabet on which some of the island's flora and fauna are pictured – "the albatross, for instance – that's a name I never would have remembered". While Bishop's Crusoe blanks at the word "solitude" in Wordsworth's "I Wandered Lonely As a Cloud" –

> "They flash upon that inward eye,
> which is the bliss ..." The bliss of what?
> One of the first things that I did
> when I got back was look it up

– Ashbery's marooned exile can only remember through the aid of his primer the most famous Romantic property of all, Coleridge's "sweet bird", Baudelaire's "prince des nuées". A storm erupts, and in the middle of a drenching rain the fantasy is reluctantly abandoned:

> Kerchoo ...
>
>   ... Good-bye, Storm-fiend. Good-
> bye vultures.

> In reality of course the middle-class apartment I live in is
>   nothing like a desert island.
> Cozy and warm it is, with a good library and record collect-
>   ion.

Dreams of escape occur throughout Ashbery's and Bishop's work. "I write mainly for escapist purposes", Ashbery commented in an interview of 1977; "I am aware of the pejorative associations of the word 'escapist', but I insist that we need all the escapism we can get and even that isn't going to be enough." The attempt fails most plangently at the end of "Self-Portrait in a Convex Mirror", as the poet realizes the limitations of his – and Parmigianino's – art:

> This could have been our paradise: exotic
> Refuge within an exhausted world, but that wasn't
> In the cards, because it couldn't have been
> The point.

Bishop's quests for an "exotic / Refuge within an exhausted world" tend to be embodied in less aesthetic terms, but dramatize essentially the same understanding. In "The End of March" she describes a walk taken with two friends along the beach at Duxbury:

> Everything was withdrawn as far as possible,
> indrawn: the tide far out, the ocean shrunken,
> seabirds in ones or twos.

The poet hopes to reach her "proto-dream-house", a tiny primitive shack perched out on the dunes:

> I'd like to retire there and do *nothing*,
> or nothing much, forever, in two bare rooms:
> look through binoculars, read long books,
> old, long, long books, and write down useless notes ...

This "waking dream", like Ashbery's, inevitably collapses, proves "perfect! But – impossible." The quixotic lion sun, the suddenly multi-coloured stones, reconnect the poet to the processes of nature, just as Ashbery is left to sift the April sunlight for clues, to readjust to the "cold, syrupy flow" of time's "pageant".

Ashbery's and Bishop's methods of relating to this "pageant" converge at many points. Both take it for granted that there is no ultimate metaphysical centre from which life's patterns become clear, "No Way of Knowing", as an Ashbery title puts it, only the "waking up / In the middle of a dream with one's mouth full / Of unknown words". Bishop's Crusoe soliloquizes in a similar vein:

> Was there
> a moment when I actually chose this?
> I don't remember, but there could have been.

Accordingly their figurations can never transcend the moment of their articulation, never aim to attain "the form, the pattern" of Eliot's Chinese jar that "moves perpetually in its stillness". Ashbery's and Bishop's properties illuminate only for the duration of their usefulness: "our knowledge", Bishop insists at the end of "At the Fishhouses", is "historical, flowing and flown". Returned to England Crusoe's flute and knife and shoes are so much "uninteresting lumber", while by the conclusion of "Self-Portrait in a Convex Mirror" Parmigianino's outsized hand has been wholly drained of purpose and memory – it "holds no chalk / And each part of the whole falls off / And cannot know it knew". From the outset of their careers Bishop and Ashbery present experience as continually inflected, even determined by, the formulations of genre; they offer us not the world but a map, or rather the world as an endless series of maps. "How", Ashbery wonders in his discussion of the opening poem of *North & South* in his 1977 essay "Second Presentation of Elizabeth Bishop", "could the map-makers' colors be more delicate than the historians'? ... Precisely because they are what is given to us to see, on a given day in a given book taken down from the bookshelf for some practical motive."

The poem "The Map" is itself a palimpsest of different kinds of maps: Bishop's speculations overlay seemingly neutral topography with erotic, domestic, and metamorphic possibilities, lovely bays one might stroke, women feeling for the smoothness of yard-goods, Norway as a scampering hare. Bishop's absorption in the map mirrors her ideal of aesthetic experience best outlined in a letter of 1964 to Anne Stevenson: "What one seems to want in art, in experiencing it, is the same thing that is necessary for its creation, a self-forgetful, perfectly useless concentration." The distance between cartography's severe codes of denotation and the poet's yearning for contact and self-expression vividly illustrates the space in which Bishop's – and Ashbery's – self-reflexive poetries both operate. "Only out of such 'perfectly useless concentration'", he suggests in his essay, "can emerge the one thing that is useful for us: our coming to know ourselves as the necessarily inaccurate transcribers of the life that is always on the point of coming into being".

Ashbery's inaccuracies ("In New York we have winter in August") are obvious, excessive, and legion, predicated on the theory that "the man who made the same mistake twice is exonerated", that two wrongs make, if not a right, at least an increased awareness of what any given discourse excludes or represses to sustain its illusions of coherence. This double vision is most literally embodied in the twin-columned "Litany", in which, as he once "half-jokingly" proposed, part of his "object was to direct the reader's attention to the white space between the columns". Bishop's "famous eye", on the other hand, would seem to leave her poetry less or even no margin for error. She fretted endlessly over minor literary transgressions – for instance her compounding of the February and March issues of the *National Geographic* in "In the Waiting Room" – and was appalled by Lowell's cavalier attitude to his originals in *Imitations* (1962). "Please forgive my sounding like French 2A", she apologizes in a letter to him, before launching into an extensive catalogue of what "*look* like mistakes".

Nevertheless, Bishop's poetry also consistently charts her longing to evade the premises and strictures of her seeing. In a 1948 article on Marianne Moore Bishop suggests that "one should constantly bear in mind the secondary and frequently sombre meaning of the title of her first book: *Observations*". In both Moore and Bishop one often feels the active gaze may be at any moment construed as its opposite, the poet become like poor Polonius at supper – "Not where he eats, but where he is eaten". This occurs most dramatically at the end of "Quai

201

d'Orléans", a poem written in the aftermath of a car accident in which Bishop and Margaret Miller, to whom the poem is dedicated, were involved. Miller was badly hurt, and part of her right arm had later to be amputated. In the poem the memory of what is seen is presented as endlessly imposing on its protagonists:

> "If what we see could forget us half as easily,"
> I want to tell you,
> "as it does itself – but for life we'll not be rid
> of the leaves' fossils."

In a mid-Thirties journal, entitled "Recorded Observations", Bishop worries about poetry's ability both to transform and control what it observes: "It's a question of using the poet's proper materials ... to express something not of them – something, I suppose, *spiritual*. But it proceeds from the material, the material eaten out with acid, pulled down from underneath, made to perform and always kept in order, in its place."

The anxiety voiced in that repetition, "in order, in its place", permeates Bishop's work. Her poetry is continually attempting to escape the principle of order and place on which it knows it depends, just as the fantasies of "The Map" depend upon topography's refusal to display "favourites". The forces of instability and disorientation – the urge "to see the sun the other way around" – express themselves in many ways in Bishop, through travel, word-play, whimsy, dreamscapes. In a number of poems in her first book, *North & South* (1946), they seem associated with Frenchness, which, like the Man-Moth's third rail, can be seen as intimating an enticing but potentially fatal realm that almost simultaneously promises and denies escape from the polarities of the book's title.

II

The Man-Moth is himself a highly Laforguian creation, a moon-haunted clown derived from the Pierrots of *L'Imitation de Notre Dame La Lune* (1886). To the Modernists Eliot and Pound, Laforgue was a sort of late-flowering metaphysical whom Eliot adjudged "nearer to the 'school of Donne' than any modern English poet", while Pound felt his work perfectly illustrated his ideal of "logopoeia" – "the dance of the intellect among words". Bishop, though, responds to less sovereign aspects of Laforgue's poetics, "the quickness, the surprise, the new sub-acid flavor". In "Rhapsody on a Windy Night" Eliot develops his Laforgue-inspired lunar cityscape into a vision of disgusted, helpless alienation. The speaker's nocturnal rambles serve to harden him for the battles ahead, almost to exorcize his individuality. The Man-Moth's antics and compulsions escape any such narrative. His frustrations are eternal and comic; after each failure he "falls back scared but quite unhurt".

As she makes clear in her 1956 review of William Jay Smith's translation of Laforgue's poems, it was Laforgue's mercurial shifts of tone, his ability to represent the mind's vacillations, that attracted her. While Pound and Eliot figured Laforgue as a master rhetorician – "a deliverer of nations ... a father of light" as Pound grandiloquently described him in 1918 – Bishop valued his undermining of rhetorics and the closeness of his poetry to the speaking voice. She stresses the sceptical wryness of his *ars poetica*, and approvingly quotes his remark that "I find it stupid to speak in a booming voice and adopt a platform manner." The Man-Moth is equally unwilling to assume a public role:

> Then from the lids
> one tear, his only possession, like the bee's sting slips.
> Slyly he palms it, and if you're not paying attention
> he'll swallow it. However, if you watch, he'll hand it over,

cool as from underground springs, and pure enough to drink.

The lines might be read as an implicit critique of the "platform manner" that had come to dominate the poetry of both of Laforgue's Modernist champions. Certainly his most complete opposite in Bishop's œuvre would be the "tragic ... talkative ... honored ... old, brave ... cruel ... busy ... tedious ... wretched man / that lives in the house of Bedlam".

If Pound and Eliot were drawn to nineteenth-century French poetry as a means of disciplining the "slushiness and swishiness of the post-Swinburnian British line", in Pound's words, Bishop and Ashbery looked to France as a means of escaping the New Critical orthodoxies instituted by Modernism. In his 1962 article "Reverdy en Amérique" (written in French), Ashbery laments the desiccated nature of most contemporary American poetry which he depicts as feebly languishing in Eliot's shadow:

> Les poètes qui lui ont succédé ont affaibli ou dénaturé le contenu intellectuel de la poésie d'Eliot, mais ils en ont retenu certains aspects superficiels: le langage sec et digne, ou le ton de J. Alfred Prufrock – celui d'un bourgeois sensible dépassé par les événements ... Pour les Français, l'expression <<poésie de l'imagination>> peut sembler redondante. En Amérique, au contraire, c'est un concept entièrement neuf. La poésie de l'imagination, bien entendu. Voilà si longtemps que cette *autre* sorte de poésie nous ennuie et nous désole!

Reverdy appeals to Ashbery for much the same reasons Laforgue appealed to Bishop, for his fluidity, his freedom from any over-determining system or purpose, his ability to surprise:

> J'ai toujours regretté que les rythmes sombres d'Eliot et

de Yeats, par exemple, soient au service d'une significa-
tion précise, et que leurs élans poétiques – différents, en
cela, du faucon de Yeats – soient comme un cerf-volant
dont le fil est fermement tenu par le poète rivé à sa terre.
Ce qui nous enchante chez Reverdy, c'est la pureté de sa
poésie, faite de changements, fluctuations, archétypes
d'événements, situatations idéales, mouvements de formes
transparentes, aussi naturels et variés que les vagues de la
mer. C'est l'étoffe même de la poésie, sa matière première
pure de toute arrière-pensée métaphysique.

Seven years later, in his 1969 review of Bishop's *The Complete Poems*,
Ashbery deliberately separates her from the dry world of the poetry
establishment to which she nominally belongs – "and the establishment ought to give thanks; she is proof that it can't be all bad" – by
highlighting the "French" aspects of her work: "Her concerns at first
glance seem special. The life of dreams, always regarded with suspi-
cion as too "French" in American poetry; the little mysteries of falling
asleep and the oddness of waking up in the morning..." He compares
her prose poems "Rainy Season; Sub-Tropics" to Jules Renard's *His-
toires Naturelles* – though in fact the prose poems of Francis Ponge
collected in *Le Parti Pris des Choses* (1942) are a more likely source
– and "The Burglar of Babylon" to Jean-Luc Godard's *Pierrot le Fou*.
   "The Man-Moth" was published in the spring of 1936, by which
time Bishop had lived half a year in France. She set sail at the beginning of August 1935, and passed the rest of the summer in Brittany
working mainly on translations of Rimbaud, now, alas, lost. She
spent the winter in Paris, a period she recalled twenty-five years later
in her letter to Lowell concerning his translations of Rimbaud and
Baudelaire: "I lived in Paris one whole winter long ago, and most
of another one [that of 1937] – and that 'endless wall of fog' [from
Baudelaire's "Le Cygne"] haunts me still." There is certainly something foggy, or at least dreamily opaque, about the poems in *North*

& South which most obviously signal their "Frenchness" – "Paris, 7 A.M.", "Quai d'Orléans", and "Sleeping on the Ceiling". These were all composed before Bishop moved to Key West in 1938, and reflect her wide reading in French poetry, particularly that of the Surrealists who dominated French intellectual life in the Thirties. In later years Bishop looked nostalgically back to this period as to a golden pre-lapsarian age: "At the time I was writing the poems I like best," she wrote to Anne Stevenson in 1964, "I was very ignorant politically and I sometimes wish I could recover the dreamy state of consciousness I lived in then – it was better for my work, and I do the world no more good now by knowing a great deal more." Other poems from the Thirties such as "The Weed", "The Unbeliever", "The Monument", "A Miracle for Breakfast", "From the Country to the City", "Sleeping Standing Up", "Love Lies Sleeping", equally reveal Bishop's ability to appropriate surrealist techniques for her own ends. "This exteriorizing of the interior, and the aliveness all through," wrote Marianne Moore to Bishop in September of 1936 on receiving "The Weed" and "Paris, 7 A.M.", "it seems to me are the essential sincerity that unsatisfactory surrealism struggles toward."

But these dreamy poems are far from innocent in their implications. The yearning for a surrealist miracle is continually played off against more quotidian concerns, the need for breakfast. The speaker's rapturous vision in stanzas five and six of Bishop's sestina may be seen as more of a parody than an endorsement of Surrealism's organicist ideal. The envoy effectively returns the miracle to the speculative world of aesthetics, far from the Depression era souplines of the poem's political context:

> We licked up the crumb and swallowed the coffee.
> A window across the river caught the sun
> as if the miracle were working, on the wrong balcony.

The wholly liberated dreamer of "Love Lies Sleeping" also ends up on

"the wrong balcony": unable to "dine" on others' hearts, he pays for
his revelation with his life:

> the image of
>
>> the city grows down into his open eyes
>> inverted and distorted. No. I mean
>>> distorted and revealed,
>>> if he sees it at all.

For such as Breton and Aragon urban existence offered a potentially
endless series of chance discoveries capable of gratifying the surrealist
urge for the marvellous. "Love Lies Sleeping", in contrast, balances
the dreamy, unlikely aspects of its immense city, imaged as "slowly
grown / in skies of water-glass" like a "little 'chemical' garden in a jar",
with its casually destructive powers that invert Nature's paradigm of
fertility:

> Then, in the West, "Boom!" and a cloud of smoke.
> "Boom!" and the exploding ball
> of blossom blooms again.

The poem's city is a place of "alarms", "stony walls and halls and iron
beds", "Danger", and "Death". In the short poem "From the Country to the City" Bishop constructs an elaborate conceit in which the
city is figured as the head tyrannically imposing its seductive anxieties
on the country's "long black length of body": "'Subside,' it begs and
begs". Bishop was happy, like the Surrealists, to use "dream-material"
as a source for poems, yet in "Sleeping Standing Up" charts the failure
of dreams – pictured as blundering "armored cars" – to yield up the
redemptive truths they promise. "How stupidly we steered", it ends,
"until the night was past / and never found out where the cottage
was."

From a different angle, however, that perhaps of the sleeper "whose head has fallen over the edge of his bed", or of the wistful protagonist of "Sleeping on the Ceiling", such poems might also be read as embodying a yearning to confound the rationalist assumptions implied by their strict and elaborate forms. They are as much an attack on the New Critical ideals of controlled wit and formal discipline as they are on the Surrealists' belief in "la liberté totale". "It is so peaceful on the ceiling. / It is the Place de la Concorde", feelingly sighs the speaker of "Sleeping on the Ceiling". Like Wallace Stevens, Bishop longs "to make the visible a little hard // To see", and thus escape being "too exactly [her]self". One technique for this borrowed from Stevens is the use of French titles as a means of complicating the reader's responses to the poem that follows; the titles of "Chemin de Fer", "Cirque d'Hiver", and "Trouvée", all impose a dandyish insouciance on the bleak narratives these poems develop. In "Paris, 7 A.M.", on the other hand, the specifying of time and place serves to counteract the poem's blurring of the distinctions between imagination and reality.

"Paris, 7 A.M.", like "Love Lies Sleeping", explores the uncertain hinterland between dreams and waking, and the odd perspectives this in-between state permits on the life of the city. The poem collapses time and space ("Time is an Etoile"), but through a method exactly opposite that of the Surrealists' liberation of the unconscious. Bishop's speaker is trapped in a constrictingly over-determined series of patterns – "circles surrounding stars, overlapping circles" – that reduces her apprehension of the weather itself to "a dead wing with damp feathers". As in "Quai d'Orléans", the poet is paralysed by the meanings relentlessly imposed by her "famous eye":

> It is like introspection
> to stare inside, or retrospection,
> a star inside a rectangle, a recollection.

The insistent rhymes mimic the poet's compulsive generation of shapes, the addiction to order that diminishes all otherness to a geometrical version of the self and its history. The city itself comes to seem an embodiment of this impulse; "childish snow-forts, built in flashier winters", are imagined hardening into houses as claustrophobic and imprisoning as the architecture of Paris:

> their walls, their shape, could not dissolve and die,
> only be overlapping in a strong chain, turned to stone,
> and grayed and yellowed now like these.

The poem finds no way of undoing the metonymic substitutions which translate the desire to create into its confining opposite – the star of the imagination into the schematic Etoile of the city, the sky into a dead pigeon. The opportunity to evade the limitations of time and space, seemingly promised by the apartment's divergent clocks, whose "ignorant faces" punningly figure the city's foreignness, in fact leads to the "endless intersecting circles" of a dizzying solipsism. Miraculously improbable as a permanent snow- or sand-fort, yet exhausting in its incessant formal repetitions, the poem's Paris oscillates between disorientating mirage and all-too-solid mausoleum, between dissolving south and freezing north, apparently stranded, despite the title's assurances, beyond the reach and records of time and place:

> When did the star dissolve, or was it captured
> by the sequence of squares and squares, and circles, circles?
> Can the clocks say; is it there below,
> about to tumble in snow?

III

John Ashbery "read, reread, studied and absorbed" *North & South* when it was published in 1946, and had the experience of "being drawn into a world that seemed as inevitable as 'the' world and as charged with the possibilities of pleasure as the contiguous, overlapping world of poetry". Like Bishop, Ashbery began writing at a time when rigid New Critical principles held sway. For Ashbery's fellow New York school poets Kenneth Koch and Frank O'Hara, certain French poets seemed to signal – and in their poems to represent – a possible means of escaping or defying the literary and social conventions they found so constricting. "I dress in oil cloth and read music / by Guillaume Apollinaire's clay candelabra", O'Hara declares with a self-conscious flourish in the early "Memorial Day 1950". The names of French poets appear regularly in O'Hara's poetry, nearly always as a talismanic source of comfort or imaginative freedom, as in the conclusion to "A Step Away from Them":

> My heart is in my
> pocket, it is Poems by Pierre Reverdy

In "Fresh Air" (1955) Kenneth Koch asks "who is still of our time?" and responds to his own question: "Mallarmé, Valéry, Apollinaire, Éluard, Reverdy, French poets are still of our time."

Ashbery, by contrast, has frequently denied the importance of French poetry to his development. Asked in a 1973 interview about the effects on his work of his expatriate years in France he insisted:

I don't think that my poetry has been much influenced by French poetry, including French surrealist poetry, as people have often said – probably because I have lived in France. I think my poetry was surrealist, in a way, from the beginning. But I don't think there is any direct influence from French surrealist poetry, which, as a rule, I am not very interested in. There are a few exceptions, such as Raymond Roussel, who is not really a surrealist, and Pierre

Reverdy. He was a surrealist of a kind, but not of the hard-core group of Breton, Éluard, and so on.

In a 1977 interview he suggests:

> The fact is, as far as European poetry is concerned, German and Slavic poetry has been much more of an influence in my work. Only Rimbaud has managed to get beyond the *lucidity* of the French language, which doesn't allow you to do much "in the shadows." It becomes very clear and classical and illuminating, even the poetry of the surrealists.

Nevertheless, allusions to and borrowings from French writers periodically surface throughout Ashbery's œuvre, from the Roussel-inspired fantasy of "The Instruction Manual" to the parody of Baudelaire's "L'Invitation au Voyage" in Part II of "The Skaters", from the Maurice Scève-influenced *dizains* of "Fragment" to the open house of the "Hotel Lautréamont", from the Surrealist-style collaborations with Kenneth Koch published in the second issue of *Locus Solus* (Summer 1961) to the version of Baudelaire's "Paysage" collected in *A Wave* (1984). In addition Ashbery has translated numerous French writers – Roussel, Reverdy, Max Jacob (also translated by Bishop), Marcelin Pleynet, Denis Roche, Arthur Cravan, Pierre Martory, André Breton, Paul Éluard, René Char – written articles on such as Michel Butor, Antonin Artaud, de Chirico's *Hebdomeros*, Roussel, and Reverdy, and written poems himself in French, which he then translated back into English. Of this last experiment he commented: "I wanted to see if my poetry would come out differently if I wrote it at one remove ... I don't think it did come out very differently."

The desire to live "at one remove" from his homeland was certainly one of the primary motivations behind Ashbery's decision to take up residence in Paris for most of the years from 1955–65. McCarthyism and the Korean War made the mid-Fifties in America "a very humili-

211

ating and cynical period, a low point ... Everyone wanted to get out of the country and the political environment", he recalled in an interview thirty years later. Ashbery looked to France, rather as Bishop had twenty years previously, as a way of discovering the fresh perspectives a foreign country inevitably forces on one's cultural and linguistic assumptions. Particularly in the radically polarized world of *The Tennis Court Oath* Ashbery presents himself responding to experience in the unsettling, self-divided, restless manner of the final stanza of Bishop's "Sleeping on the Ceiling":

> We must go under the wallpaper
> to meet the insect-gladiator,
> to battle with a net and trident,
> and leave the fountain and the square.
> But oh, that we could sleep up there ...

That any attempt to satisfy the need to escape is as likely to result in disorientation as peaceful sleeping upside down is one of the lessons repeatedly taught by Bishop's and Ashbery's poetries. Imaginary and real journeys alike end up posing Bishop's fundamental questions of travel:

> *Continent, city, country, society;*
> *the choice is never wide and never free.*
> *And here, or there ... No. Should we have stayed at home*
> *wherever that may be?*

Ashbery's voyages are never as literal as those of Bishop's South American poems. An early unpublished piece, "Embarkation for Cythera", based on Baudelaire's "Voyage à Cythère", turns on a couple of puns that unite travelling and music:

> Now the bow dragged over mournful strings

> Expands and breathes the tints of Cythera
> Into the fever's beat.

In a similar fashion map and landscape prove inseparable in "Rivers and Mountains" ("you found / It all on paper but the land / Was made of paper processed / To look like ferns, mud"), and the high Symbolist sea-journeying of Part II of "The Skaters" flagrantly reveals its source in a pored-over atlas – "And we finger down the dog-eared coasts". As in Bishop's "The Map", cartography assumes an unpredictable life of its own. The early poem "The Instruction Manual" parades even more explicitly the extent to which Ashbery's travels are "at one remove".

"The Instruction Manual", composed in September of 1955, clearly reflects the influence of Raymond Roussel, as Ashbery has acknowledged. Ashbery was introduced to Roussel by Kenneth Koch, who returned from his trip to France in 1951 with a copy of Roussel's *La Vue* (1904). This volume consists of three enormously long poems in which Roussel describes in exhaustive, indeed impossible, detail three miniature representations. The 4,000 lines of "La Vue" depict a beach scene set in the lens of a pen-holder, "La Source" presents the spa pictured on the label of a bottle of mineral water, while "Le Concert" is based on the sketch of a hotel adorning the heading of a letter written on the hotel's writing paper. Like "The Instruction Manual", each begins with a short portrayal of the solitary poet's immediate circumstances and ends by returning to this stark reality. The view in the lens clouds over, and Roussel is left only the

> souvenir vivace et latent d'un été
> Déjà mort, déjà loin de moi, vite emporté.

In "Le Concert" he turns from the letter's heading to the letter itself:

> Puis, tous bas, je relis pour la centième fois,
> Essayant d'évoquer, à chaque mot, la voix.

Ashbery seems to have been intrigued not only by the obsessive metic-
ulousness of Roussel's imagination – for instance he observes of the
eyebrows of a rower way out at sea that

> son sourcil gauche n'est pas pareil
> Au droit; il est plus noir, plus important, plus dense
> Et plus embroussaillé dans sa grande abondance

– but by the odd fusion the poems establish between the utilitarian
and the fantastic: "the poet," he writes in his essay entitled "Re-
establishing Raymond Roussel", "like a prisoner fascinated by the
appearance of the wall of his cell, remains transfixed by the spectacle
before his eyes, which is not even a real scene but a vulgar reproduction." Roussel's "self-forgetful, perfectly useless concentration" on the
tiny mass-produced images mirrors Bishop's absorption in the "commercial colors" of the map, which are, as Ashbery points out in his
second Bishop essay, "the product, after all, of the expediencies and
limitations of a mechanical process". In "The Instruction Manual"
too, the world of fantasy is presented as dependent upon the "press",
the peremptory laws of commercial publishing:

> City of rose-colored flowers!
> City I wanted most to see, and most did not see, in Mexico!
> But I fancy I see, under the press of having to write the instruc-
> tion manual,
> Your public square, city, with its elaborate little bandstand!

Ashbery's pun deftly encapsulates the antithetical realms of instruction manual and pastiche travelogue, and also implies that each is
governed by an equally rigid code that makes them suitable for mass
circulation. As in Bishop and Roussel, it is the uniting of seemingly
incompatible genres that prompts speculation on what Ashbery has
called the "confessional" aspect of the poem. Its conclusion, however,

grimly insists that the publisher's pressing deadlines and the cornball rose-coloured city are part of the same interminable loop:

> And as a last breeze freshens the top of the weathered old tower,
>   I turn my gaze
> Back to the instruction manual which has made me dream of
>   Guadalajara.

The poem's double-take leaves one marooned, rather as Bishop's "Paris, 7 A.M." does, neither reconciled to the schedule of instruction manuals, nor believing in the possibility of escaping them.

This dilemma is charted throughout Ashbery's œuvre, but is most explosively dramatized in the poems written mainly in France and collected in his second volume, *The Tennis Court Oath* (1962). Here *d'espoir* and despair collide at frightening velocity, at once polarized and inseparable: "This honey is delicious", observes a character in "They Dream Only of America", *"Though it burns the throat"*. Ashbery's language, suddenly unleashed from symbolic and narrative constraints, evolves its own secret methods of connection and disjunction that aggressively refuse to be plotted according to pre-existing schema or value systems. The effect might be compared to that Ashbery experienced reading Reverdy: "C'est comme si on voyait pour la première fois un paysage naturel, n'ayant vu jusque là que des paysages peints." The poems insistently juxtapose the forces of obsession and dispersal, desire and flux, as "To Redouté" graphically illustrates:

> My first is a haunting face
> In the hanging-down hair.
> My second is water:
> I am a sieve.

Ashbery's essay on Reverdy also helps make clear the extent to which the radical techniques of *The Tennis Court Oath* may be construed as a reaction against the stifling, overweening claims of Modernism:

> A l'inverse des écrivains importants de langue anglaise
> de ce siècle (Eliot, Pound, Yeats, Joyce), Reverdy parvi-
> ent à restituer aux choses leur vrai nom, à abolir l'éternel
> poids mort de symbolisme et d'allégorie qui excède chez
> les auteurs que j'ai cités. Dans *The Waste Land* d'Eliot, le
> monde réel apparaît avec les rêves qui lui sont propres,
> mais il est toujours artificiellement lié à une signification
> allégorique – l'usine à gaz et le <<dull canal>>, par exem-
> ple. Tandis que chez Reverdy un canal ou une usine sont
> des phénomènes vivants, ils font partie du monde qui nous
> entoure, dont le souffle cru se fait sentir partout dans sa
> poésie.

The landscapes and mindscapes of *The Tennis Court Oath* similarly
resist being formulated in terms other than their own, like Reverdy
seem "pure de toute arrière-pensée métaphysique", though Ashbery
is not above the occasional sly jab at his precursors, as in "The Suspended Life": "In the hay states of Pennsylvania and Arkansas / I lay
down and slept".

The vertiginous, disruptive, all-over poetics of *The Tennis Court
Oath* can be traced back to any number of sources – Gertrude Stein's
Stanzas in Meditation, the drip-paintings of Jackson Pollock, the musical experiments of Webern, Berio, or John Cage – but the dominant
influence is surely again the work of Raymond Roussel, and in particular his late extremely rebarbative poem in four cantos, *Nouvelles
Impressions d'Afrique* (1932), considered by Ashbery to be Roussel's
"masterpiece". *Nouvelles Impressions* was originally intended to be a
follow-up to *La Vue*. Roussel planned to describe "une minuscule lor-
gnette-pendoloque, dont chaque tube, large de deux millimètres et
fait pour se coller contre l'oeil, renfermait une photographie sur verre,
l'un celle des bazars du Caire, l'autre celle d'un quai de Louqsuor."

After five years work, however, Roussel abandoned this idea, and began the poem all over again. Though still set in Egypt, it develops a methodology wholly its own, for Roussel fractures its progress every few lines with a parenthetical thought, introduced by a bracket, which is itself interrupted by a new parenthesis, and so on and so on. The poem's Chinese box effect constitutes a further evolution of Roussel's *"procédé"* which generated the elements of the narratives that make up his novels and plays. "The result", Ashbery argues in "Re-establishing Raymond Roussel" "is a tumultuous impression of reality which keeps swiping at one like the sails of a windmill... In *Nouvelles Impressions* the unconscious seems to have broken through the myths in which Roussel had carefully encased it: it is no longer the imaginary world, but the real one, and it is exploding around us like a fireworks factory, in one last dazzling orgy of light and sound." As in his discussion of the poetry of Bishop, which seems to present a world "as inevitable as 'the' world", or his praise for the "paysage naturel" embodied by the work of Reverdy, or his admiration for the "counterfeit of reality more real than reality" offered by Stein's *Stanzas in Meditation*, Ashbery celebrates Roussel's power to create a poetry whose strangeness seems analogous in the fullest possible way to the strangeness of experience. Roussel's writings consistently defeat all expectations of purpose and meaning:

> What he leaves us with is a body of work that is like the perfectly preserved temple of a cult which has disappeared without a trace, or a complicated set of tools whose use cannot be discovered. But even though we may never be able to "use" his work in the way he hoped, we can still admire its inhuman beauty, and be stirred by a language that seems always on the point of revealing its secret, of pointing the way back to the "republic of dreams" whose insignia blazed on his forehead.

A Driftwood Altar

The fragmentations of *The Tennis Court Oath* seem motivated by just such ideals. "There was no longer any need for the world to be divided", he declares in "Measles", the implication being that the principle of endless division may itself become a totalizing force. Ashbery's collaged cut-ups such as "Europe" or "Idaho" or "America" seek in "the hazards of language" the sorts of juxtapositions he finds so convincing in *Nouvelles Impressions*, of which he observes: "The logic of the strange positions [a rephrasing of a line from his own *"Le livre est sur la table"*] of its elements is what makes the poem so beautiful. It has what Marianne Moore calls 'mysteries of construction'."

To many, including Ashbery himself, the "mysteries of construction" shaping *The Tennis Court Oath* have remained that bit too mysterious. Its most vociferous supporters, the L=A=N=G=U=A=G=E poets, dislike much of the rest of Ashbery's poetry, while for critics eager to place Ashbery in the central traditions of American poetry such as Harold Bloom and Helen Vendler, the book is "a fearful disaster", "a mixture of wilful flashiness and sentimentality." No other Ashbery volume has excited such conflicted responses, such *d'espoir* and despair, for this particular Crusoe has no time to play with names, only to live them:

> Everything is being blown away;
> A little horse trots up with a letter in its mouth, which is read
>   with eagerness
> As we gallop into the flame.

P.N. Review, 1995

A Wide and Wingless Path to the Impossible: The Poetry of F.T. Prince

F.T. Prince's first collection, austerely entitled *Poems*, was published by Faber & Faber in 1938. Its editor was of course T.S. Eliot, who over the previous 13 years had established Faber as the market leader in modern poetry. The 26-year old Prince was joining a stable that included the likes of Ezra Pound, W.H. Auden, Louis MacNeice, Stephen Spender and Marianne Moore. Until the Eliot archives finally open at some unforeseeable date in the future, we won't know exactly what appealed to the Pope of Russell Square about this diverse, dense often bewildering volume, whose contents include a sinuously complex dramatic monologue by Edmund Burke, an elaborate mock seventeenth-century epistle to a supposed patron, a Stevensian address to the Muse of America, a five part recreation of the reign of the Zulu king Chaka, and a number of beautiful – but at times almost unfathomable – shorter lyrics.

One can guess, however, at the reasons behind Prince's decision to call the collection simply *Poems*. Its various styles seem to have developed in total isolation from each other, and to pull in completely different directions: it establishes no unifying set of concerns, and no readily identifiable poetic persona. Each poem appears wholly self-contained, as if answerable only to itself. In this Prince's debut might be seen as the polar opposite of another volume edited and published by Eliot eight years earlier, and also called *Poems*: in his first Faber collection Auden appears determined almost to abolish the gap between the individual poems, which were presented without titles; from the book's urgent opening lines ("Will you turn a deaf ear / To what they said on the shore") to its closing promise of "new styles of architecture, a change of heart", we feel ourselves addressed by an absolutely distinctive voice whose eloquence and authority are far more important than the subject matter or angle of perception explored in any given lyric. Prince's voice, on the other hand, even when he is at his most seemingly autobiographical in poems such as "The Babiaantje" or "Cefalù", continually eludes definition. His attention is so wholly on the poetic matter at hand, on the "rich web" – to borrow a phrase from the Burke poem – he is intent on weaving, that he seems altogether incapable of either self-display or large-scale cultural generalization.

It's interesting, further, to compare the uses to which Prince and Auden put earlier poetic styles. The early Auden was peculiarly adept at appropriating random phrases and making them seem an unquestionable aspect of his own poetic terrain: scraps lifted even from Anglo-Saxon poems such as "The Battle of Maldon" or "Wulf and Eadwacer" come to seem pure embodiments of the Audenesque. Prince's historical poems attempt something very different –to explore the past for its own sake, or perhaps rather, for the sake of poetry *per se*. The virtuosity of his early monologues, or later longer poems like "Afterword on Rupert Brooke" or his account of Laurence Sterne's late love for Eliza Draper ("A Last Attachment"), can perhaps best be conveyed through negatives, that is by stressing their rigorous avoidance of pastiche, of satire, of aesthetic or political theorizing, and of overt – or, for that matter, covert – self-revelation.

It is the lack of a discernible ulterior motive which makes Prince's use of masks and personae so original. Though passages, particularly in his first two books, deliberately echo the cadences of the Victorian dramatic monologue as developed by Tennyson and Browning, Prince is never, so to speak, smirking at us behind their backs:

> Often night lets down darkness upon me,
> And every kind of doubt to weigh upon me. Then

I have cried to him, as he thrust out his breast,
As he leapt forward like a pitch-black bullock ...

The lines glide from languorous Tennysonian gloom to Browningesque
bluster, but refuse to invite the kinds of critical mirth or censure
routinely directed at Victorianisms by the likes of Pound and Eliot.
Pound invented the concept of "logopoeia" to define the sort of linguistic awareness he felt was needed to purge the archaic and forge the
new. He defined this as

> "the dance of the intellect among words," that is to say,
> it employs words not only for their direct meaning, but
> it takes count in a special way of habits of usage, of the
> context we *expect* to find with the word, its usual concomi-
> tants, of its known acceptances, and of ironical play.

Prince blithely dissents from what had become, by the Thirties,
Modernist orthodoxy; the archaic well done, he suggests, can be just
as effective as contemporary idioms, and much more so than the
aggressively or complacently up-to-date. And while the "logopoi-
eac" sensibility continually obtrudes upon the reader its awareness
of its own critical sophistication, Prince's poetry seems inspired by its
antithesis, a longing for complete absorption in the language of the
poem he is at this moment writing.

This is not, I hope, to make him sound either a naïve romantic or
a proto-Postmodernist. Prince, unusually for his era, seems to me a
poet both supremely conscious of the conventions within which he
presents a given poem as operating, and determined never to mock
or undermine those conventions through irony. Clearly we are not
meant to think the Zulu king Chaka, the supposed speaker of the
lines quoted above, really mused on his life in terms derived from a
mid-Victorian dramatic monologue. The poem refuses, however, to
appeal to anything outside its own effects for the justification of its

means – and the same applies even to Prince's most insistently literary works, like the Sterne or Brooke sequences, or *Drypoints of the Hassidim* (1975), which is based on numerous primary and secondary Hassidic texts.

It is this lack of irony which sets apart his "Soldiers Bathing" from most other Second World War poems. "I see men as trees suffering / or confound the detail and the horizon", observed Keith Douglas laconically in "Desert Flowers". Prince is no less separated from his men, as they "shout and run in the warm air" before plunging into the sea to bathe, and no less aware of the "terrible pressure that begets / A machinery of death and slavery." There is something touchingly tentative, however, about the poem's flirtation with the Nietzschean / Yeatsian ideals of the warrior developed by such as Douglas into a private code of honour:

> Yet, as I drink the dusky air,
> I feel a strange delight that fills me full,
> Strange gratitude, as if evil itself were beautiful,
> And kiss the wound in thought, while in the west
> I watch a streak of red that might have issued from Christ's
>   breast.

Prince's "strange delight", hedged round with hypothetical qualifiers ("as if ... in thought ... that might ..."), is far removed from Yeats's provocative tub-thumping in "Under Ben Bulben":

> Know that when all words are said
> And a man is fighting mad,
> Something drops from eyes long blind,
> He completes his partial mind,
> For an instant stands at ease,
> Laughs aloud, his heart at peace.

Indeed Prince's evocation of Christ might be said to overturn one of Yeats's most deeply held credos: "Passive suffering is not a theme for poetry", he declared in his introduction to his 1936 *Oxford Book of Modern Verse* to justify his exclusion of First World War poets such as Wilfred Owen: Prince's streak of red that links the poet's imagined future wound to Christ's implies exactly the reverse.

Passive suffering is very much the dominant theme of Prince's most ambitious and – to my mind – successful early poem, "Apollo and the Sibyl", collected in *Soldiers Bathing* (1954). The Sibyl of Cumae, he explains in a note, "was loved in her youth by Apollo, who offered to grant any wish she might express. She asked to live as many years as there were grains in a certain heap of dust, but forgot to ask for enduring youth. This too would have been granted her, if she had accepted Apollo's love. Refusing it, she lived on to become a prophetess, and at last only a voice, haunting her cave at Cumae." Her narrative appears in Book XIV of Ovid's *Metamorphoses*, and a reference to her made in Petronius's *Satyricon* was used by T.S. Eliot as the epigraph to *The Waste Land*. Translated it reads

> For once I saw with my very own eyes the Sibyl at Cumae
> hanging in a cage, and when the boys said to her, "Sibyl,
> what do you want?" she answered, "I want to die."

Prince's Sibyl, however, does not want to die. She is not even sure she regrets her rejection of Apollo's advances:

> My mournful calcined life
> Half-eaten by desires,
> Brimming with light and sorrow,
> Yet I do not repent me;
> I remain in my pain that is
> A golden distance endlessly,
> And with my head bent, and my eyes

That follow down and stare
As with a dreaming stare, I gaze
Until the noon that climbs the air
Troubles, makes more than ever now excessive
– Rubbed and ruffled, thumbed –
Outrageously more beautiful
The burning young tumescent sea ...

The movement from self-pity to an exhilarating vision of noon and sea as lovers typifies the centrifugal drive of Prince's imagination, paradoxically released by his dramatic use of the decaying Sybil imprisoned in her fate. Throughout, radiant landscapes and seascapes are played off against her physical decrepitude and insistent doubts:

And now a low brown person, shrinking slowly to a bag of skin,
I wonder at myself, and even more that, were I to begin,

I think that I should do what I have done.

And gulls, swallows, turn down wind,
The sea toils, grinds and crushes
Marble to milk at cliff-base.
                                        And the air,
The air is stirring, everywhere
A sweetness dignifies the air:
The broom, that tanned and dusty angel,
Bound down, is taken by the hair
And rifled, and blown lingeringly, or plunged
By the wind's tooth and talon, torn
But living and enduring ...

The exquisitely subtle power of such passages derives from Prince's immaculate control of sound, rhythm, and the energies of syntax.

A Wide and Wingless Path to the Impossible

Though in comparison with such as Eliot, Pound, or Auden he can seem a somewhat unassuming poet, while reading him one is periodically struck by the sublime sweep of his metaphors – the streak of sunset compared to Christ's wound at the end of "Soldiers Bathing", for instance, or, in the lines above, the broom figured as an angel through whose hair a playful or savage wind streams. At his best he swings mercurially from suggestively abstract formulations ("Dead thistledowns of bitterness") of the kind Pound abhorred, to daunting tautologies and paradoxes that verge on the metaphysical:

> Moving motionless to death, I see
> That one must suffer what one sees ...

The Sibyl may, as Prince informs us in his note, age and diminish in her lonely cave at Cumae to a mere voice, but what a voice!

> And the sky opens
> Like a fan its vault of violet light, unfolding
> A wide and wingless path to the impossible.

P.N. Review, 2002

Charles Simic

Charles Simic's collection of autobiographical fragments, *A Fly in the Soup* (2000), concludes with one of his earliest memories. It is 1942 or '43, so he is four or five years old. Despite the war, operas are still being performed in Belgrade, and his mother has taken him to a performance of *The Marriage of Figaro*:

> It's the first act, and Susanna and Figaro are in an eighteenth-century salon, pacing up and down. At one point Susanna brushes against one of the candles, and the long scarf she is wearing over her shoulders catches fire. The audience gasps. She stops singing and stands clutching her head in terror while the flames get bigger and bigger. Figaro, without missing a beat, quickly snatches the scarf, throws it on the floor, and stamps on it like a Spanish dancer. All along he's singing that beautiful music ...

Simic's poetry has always been fascinated by the borderline between art and violence. "So I sat between the word *truth*", he writes in the very early "Pastoral" (1969), "And the word *gallows* / Took out my tin can / And spoon". Reflecting on the opera singer's presence of mind in the course of his conversation with Michael Hulse (the English poet and translator of W.G. Sebald), Simic marvels again at "the way he kept the comic spirit of the performance uninterrupted while the audience gasped in horror. Outside, the war was on. We were an occupied country. People were arrested, disappeared or were sent to

226

camps. There were public executions. That's how art exists in this world of ours – a clear head in the face of calamity." Yet at the same time his poetry shows itself constantly aware of how its own energies and patterning are determined by the "calamity" from which it derives its origin. The *locus classicus* of this theme in Simic's work is still his earliest expression of it, the final stanza of "Butcher Shop" of 1967:

> There is a wooden block where bones are broken,
> Scraped clean – a river dried to its bed
> Where I am fed,
> Where deep in the night I hear a voice.

There can be no complete description of the sources or evolution of any good poet's "voice", and poets themselves are rarely willing to reduce their *alchimie du verbe* to a scientific formula. (I once wearied the preternaturally patient Allen Ginsberg with what must have seemed an endless series of silly questions about his style until he finally snapped, "I can't tell you why I write the way I do. I just do!") Simic is particularly wary of imposing on his imagination, the voice at 3.00 A.M., any kind of agenda; "the most beautiful riddle has no answer", he has his muse figure say in his densest and most elaborate embodiment of the mysteries of the imagination, and his longest ever poem, "White", first issued in 1972, and then revised and republished in four different versions.

But Simic's riddles, however unanswerable, tend to be ways of engaging, rather than avoiding, history; they seem driven primarily by the urge to present what he calls in a 1986 essay, "Poetry and History", reprinted in his latest collection of prose pieces, *The Metaphysician in the Dark* (the title is borrowed from Wallace Stevens), "a kind of reverse history of what in the great scheme of things are often regarded as 'unimportant' events, the image of a dead cat, say, lying in the rubble of a bombed city, rather than the rationale for that air campaign." He quotes a line by the Italian poet Salvatore Quasimodo, who writes of "the black howl of the mother gone to meet her son crucified on a telephone pole". "Perhaps only in lyric poetry", Simic comments, "can that mother's howl be heard as loudly as it ought to be."

Certainly Simic's own poetry is best approached as a kind of "reverse history"; his laconic, bleached, often puzzling lyrics avoid pointing morals or extracting clear meanings from the scenes they enact; instead they skilfully create the illusion they have just stumbled over or backed into bizarre juxtapositions that startle and unnerve – or at the very least invite the reader to pause for thought. The tiny opening piece in this selection of Simic's work of the last two decades typifies his most basic manoeuvre:

DECEMBER

It snows
and still the derelicts
go
carrying sandwich boards –

one proclaiming
the end of the world
the other
the rates of a local barbershop.

His poems often swing in this manner between the ordinary and the ultimate, like updated versions of Emily Dickinson's darting, dizzying transitions from the quotidian to the sublime:

A Clock stopped –
Not the Mantel's –
Geneva's farthest skill
Can't put the puppet bowing

That just now dangled still –
An awe came on the Trinket!
The Figures hunched, with pain –
Then quivered out of Decimals –
Into Degreeless Noon –

"Well, where shall I begin?" Simic responds when asked by Hulse about the influence of Dickinson's work on his own development. "She writes short poems and I write short poems. She speculates about ultimate things and so do I. She thrives on paradoxes and contradictions and so do I. She felt like an outsider and so do I."

Simic has lived in America for fifty years, and frequently insists he is much more an American poet – one in the tradition of New England writers such as Dickinson, Thoreau, Emerson, Melville, William James and Robert Frost – than a Serbian or European one. He has never attempted to compose poems in his mother tongue, and even found himself unable to translate his own work into Serbian ("I knew all the words, of course, but had lost the feel for what they do to the native speaker"). On the other hand, as he also acknowledges to Hulse, the vision of history articulated by his poems runs directly counter to ideals of American election: "I'm a poet haunted by history," he declares, "writing in a country which long ago replaced history with utopia."

All Simic's writing is strongly, often virulently, anti-utopian. In terms of the nineteenth-century American writers who mean so much to him, he is much closer to the Melville of *The Confidence-Man* or the darker chapters of *Moby-Dick* than the Emerson of *Nature*. In a poem such as "Two Dogs" (1990), for instance, Simic takes an anecdote that might have furnished Mark Twain with an episode or short story in a wholly surprising direction:

An old dog afraid of his own shadow
In some Southern town.

> The story told me by a woman going blind,
> One fine summer evening
> As shadows were creeping
> Out of the New Hampshire woods,
> A long street with just a worried dog
> And a couple of dusty chickens,
> And all that sun beating down
> In that nameless Southern town.

The contrasting scenes of this opening stanza suggest the poem is working towards a meditation on the difference between New England and the deep South. There is a picture postcard quality to both depictions that is heightened by the absence of a main verb from its two sentences. While the first two lines promise some kind of anecdote, that promise is diffused in the eight that follow into quietly clichéd scene-painting: the story of the paranoid hound allows the poet's imagination to rove from his fine New Hampshire evening to its Southern opposite, a baking street, some dusty (Simic's all-time favourite adjective) chickens, and the slightly freakish worried dog. The stanza gently activates the myths of north and south, and both dog and nearly blind woman tremble on the threshold of the archetypal. The second stanza is also ten lines long:

> It make me remember the Germans marching
> Past our house in 1944.
> The way everybody stood on the sidewalk
> Watching them out of the corner of the eye,
> The earth trembling, death going by ...
> A little white dog ran into the street
> And got entangled with the soldier's feet.
> A kick made him fly as if he had wings.
> That's what I keep seeing!
> Night coming down. A dog with wings.

There are many good American poems written by such as Anthony Hecht, Louis Simpson, and Randall Jarrell about the Second World War, but none that captures the experience of passive, terrified civilians with this kind of subtlety and force. While the dog of the first stanza seems on the point of sliding into the mythology of Southern Gothic, the soaring white mutt of the second illustrates exactly the kind of "reverse history" that Simic believes is the domain of lyric poetry. This dog has more than his own shadow to worry about. But it's also worth pointing out how deftly "Two Dogs" avoids triggering the repository of emotions war stories normally exploit. The image of German troops marching through a cowed populace, familiar from so much newsreel footage, is unobtrusively but firmly focused by "our house", then brilliantly disrupted by that of the kicked dog: "That's what I keep seeing! / Night coming down. A dog with wings." As in the first stanza, we are not allowed to forget the part played by the poet's own imagination in the scene the poem describes: it is the helplessness of the six year old boy forced to watch death march by which begets the transfiguring, compensatory fantasy of flight.

One of the most striking episodes in *A Fly in the Soup* concerns a conversation Simic had in 1972 with the poet Richard Hugo, whom he ran into in a restaurant in San Francisco. Simic tells Hugo he has just returned from a trip to Belgrade:

> "Oh yes," he said, "I can see the city well."
> Without knowing my background, he proceeded to draw on the tablecloth, among the breadcrumbs and wine stains, the location of the main post office, the bridges over the Danube and Sava, and a few other important landmarks. Without a clue as to what all this meant, supposing that he had visited the city as a tourist at one time, I inquired how much time he had spent in Belgrade.
> "I was never there," he replied. "I only bombed it a few times."

When absolutely astonished, I blurted out that I was there at the time and that it was me he was bombing, Hugo became very upset. In fact he was deeply shaken.

Simic reassures him that he bears no grudge, that both were just "two befuddled bit players in events beyond our control". The cinematic metaphor of the bit player is taken up in a 1996 poem, "Cameo Appearance", inspired by a documentary film about the bombing of Belgrade:

> I had a small, nonspeaking part
> In a bloody epic. I was one of the
> Bombed and fleeing humanity.
> In the distance our great leader
> Crowed like a rooster from a balcony,
> Or was it a great actor
> Impersonating our great leader?

And yet, although he points himself out to his children, "squeezed between the man / With two bandaged hands raised / And the old woman with her mouth open / As if she were showing us a tooth // That hurts badly," he can't get them to spot him in the "huge gray crowd, / That was like any other gray crowd":

> Trot off to bed, I said finally.
> I know I was there. One take
> Is all they had time for.
> We ran, and the planes grazed our hair,
> And then they were no more
> As we stood dazed in the burning city,
> But, of course, they didn't film that.

For Simic, then, poetry is a means of recording what doesn't get filmed,

232

whatever eludes or is suppressed by the kinds of narrative that offer to make sense of our lives only at the cost of dangerously simplifying the contradictory, incomplete, and random nature of experience. The voice at 3 A.M. refuses to allow any single discourse or genre to hold sway: "Who put", runs the two-line poem of that title, "canned laughter / Into my crucifixion scene?" Although not many of Simic's poems end up turning the page, and he specializes in radical acts of ellipsis and foreshortening ("O you simple, indefinable, ineffable, and so forth" ("Beauty"), or "You're the famous torturer much feared / I beg you to spare my love / Who is in your darkest prison cell / I wish to marry him etc." ("Rough Outline")), central to his *ars poetica* is the ideal of an almost Whitmanesque expansiveness; the surest way of freeing oneself from the limitations of a particular mind-set or discourse is to juxtapose it with a different or even contradictory one. Like Whitman, Simic is drawn to lists and catalogues, to poems scavenged from the random collisions of the streets:

> The curtains of cheap hotels flying out of windows
> Like seagulls, but everything else quiet ...
> Steam rising out of the subway gratings ...
> Bodies glistening with sweat ...
> Madness, and you might even say, paradise!
>
> ("Paradise" – his ellipses)

The enthusiasm of the first generation immigrant for American diversity and possibility shines undimmed through such lines. The erotically glistening bodies contrast sharply with the maimed and traumatized, "the cripple and the imbecile", who inhabit his war and post-war Belgrade city-scapes. Asked by Hulse to describe his ideal city, Simic replies: "My ideal city already exists. It is New York. New York is the place where my imagination and intellect are at home. I'm not surprised various religious fundamentalists and nationalists hate it. To see different races and ethnic groups work together and get along terrifies them since it goes against everything they believe. The revenge of the small town bullies, village priests, and provincial fascists has been the secret force behind so much recent history. They all dream of burning down the cities. What frightens them and makes them froth with hatred are the things I adore."

Simic's minimalism, then, is of a particularly impure kind. This is what so distinguishes his work from that of Yugoslavian poets such as Ivan Lalic and Vasko Popa, whose work he first began translating in the early Sixties. The riddles of Popa, for instance, seem to evolve wholly on their own terms, to emerge from his severe, deadpan conjugations of language like some irrefutable, if obscure, mathematical formula. "The usual drama of the self", as Simic notes in his introduction to his versions of Popa's work collected in *Homage to the Lame Wolf* (1987), "is completely absent." Popa, and Lalic after him, set about fusing the technical innovations of twentieth-century poetry – in particular French Surrealism – with the traditions of Serbian folklore, to create a poetry at once modern and archetypal. Simic freely acknowledges his debt to their work, but perhaps equally significant to his development was his purchase in 1959 of a second-hand copy of Dudley Fitts's New Directions *Anthology of Contemporary Latin-American Poetry* (1942). In a review of a selection of the poetry of Pablo Neruda, Simic recalls the impact made on him of the work of such as Borges, César Vallejo, Carlos Drummond de Andrade, Nicolás Guillén, and Neruda himself:

> I remember turning its pages in the store, realizing what a valuable book it was, paying for it quickly, and rushing home to read all of its 666 pages that very night. It was like reading Eliot's "Love Song of J. Alfred Prufrock" for the first time, seeing a Buster Keaton movie, hearing Thelonius Monk, and making other such exhilarating discoveries.

It is perhaps a typical immigrant paradox that the major poetic influences on Simic's evolution into an American poet were not American. He was not, however, alone in turning to foreign models in his search for ways of escaping the strait-jacket of the dry, New Criticism-friendly lyric that dominated the American poetry establishment of the Fifties. The prevailing tone of the official poetry world is nicely captured in his description in *A Fly in the Soup* of a reading he attended at NYU some time in the late Fifties:

> Just as the professional lovers of poetry in the audience were already closing their eyes blissfully in anticipation of the poet's familiar, soul-stirring clichés, there was the sound of paper being torn. We all turned around to look. A shabby old man was ripping newspapers into a brown shopping bag. He saw people glare at him and stopped. The moment we turned back to the poet, who went on reading oblivious to everything, in a slow monotone, the man resumed ripping, but now more cautiously, with long pauses between rips.
>
> And so it went: the audience would turn around with angry faces, he'd stop for a while and then continue, while the poet read on and on.

The Beats, the New York School Poets, Deep Image poets such as Robert Bly and W.S. Merwin had all made use of the techniques of European Surrealism in their various attempts to rip apart the prevailing poetic conventions. Simic was perhaps fortunate to begin writing in the wake of the poetry wars which invited all poets to identify themselves either with the "cooked" (i.e. the formal) or the "raw" (i.e. the experimental), and he has cleverly avoided allowing his work to be co-opted by any group since. He seems as aware as Dickinson, or another of his heroes, Joseph Cornell, that his art depends on protecting at all costs his status as an "outsider". In his introduction to his translations of the poetry of Ivan Lalic, *Roll Call of Mirrors* (1988), he quotes with approval a declaration by the American poet Charles Wright: "Poetry is an exile's art. Anyone who writes it seriously writes from an exile's point of view."

There is a political dimension to this ideal of non-alliance which was thrown into particular relief by the civil war that tore apart the former Yugoslavia in the Nineties. The opposite of non-alliance, of art's "clear head in the face of calamity", is the kind of murderous nationalism that rejects "the possibility of any kind of choice", as he puts it in one of a number of pieces on the conflict reprinted in *The Metaphysician in the Dark*, "believing instead in the iron law that says we must either kill or be killed." Much of his invective in these articles is directed at the idiocies pronounced by ignorant American and British political commentators on Balkan issues, who, Simic argues, ended up colluding with, rather than attempting to expose, the discourses of ethnicity unleashed by various demagogues who fomented the break-up and ethnic cleansing that followed. "The approach of the West to the crisis", he tells Hulse, "emphasized tribal rather than individual rights. In other words, they repudiated their own democratic values."

And there is no doubt the approach of war and the war itself reactivated in his imagination the vision of history inculcated by his formative years in Belgrade:

> History practicing its scissor-clips
> In the dark,
> So everything comes out in the end
> Missing an arm or a leg.
>
> Still, if that's all you've got
> To play with today ...
> This doll at least had a head
> And its lips were red!
>
> ("Frightening Toys" – his ellipsis)

The transition from a bleakly unillusioned diagnosis to a determination to make do with what's left "to play with today" is characteristic of the movement of many of Simic's poems of recent years. Political and journalistic commonplaces are undercut, or rendered weightless by the incongruous contexts into which he slides them. The poems move insistently towards what is available in the here and now,

> the small arcana of the frying pan,
> The smell of olive oil and garlic wafting
> From room to empty room, the black cat
> Rubbing herself against your bare leg
> While you shuffle toward the distant light
> And the tinkle of glasses in the kitchen.
>
> ("The Lives of the Alchemists")

"Sunday Papers", from the same volume, *Night Picnic* (2001), opens with a moment of complacent sententiousness, "The butchery of the innocent / Never stops. That's about all / We can ever be sure of, love," but ends up celebrating the end product of a different kind of butchery, a lamb roast "In your outstretched hands / Smelling of garlic and rosemary."

Simic has written often and expansively of the delights of food. "What's a poem", he asks Hulse when quizzed about the numerous references to meals and restaurants in his work, "but a well-prepared dish served on a plate?" Simic has been uninhibited in celebrating his favourite dishes in both poetry and prose. *The Metaphysician in the Dark* expands our knowledge of his culinary preferences with an essay, first published in *Food and Wine* in 2000, called "Self-Portrait with a Bowl of Spaghetti" which includes a versified dream-menu:

> Give me your tongue tasting of white beans and garlic,
> Sexy little assortment of formaggi and frutta!
> I want to drown you in red wine like a pear ...

Food provides many of the hedonistic moments that dissolve, temporarily at least, the historical and existential anxieties mapped by Simic's poems. Even the most venerable figures of literature can be cut down to size by a culinary metaphor:

> O King Oedipus, O Hamlet,
> Fallen like flies
> In the pot of cabbage soup,
> No use beating with your fists,
> Or sticking your tongues out.
>
> ("Folk Songs")

And the most memorable of his portraits of the members of his family in *A Fly in the Soup* (the ultimate comic abomination) occur in the course of his descriptions of prolonged, argumentative meal-times. "Would Kant", he wonders, "have been a better philosopher if he had worried about sausages as much as he did about the critique of judgement?" Well, we'll never know, but it's the kind of question only Simic would think of asking.

New York Review of Books, 2003: Review of Charles Simic's *The Voice at 3.00 A.M.: Selected Late and New Poems* (Harcourt, 2003) and *The Metaphysician in the Dark* (University of Michigan Press, 2003), and *Charles Simic in Conversation with Michael Hulse* (Between The Lines, 2002).

Inventions of Solitude:
Henry David Thoreau and Paul Auster

In *Ghosts*, the second part of Paul Auster's *The New York Trilogy*, a private eye called Blue is hired by a certain White to shadow a man called Black. Black lives in a small apartment in Brooklyn; Blue moves into an equally small apartment just across the street from Black. He is alarmed to discover that Black spends most of his time at his desk by the window, writing in a notebook with a red fountain pen. In the evenings Black reads, and through his binoculars Blue can just make out the title of Black's book: *Walden*, by Henry David Thoreau.

Accordingly Blue obtains his own copy of *Walden* – a 1942 edition published, by coincidence, by one Walter J. Black – thinking it might help him solve the mystery of his assignment. But like almost every reader of *Walden*, from Emerson to Stanley Cavell to Auster himself, Blue finds reading this book is "not a simple business":

> Whole chapters go by, and when he comes to the end of them he realizes that he has not retained a thing. Why would anyone want to go off and live alone in the woods? What's all this about planting beans and not drinking coffee or eating meat? Why all these interminable descriptions of birds? Blue thought that he was going to get a story, or at least something like a story, but this is no more than blather, an endless harangue about nothing at all.

The next day Blue tries the book again, and finally comes across a sentence he can understand: "Books must be read as deliberately and

239

reservedly as they were written." Blue realizes that "the trick is to go slowly, more slowly than he has ever gone with the words before." Nevertheless, he still finds the whole business excruciatingly painful, and curses Black for torturing him in this way. "What he does not know", the anonymous narrator remarks, "is that were he to find the patience to read the book in the spirit in which it asks to be read, his entire life would begin to change, and little by little he would come to a full understanding of his situation – that is to say, of Black, of White, of the case, of everything that concerns him." Instead, Blue throws the book aside in disgust and goes out for a walk, not realizing "that this is the beginning of the end."

The difficulties posed by *Walden* to Blue, and any number of readers from 1854 to the present day, derive largely from its refusal to ground itself in a stable terminology. As Stanley Cavell points out, "the writer of *Walden* is not counting on being believed; on the contrary, he converts the problem or condition of belief into a dominant subject of his experiment." The book's canonical status is inextricably bound up with its near unreadability, which in turn accounts for its "all but inevitable neglect", to quote Cavell again. *Walden* avoids identifying itself with any recognizable genre: it glides from spiritual confession to speculative linguistics, from wilderness narrative to jeremiad, from pastiche epic to heroic apologia, from fable to social history. In the process the literal and metaphorical are insistently confused:

> Not that I wanted beans to eat, for I am by nature a Pythagorean, so far as beans are concerned, whether they mean porridge or voting, and exchanged them for rice; but, perchance, as some must work in fields if only for the sake of tropes and expression, to serve a parable-maker one day.

The vagaries of Thoreau's approach particularly infuriated Emerson, who in his Journal compared him to "the woodgod who solicits the wandering poet & draws him into antres vast & desarts idle, & bereaves him of his memory, & leaves him naked, plaiting vines & with twigs in his hands. Very seductive are the first steps from the town to the woods, but the End is want & madness." For Emerson a crisis ought to result not in a dispersal of the self, but a rediscovery of one's origins: "We must hold hard", he writes in "Experience", "to this poverty, however scandalous, and by more vigorous self-recoveries, after the sallies of action, possess our axis more firmly." *Walden* rejects this archetypal romantic narrative of return, insisting instead on a continuous and paradoxical tension between what can and cannot be known: "At the same time that we are earnest to explore and learn all things, we require that all things be mysterious and unexplorable, that land and sea be infinitely wild, unsurveyed and unfathomed by us because unfathomable." It is, therefore, impossible to identify the stages of the quest for selfhood that *Walden* promises to enact. Far from conclusively proving the virtues of self-reliance, *Walden* reveals the impossibility of abstracting from the experiences it describes. Its relentless contradictions and evasions, its elaborate metaphorical expansions and sudden shifts of register, make it virtually impossible to know how to respond to its propositions. In this it closely resembles the reading experience offered by Fanshawe's notebook at the end of *The New York Trilogy*:

> All the words were familiar to me, and yet they seemed to have been put together strangely, as though their final purpose was to cancel each other out. I can think of no other way to express it. Each sentence erased the sentence before it, each paragraph made the next paragraph impossible. It is odd, then, that the feeling that survives from the notebook is one of great lucidity. It is as if Fanshawe knew his final work had to subvert every expectation I had for it. These were not the words of a man who regretted anything. He had answered the question by asking another

question, and therefore everything remained open, unfinished, to be started again.

We are told nothing specific of the contents or genre of this work, yet
like *Walden* – at least in Blue's frustrated reading of it – this elusive
text also seems to be "about nothing at all."

The protean methodology adopted by the Thoreau persona in
Walden and by Fanshawe in his red notebook can be seen as directly
challenging Emerson's belief in "self-recovery". Both *Walden* and the
red notebook articulate visions of "poverty" less open than Emerson's
to the recuperative forces of integration. Fanshawe refuses to emerge
from his locked room, and threatens the narrator with a gun when he
attempts to break down the door. Though Thoreau counsels his readers to "simplify, simplify", his own "*extra-vagant*" word-plays embody
a linguistic doubleness that mirrors society's schizophrenic demands:
"For the most part, we are not where we are, but in a false position.
Through an infirmity of our natures, we suppose a case, and put ourselves into it, and hence are in two cases at the same time, and it is
doubly difficult to get out." In *Ghosts* Blue cannot work out whether
his employer White or his quarry Black poses the greater threat; he
remembers these lines from *Walden* which perfectly express his situation, "thwarted in front and hemmed in on the rear". The first novel
in the trilogy, *City of Glass*, offers an even more dramatic instance of
the extent to which any situation must "admit of more than one interpretation". The crime novelist turned detective, Quinn, is required to
track down and tail Peter Stillman senior. He is given a photograph
and informed that Stillman will be arriving at Grand Central Station
on the 6.41 from Poughkeepsie. Quinn has no trouble recognizing
Stillman as a stooping, seedily dressed man in his sixties. Before setting off in pursuit, he glances over the rest of the crowd "to be doubly
sure he had made no mistakes":

What happened then defied explanation. Directly behind

Stillman, heaving into view just inches behind his right
shoulder, another man stopped, took a lighter out of his
pocket, and lit a cigarette. His face was the exact twin of
Stillman's. For a second Quinn thought it was an illusion,
a kind of aura thrown off by the electromagnetic currents
in Stillman's body. But no, this other Stillman moved,
breathed, blinked his eyes; his actions were clearly independent of the first Stillman. The second Stillman had a
prosperous air about him. He was dressed in an expensive
suit; his shoes were shined; his white hair was combed; and
in his eyes there was the shrewd look of a man of the world.
He, too, was carrying a single bag: an elegant black suitcase, about the same size as the other Stillman's.

Quinn craves "an amoeba's body, wanting to cut himself in half and
run off in two directions at once," for he is literally "in two cases at
the same time."

Both Thoreau and Auster are obsessively concerned with the powers
of solitude to convert the socially-induced anxieties of self-division
into the creative forces of self-awareness. In their writings solitude
is frequently presented as enabling a dream-like schism of the self
that allows one to follow, so to speak, both Stillmans at once. In the
chapter on "Solitude" in *Walden* Thoreau remarks that when alone
he becomes "sensible of a certain doubleness by which I can stand as
remote from myself as from another":

However intense my experience, I am conscious of the
presence and criticism of a part of me, which, as it were, is
not a part of me, but spectator, sharing no experience, but
taking note of it; and that is no more I than it is you. When
the play, it may be the tragedy, of life is over, the spectator
goes his way. It was a kind of fiction, a work of the imagination only, so far as he was concerned. This doubleness may

easily make us poor neighbors and friends sometimes.

Auster's "The Book of Memory" in *The Invention of Solitude* operates according to the same principle. In a 1987 interview Auster revealed that he spent months attempting to write these autobiographical reflections in the first person, to no avail: "The more deeply I descended into the material, the more distanced I became from it. In order to write about myself, I had to treat myself as though I were someone else." For Auster as for Thoreau, solitude fundamentally alters the relationship between reading, writing, and living, between the text and the world, for while "every book is an image of solitude", "The Book of Memory" is also, like *Walden* and *A Week on the Concord and Merrimack Rivers*, a crazy quilt of others' writings, a palimpsest of memories, anecdotes, and quotations. In a later interview Auster explained how in "The Book of Memory" he was trying to explore "both sides of the word 'solitude'. I felt as though I were looking down to the bottom of myself, and what I found there was more than just myself – I found the world." In a similar vein Thoreau cheerfully declares: "I have a great deal of company in my house; especially in the morning, when nobody calls."

Paradoxically, then, solitude, rather than offering a stable grounding of experience in a single autobiographical discourse, is construed by Thoreau and Auster as a means of connecting with the world through multiple, metamorphic selves. Only by losing ourselves, Thoreau argues in "The Village", can we realize "the infinite extent of our relations". Thoreau removes to the woods in search of "the essential facts of life", determined "to drive life into a corner, and reduce it to its lowest terms, and, if it proved to be mean, why then to get the whole and genuine meanness of it, and publish its meanness to the world; or if it were sublime, to know it by experience, and be able to give a true account of it in my next excursion." Yet life proves unknowable, irreducible, neither mean nor sublime, but both. Thoreau discovers that Walden Pond has "a reasonably tight bottom" and its greatest depth is "exactly one hundred and two feet", yet the pond is also "God's Drop", "earth's eye", "sky water", "made deep and pure for a symbol". Rather than the "essential facts of life", Thoreau discovers in solitude, or rather in the process of writing his solitude, a figurative space capable of accommodating both the mean and the sublime, and which consequently allows him "to coexist with the forces of [his] own uncertainty."

Thoreau's self-divisions are mirrored in some of the other nineteenth-century American texts to which Auster alludes in *The New York Trilogy*. In *City of Glass* Quinn publishes his detective novels under the pseudonym of William Wilson, a name borrowed from a short story of 1839 by Edgar Allan Poe. "Let me call myself, for the present, William Wilson", Poe's tale begins. Quinn, we are told, "never went so far as to believe that he and William Wilson were the same man" but that is of course exactly what Poe's protagonist discovers about his hated doppelgänger, though only by murdering him, and thereby himself: "Not a thread in all his raiment – not a line in all the marked and singular lineaments of his face which was not, even in the most absolute identity, *mine own!*" While waiting for Stillman at Grand Central Station Quinn ponders an advertisement featuring a New England fishing village, which reminds him of a visit he once made to Nantucket, the port from which the *Pequod* sails in Melville's *Moby-Dick*:

> From there his mind drifted off to the accounts he had read of Melville's last years – the taciturn old man working in the New York customs house, with no readers, forgotten by everyone. Then, suddenly, with great clarity and precision, he saw Bartleby's window and the blank brick wall before him.

Like William Wilson, Melville's Bartleby is terminally polarized, at war with his own body. His gradual self-starvation shadows Quinn's equally extreme refusals and mortifications, undertaken in the hope of liberating the spiritual from the physical: "He did not want to starve himself to death – and he reminded himself of this every day – he simply wanted to leave himself free to think of the things that truly concerned him."

The radical disjunctions and inner conflicts enacted in the narratives of "Bartleby" and "William Wilson" register in *City of Glass* as cautionary tales that illustrate what happens to those unable to live with their own uncertainties. In *Ghosts*, on the other hand, Auster explores the ways in which American Renaissance writers attempted to negotiate the forces of self-division inherent in mid-nineteenth-century economic and cultural relations. Exasperated by his inconclusive assignment, one day Blue dresses up as a tramp by the name of Jimmy Rose, a local character he remembers from his childhood. As Jimmy Rose he is "not a scrofulous down-and-outer so much as a wise fool, a saint of penury living in the margins of society". Like Bartleby, Melville's Jimmy Rose, in the 1855 short story of that name, is condemned to the "margins of society", but he manages to find ways of balancing the conflicting aspects of his identity. He avoids Bartleby's suicidal endgame by accepting the compromises entailed by his financial ruin. The narrator is astonished when he meets Jimmy Rose twenty-five years after his "clean smash":

> He whom I expected to behold – if behold at all – dry, shrunken, meagre, cadaverously fierce with misery and misanthropy – amazement! the old Parisian roses bloomed in his cheeks. And yet poor as any rat ...

Jimmy Rose has adapted to his diminished circumstances as best he could, and the wallpaper with which the story begins and ends serves as an emblem for his ability to accommodate these melancholy but unfatal contradictions:

And every time I look at the wilted resplendence of those proud peacocks on the wall, I bethink me of the withering change in Jimmy's once resplendent pride of state. But still again, every time I gaze upon those festoons of perpetual roses, mid which the faded peacocks hang, I bethink me of those undying roses which bloomed in ruined Jimmy's cheek.

Analogously, it is by pretending to be a wise fool that Blue avoids Quinn's disintegration into a scrofulous down-and-outer. Self-division becomes a source of comedy rather than tragedy. If Auster again uses nineteenth-century American literature as a means of figuring the interplay of competing selves, the anecdotes and allusions incarnate a wholly different perspective. In the course of their conversation Black tells Blue about the farcical fate of Whitman's brain, dropped by an assistant of the American Anthropometric Society while in the process of being measured and weighed. The story provokes "several wheezing laughs" from Blue as Jimmy Rose. Black compares the shattered brain to the excrement in the chamber pot legendarily present during Thoreau and Alcott's visit to Whitman in the family house on Myrtle Avenue. "There's a definite connection," he asserts, "Brains and guts, the inside of a man". And finally he relates the story of Hawthorne's "Wakefield", and the "little joke" Wakefield plays on his wife. By "stepping aside for a moment" Wakefield risks becoming, like Quinn or Bartleby or William Wilson, an "Outcast of the Universe", and yet in the end he returns with a "crafty smile" and recovers his other life.

Blue's efforts to generate a fantasy of perfect solitude are similarly broken down. He tries to picture himself escaping his case and leading a mythical Thoreauvian existence "free and uncommitted" on the frontier:

He imagines himself somewhere else, far away from here,

walking through the woods and swinging an axe over his shoulder. Alone and free, his own man at last. He would build his life from the bottom up, an exile, a pioneer, a pilgrim in the new world. But that is as far as he gets. For no sooner does he begin to walk through these woods in the middle of nowhere than he feels that Black is there too, hiding behind some tree, stalking invisibly through some thicket, waiting for Blue to lie down and close his eyes before sneaking up on him and slitting his throat.

Detective and wilderness discourses incongruously merge to create a ludicrous parody of Thoreau's figurative frontier and the exhilarating range of tropes it affords the self. For it is Thoreau's multiple layerings and contradictions that allow *Walden* to evade the constraints of the various terminologies he exploits. Although Thoreau is consciously acting out the central American myth that stipulates one can only achieve selfhood by immersion in the wilderness, he continually blurs both this narrative and its familiar implications. By allowing the book's structure to be determined by the seasons, Thoreau seems to abdicate responsibility to forces beyond him, eliding the active into the passive. For all his moral earnestness, the lofty rejections, the vatic exhortations, the severe disciplines ("think of dashing the hopes of a morning with a cup of warm coffee, or of an evening with a dish of tea! Ah, how low I fall when I am tempted by them!"), Thoreau seems above all concerned to elude definition, to escape being imprisoned within the various myths and rhetorics he appropriates. Thoreau may, as Auster suggests in "Portrait of an Invisible Man", have "exil[ed] himself in order to find out where he was", but only so he might move on from there: "I left the woods for as good a reason as I went there. Perhaps it seemed to me that I had several more lives to live, and could not spend any more time for that one." *Walden* offers us no final perspective that makes triumphant sense of Thoreau's experiment, and he advises readers against attempting anything too similar themselves: "I would not have anyone adopt *my* mode of living on any account." As hero of his own book Thoreau is thus at once exemplary and inimitable, while his life in the woods, rather than defining a solid basis for action, is only justified by its provisionality: "Perhaps if I lived there much longer," he ruminates in a Journal entry of January 1852, "I might live there forever. One would think twice before he accepted heaven on such terms."

Thoreau's clarion calls for spiritual reform, for constant self-awareness, for abstinence, belie a certain arbitrariness that permeates his presentation of his enterprise. How, for instance, are we to respond to the reference he makes to chance when describing the first night he spent in his cabin, "which, by accident, was on Independence Day, or the Fourth of July, 1845"? Is this the dry wit of a national redeemer, or a disarming disclaimer? And if we are not to follow Thoreau's example, what exactly *are* we supposed to do? It is this confusion which allows critics like Sacvan Bercovitch to argue that *Walden*, rather than radically challenging the dominant political culture, merely updates the analogies between moral, spiritual, and material progress first sanctioned by the doctrines of Puritanism, while such as Lawrence Buell now claim Thoreau as America's first eco-saint, a prophetic defender of the wilderness against the encroachments of capital. The book's "obscurity", to use Thoreau's own term, seems to encourage any number of conflicting readings, as Emerson first pointed out in a Journal entry: "The trick of his rhetoric is soon learned; it consists in substituting for the obvious word & thought its diametrical antagonist ... It makes me nervous and wretched to read it."

These contradictions may be seen as emerging out of what Auster defines in an interview as Thoreau's "passionate excess". In the economy of *Walden*, however, the excess of Thoreau's figurations is dependent on the deprivation of his body: "I believe that every man who has ever been earnest to preserve his higher or poetic faculties has been particularly inclined to abstain from animal food, and from much food of any kind." Auster's characters are also prone to pursuing illumination through the rituals of self-denial. Like Thoreau, "by accident" they find themselves declaring independence and embracing the austere *via negativa* of the American hermit.

Auster's protagonists are persistently driven to embrace "a primitive and frontier life, though in the midst of an outward civilization". Quinn's assignment in *City of Glass* soon develops into a Thoreauvian quest for "spiritual grace" that involves ever more extreme forms of asceticism. Quinn is eventually reduced to the barest essentials, holed up in an alley, hardly eating or sleeping, and sheltering from the weather in a large metal garbage bin. It is at this point that he begins "to understand the true nature of solitude". He spends most of his time watching the sky, noting each shift in conditions as thoroughly as the "self-appointed inspector of snowstorms and rainstorms":

> He became familiar with the cirrus, the cumulus, the stratus, the nimbus, and all their various combinations, watching for each one in its turn, and seeing how the sky would change under its influence. Clouds, too, introduced the matter of colour, and there was a wide range to contend with, spanning from black to white, with an infinity of greys between. These all had to be investigated, measured, and deciphered.

Quinn gives up writing about the case in his journal, and instead notes down observations "about the stars, the earth, his hopes for mankind." His words no longer seem to belong to him; they seem instead wholly dispersed, "a part of the world at large, as real and specific as a stone, or a lake, or a flower."

The narrator of *Moon Palace*, Marco Stanley Fogg, is also driven to discard his possessions and repudiate society. Like Thoreau seeking out "the hidden advantage that each deprivation produced", Fogg is determined to interpret his successive humiliations and terrible hunger pangs as "spiritual initiations, as obstacles that had been thrown across my path to test my faith in myself. If I learned how to overcome them, I would eventually reach a higher stage of consciousness." Evicted from his apartment, down to his last few dollars, Fogg takes up residence in Central Park where he scrounges food from litter baskets and ponders the Higher Laws. "Once you throw your life to the winds," he asserts, "you will discover things you had never known before, things that cannot be learned under any other circumstances." He too experiences the double consciousness of solitude, the pure detachment of the self-exiled: "This is human loneliness, I said to myself. This is what it means to have no one. I was not angry anymore, however, and I thought these words with a kind of brutal candor, an absolute objectivity." But whereas Quinn and Blue found themselves in stories whose generic conventions relentlessly widen and finally dissolve into the imponderables of metaphysics, Fogg manages to return from his moon-voyaging to the narratives of national history and myth. On the verge of starvation, Fogg falls asleep and begins to dream of Indians:

> It was 350 years ago, and I saw myself following a group of half-naked men through the forests of Manhattan. It was a strangely vibrant dream, relentless and exact, filled with bodies darting among the light-dappled leaves and branches. A soft wind poured through the foliage, muffling the footsteps of the men, and I went on following them in silence, moving as nimbly as they did, with each step feeling that I was closer to understanding the spirit of the forest.

He wakes from this dream-induction to discover he has been rescued by his two friends, Zimmer and Kitty Wu. Kitty is wearing a Navaho head band, and Fogg is initially convinced that she is Pocahontas.

"He has repudiated all regular modes of getting a living, and seems inclined to lead a sort of Indian life among civilized men," Hawthorne wrote of Thoreau in *The American Notebooks*. Auster has suggested this "sums up [Thoreau's] project better than anything else". During the period in which *Moon Palace* is set (1965–71), Thoreau's example and writings were frequently invoked by apologists for the counter-culture as a precedent for their experiments and defiances. While the violent aspects of frontier initiation were being re-enacted in Vietnam, Thoreau's spiritual internalization of the pioneer spirit – "Explore thyself" – served as a paradigm for all those travelling to the beat of a different drum, to borrow the best known reworking of a Thoreauvian aphorism. In his recent memoir, *Hand to Mouth*, Auster narrates his own experience of this period as a series of economic failures and political refusals roughly equivalent to those described in *Moon Palace*. His identity seems mainly predicated on his "need to affirm myself as an outsider", and his "downfall" derives from his attempts to preserve his personal integrity at all costs:

> My life would be good if and only if I stuck to my guns and refused to give in. Art was holy, and to follow its call meant making any sacrifice that was demanded of you, maintaining your purity of purpose to the bitter end.

At the same time Auster is uneasily aware that it is exactly these exemplary acts of resistance which have helped win for him the institutional status that enables him to present these failures as an integral part of his American success story. "So much for selling out", the memoir concludes, dubiously punning on moral and economic values, just as Thoreau does throughout *Walden*.

"I simply wish to refuse allegiance to the State, to withdraw and stand aloof from it effectually", Thoreau proclaims in "Resistance to Civil Government"; "In fact, I quietly declare war with the state, after my fashion." As with Auster, this radical rejection of his country's institutions does not, however, open him to the charge of being anti-American, for resistance has always been one of the primary markers of Americanness. "No truer American existed than Thoreau", insists Emerson in his 1862 memorial essay on his fellow townsman. Indeed Thoreau presents his own independence as a redemptive recreation of American ideals, arguing that "a really free and enlightened State" would "recognize the individual as a higher and independent power from which all its own power and authority are derived". Thus for Thoreau resistance is a patriotic duty, one of the crucially defining features of the American hero, as he most clearly explains in his idealized portrait of John Brown. Feverishly inspired by Brown's example, Thoreau delivered his lecture, "A Plea for Captain John Brown", just two weeks after Brown's attack on the federal arsenal at Harpers Ferry:

> He did not value his bodily life in comparison with ideal things. He did not recognize unjust human laws, but resisted them as he was bid. For once we are lifted out of the trivialness and dust of politics into the region of truth and manhood. No man in America has ever stood up so persistently and effectively for the dignity of human nature, knowing himself for a man, and the equal of any and all governments. In that sense he was the most American of us all.

Brown is praised for a variety of other Thoreauvian virtues – not eating much, self-culture, surviving in the wilderness, and being considered insane by the majority of his fellow countrymen. A further sign of his genius is his ability to create his own solitude wherever he goes: like Thoreau running "the gauntlet" of the inhabitants of Concord on his visits to the village, or Fogg "blending into the environment" in Central Park, Brown is adept at preserving his separateness; he "becomes a hermit in the thoroughfares of the market-place".

While Thoreau's rhetorical elusiveness brilliantly exemplifies this ideal of political and social standoffishness, it has also meant that even

253

his most overtly polemical writings can be appropriated in the name of widely divergent causes. Thoreau was himself, in Emerson's words, "not only unrepresented in actual politics, but almost equally opposed to every class of reformers". Emerson also frequently worried about the dangers posed to the self's integrity by reform movements, and always insisted on the "paramount duties of self-reliance". He was more willing than Thoreau, however, to try to sift the good from the bad; in his lecture "New England Reformers", delivered in 1844, he evenly observes:

> With this din of opinion and debate, there was a keener scrutiny of institutions and domestic life than any we had known, there was sincere protesting against existing evils, and there were changes of employment dictated by conscience. No doubt, there was plentiful vaporing, and cases of backsliding might occur. But in each of these movements emerged a good result, a tendency to the adoption of simpler methods, and an assertion of the sufficiency of the private man.

Thoreau, on the other hand, trenchantly attributed all enthusiasm for reform to "some obscure, and perhaps unrecognized private grievance":

> Now, if anything ail a man so that he does not perform his functions; especially if his digestion is poor, though he may have considerable nervous strength left; if he has failed in all his undertakings hitherto; if he has committed some heinous sin and partially repents, what does he do? He sets about reforming the world.

Thoreau is anxious in his essay on Brown to insist on his hero's indifference to all institutions and movements: "This man was an exception, for he did not set up even a political graven image between him and his God."

It is with John Brown – as well as Irving's Ichabod Crane – that the writer Peter Aaron initially compares Benjamin Sachs at their first meeting in Auster's *Leviathan*:

> In spite of his ridiculous get-up, there was something fierce in his eyes, an intensity that quelled any desire to laugh at him. He resembled Ichabod Crane, perhaps, but he was also John Brown, and once you got past his costume and his gangly basketball forward's body, you began to see an entirely different sort of person: a man who missed nothing, a man with a thousand wheels turning in his head.

Thoreau, however, soon emerges as Sachs's ultimate exemplar. Like Fogg's, Sachs's "challenge to the American way" is based on the principle of refusal. Called up for service in the U.S. Army in 1968, Sachs, rather than fleeing to Canada or Europe, opts to stand trial and go to jail. "If I had to sum up his attitude towards his own beliefs," Aaron muses,

> I would begin by mentioning the Transcendentalists of the nineteenth century. Thoreau was his model, and without the example of *Civil Disobedience*, I doubt that Sachs would have turned out as he did. I'm not just talking about prison now, but a whole approach to life, an attitude of remorseless inner vigilance. Once, when *Walden* came up in conversation, Sachs confessed to me that he wore a beard "because Henry David had worn one" – which gave me a sudden insight into how deep his admiration was. As I write these words now, it occurs to me that they both lived the same number of years. Thoreau died at forty-four, and Sachs wouldn't have passed him until next month. I don't

suppose there's anything to be made of this coincidence, but it's the kind of thing that Sachs always liked, a small detail to be noted for the record.

By grounding Sachs's opposition in the Thoreauvian tradition of civil disobedience, Auster creates a context for his resistance within the overall development of American history. During his seventeen months in prison Sachs composes his first novel, *The New Colossus*, set in America between 1876 and 1890, and featuring a vast range of historical and fictional characters – Emma Lazarus (from whose poem on the Statue of Liberty Sachs's title is borrowed), Sitting Bull, Huckleberry Finn, Emerson, Buffalo Bill Cody, Ishmael, Walt Whitman, Raskolnikov... Thoreau, though dead fourteen years when the book opens, seems yet to be its presiding spirit. In the Friday chapter of *A Week on the Concord and Merrimack Rivers* he laments: "the land is lost sight of, the compass varies, and mankind mutiny; and still history accumulates like rubbish before the portals of nature." Sachs's *The New Colossus* further develops this prophecy. Ellery Channing and Emma Lazarus visit Walden Pond together. As a parting present Channing gives Lazarus a parcel containing his book on Thoreau and Thoreau's pocket compass:

> It's a beautiful moment, very sensitively handled by Sachs, and it plants an important image in the reader's head that will recur in any number of guises throughout the book. Although it isn't said in so many words, the message couldn't be clearer. America has lost its way. Thoreau was the one man who could read the compass for us, and now that he is gone, we have no hope of finding ourselves again.

Emerson declared of Thoreau that "he did not feel himself except in opposition". Sachs's life is similarly determined by his search for ways of undermining authority and institutions. *The New Colossus* is dominated by Sachs's "anger against America, anger against political hypocrisy, anger as a weapon to destroy national myths". We learn less of his unfinished second novel, *Leviathan*, written while Sachs was "living like a hermit in the woods" of New England, but its title suggests that this book was also fundamentally concerned with matters of state. In the end, however, the iconoclastic Sachs realizes his perfect mode of self-expression lies not in creating books, but in destroying the political images that stand between him and his God, or rather Goddess.

With a third of *Leviathan* written, Sachs goes for a walk in the woods – without a compass – and gets lost. Next morning he is picked up by a young truck driver. On a back road they stop to help a man whose car appears to have broken down. Far from welcoming their assistance, he shoots the truck driver dead, and is in turn killed by Sachs who smashes him on the head with a baseball bat. Sachs discovers that the man he has killed, Reed Dimaggio, belongs to a left-wing ecology group. Dimaggio is an eco-terrrorist – "a crazed idealist, a believer in a cause, a person who had dreamed of changing the world ... He and Sachs had stood for the same things." He finds in Dimaggio's car a suitcase full of bomb-making equipment and a bowling bag containing $165,000. Sachs at first attempts to redeem himself by fulfilling the social responsibilities that Dimaggio had neglected. He tracks down Dimaggio's ex-wife, insinuates himself into her household, and becomes a surrogate father to their child. He hopes his conduct will "embody an ideal of goodness that would put him in an altogether different relation with himself".

Thoreauvian idealists like Dimaggio and Sachs can only achieve this "different relation", however, through opposition and solitude. Contemplating the drawing of the Statue of Liberty on the cover of his own novel, *The New Colossus*, in a book store, Sachs suddenly understands his mission: he realizes he is at last "ready to march out into the wilderness and spread the word, ready to begin all over again". He renounces domesticity, and decides to dedicate his life to blowing up as many as possible of the 130 or so scale-model replicas of the Statue of Liberty that adorn public spaces across America. This programme of mini-terrorism, of civil disobedience, is to remind the nation of its failure to live up to its own principles. The Phantom of Liberty's accompanying messages combine, in Thoreauvian fashion, exhortatory rhetoric and puzzling conundrums: "Wake up, America. It's time to start practicing what you preach ... Each person is alone, and therefore we have nowhere to turn but to each other ... We exist in the present only to the degree that we put our faith in the future." The demolished Statues of Liberty represent the ideals from which America has fallen, a betrayal that is mirrored by Sachs's own fall from a fire-escape while watching the fireworks illuminating the original Statue of Liberty at an Independence Day party. This accident – which he later claims was no accident at all – initiates the process of self-exploration which finally results in his transformation into the Phantom of Liberty, the Statue's shadowy living counterpart.

"I am under an aweful necessity", Thoreau reflects in an 1851 Journal entry, "to be what I am." Ultimately the authority of *Walden* rests on this belief. Sachs makes his case to Aaron in equivalent terms: "I've become who I am now, and there's no going back." It is this fully achieved sense of self and purpose which justifies both their ever-changing self-figurations and their solitary freedom. After realizing his vocation, Sachs assumes any number of identities, at one point even posing as a journalist writing an article on responses to the Phantom. His powers of self-creation enable him to feel "equally at home anywhere", like the Saunterer of Thoreau's "Walking", or the ideal self projected in the image of the heroic hawk of *Walden*, "sport[ing] with proud reliance in the fields of air".

If reading *Walden* often feels like searching for footholds in "fields of air", that is because Thoreau wants to confuse and multiply the reader's "order of understandings":

> I fear chiefly lest my expression may not be *extra-vagant*
> enough, may not wander far enough beyond the narrow
> limits of my daily experience, so as to be adequate to the
> truth of which I have been convinced. *Extra vagance!* it
> depends on how you are yarded.

Thoreau's linguistic wandering unsettles like the loon in "Brute
Neighbors" who mocks Thoreau's attempts to predict his movements. It is the primary means by which he hopes to "wake [his]
neighbors up". The indeterminate range of *Walden's* possible meanings compels us "to witness our own limits transgressed", which in
turn makes us realize "the necessity of being forever on the alert".
For *Walden* insists we be aware that "[e]verything, in some sense,
can be read as a gloss on everything else". The thawing bank of
"Spring", for instance, which occasions Thoreau's hypotheses on
the relations of lobe, drop, lip, *labium*, lapse, serves to illustrate
"the principle of all the operations of Nature". Language, Thoreau
suggests, may encode similarities between these operations.

It is just this possibility which obsesses the older Peter Stillman in
City of Glass. Stillman's doctoral thesis concerned the work of the
fictitious Henry Dark – supposedly for a time secretary to Milton
– who emigrated to the New World in 1675. His only surviving
pamphlet, *The New Babel*, argues that in America language will
finally be redeemed from its fallen state, and heaven and earth be
reunited. In the hope of fulfilling this prediction, Stillman impris-
ons his infant son for nine years in a boarded up room, believing the
younger Stillman will naturally begin to speak this pure Utopian
language. Eventually the older Stillman's mad scheme is exposed,
and he is sent to an insane asylum. On his release, however, he
immediately takes up his project again: he spends his days collect-
ing debris from the streets and invents new names for each find,
"words that will correspond to the things". The routes he follows
on his walks also spell out his undertaking: Quinn traces the course
of Stillman's wanderings in his notebook, and finds they resemble

the words TOWER OF BABEL. However, when Quinn asks for an example of this new, primary language, Stillman refuses: "I'm sorry, but that won't be possible. It's my secret, you understand."

Stillman's Utopian fantasies derive from his consuming desire – shared with Sachs and Thoreau – that vision and expression be fused, even if the resultant work must remain either wholly private, or indistinguishable from life itself. "The true poem is not that which the public read", Thoreau argues in *A Week*:

> There is always a poem not printed on paper, coincident with the production of this, stereotyped in the poet's life. It is *what he has become through his work*. Not how is the idea expressed in stone, or on canvass or paper, is the question, but how far it has obtained form and expression in the life of the artist. His true work will not stand in any prince's gallery.

> My life has been the poem I would have writ,
> But I could not both live and utter it.

It is this compulsion constantly to refigure the relations and divisions between living and writing that underlies the long gestation of *Walden*, and accounts for the book's kaleidoscopic multiplicity that so baffles Blue in *Ghosts*, and rendered Emerson so "nervous and wretched". Equally, Auster's self-reflexive narrative strategies repeatedly illustrate the impossibility of separating autobiography from fiction, or vice versa. "My dear Henry," Emerson wrote in a mock letter to Thoreau in his Journal, "A frog was made to live in a swamp, but a man was not made to live in a swamp. Yours ever, R." Neither Thoreau nor Auster can resist exploring that swamp in search of its mysterious "solid bottom", and as part of this process each is driven to relate the dizzying inventions of solitude.

Journal of American Studies, 1999

Paul Muldoon's Nose for Trouble

Paul Muldoon was born in Co. Armagh in Northern Ireland in 1951. His father was a farm labourer and market gardener, and his mother a schoolteacher: "She had read one volume of Proust," he writes in "The Mixed Marriage", "He knew the cure for farcy. / I flitted between a hole in the hedge / And a room in the Latin Quarter."

Analogous hybrids of all sorts abound in Muldoon's all-accommodating narratives: mules, talking horses, skywomen, a coney who dissolves into honey, a pig made of soap, an Apache / Irish terrorist, a man-ox, a fish with three gold teeth, a flute fashioned from a missionary's tibia on which the poet hears "The Lass of Aughrim" played during a trip down the Amazon. And Muldoon's forms and plots seem to derive from a similar compulsion to bring together the unlikely: his longest poem to date, for instance, "MADOC – A Mystery", purports to describe the adventures of Coleridge and Southey in America in the 1790s, as if those two ardent pantisocrats, as they called themselves, really had set sail, as they for awhile intended, to found a Utopian colony in the New World. To complicate matters further: 1) a science fiction framing device presents the narrative of their journey as in fact a transcription made during the middle of the 21st century by a retinagraph of the right eyeball of a character called John South, a shadowy terrorist figure possibly working to overthrow the power of a futuristic conglomerate called Unitel; 2) each of the 233 sections of the poem is introduced by the name of a philosopher in square brackets, inviting us to connect some aspect of the section with the given philosopher's life or philosophy. In the [Diogenes] poem we find Southey in his tent on the banks of the Susquehanna bathing in a "claw-foot tub", and in the [Erasmus] section a reference to a ship from Rotterdam; but, as always in Muldoon, for every ladder there are a multitude of snakes, and even experts in the thought of the 3rd century BC Greek peripatetic philosopher, Theophrastus, might, one imagines, have trouble meaningfully linking his work to his section in the poem, which consists of this single line: "De dum de dum de dum de dum de dum."

Muldoon is not himself prone to falling into the jogtrot of the iambic pentameter, and the traditional forms of British poetry suffer at his hands a transformation into something sometimes rich and always strange. Consider, for example, the title poem of his fourth collection, *Quoof* (1983), a typical Muldoon sonnet:

> How often have I carried our family word
> for the hot water bottle
> to a strange bed,
> as my father would juggle a red-hot half-brick
> in an old sock
> to his childhood settle.
> I have taken it into so many lovely heads
> or laid it between us like a sword.
>
> A hotel room in New York City
> with a girl who spoke hardly any English,
> my hand on her breast
> like the smouldering one-off spoor of the yeti
> or some other shy beast
> that has yet to enter the language.

Here again we have the theme of the mixed marriage: it is his father whom the poem connects with the domestic rites and private language of the family. Adrift in the wide, adult world of strange beds, sexual partners, and New York hotel rooms, the word "quoof" becomes a talismanic signifier of both the losses and excitements implicit in his engagement with the exotic world beyond his parochial upbringing – the "Latin Quarter" life yearned for by his mother. It at once dramatizes the distance he has travelled from his father's simple rural roots, and allows him to defend his most primary sense of self from the threat of erotic entrapment and dissolution inherent in his cosmopolitan philandering.

This, at least, seems to be the theory of the octet, that the lucky product of the mixed marriage might, in the words of the title poem of his 1977 collection, *Mules*, "have the best of both worlds." The verbless sestet that follows, however, seems to tell a different story. The sexual encounter with a girl who speaks hardly any English leads to a sense of freakishness and detachment: his very hand metamorphoses into the smouldering "one-off spoor" of some chimerical beast – the antithesis of the warm brick juggled by his father in his homely nightly ritual. And if it is the scene's stalled randomness and uniqueness that makes it uninterpretable, yet one cannot help parsing it in relation to the octet in the hope of solving the poem's puzzle, and achieving the momentary "clarification of life" in which Robert Frost – to whose work Muldoon insistently alludes – claimed a poem should end.

Muldoon has frequently praised Frost's devious ability to say one thing and mean another, and from Frost he learned how to use form as a means of evading self-revelation. The persona of "Quoof", though willing to disclose a secret word from his family's private lexicon, nevertheless refuses to relate his experience in a way that allows it to be classified; and while the poem is a sonnet in rhymes and length, it might more accurately be described as an anti-sonnet in its refusal of all the traditional resources of the form, and in its almost mocking half-rhymes: bottle / settle, City / yeti, English / language.

It is to this ventriloquistic elusiveness that Seamus Heaney calls attention in his tiny poem, "Widgeon", dedicated to Muldoon and collected in his *Station Island* volume of 1984:

> It had been badly shot.
> While he was plucking it
> he found, he says, the voice box –
>
> like a flute stop
> in the broken windpipe –
>
> and blew upon it
> unexpectedly
> his own small widgeon cries.

Muldoon appears to consider this poem a good one, for he included it in his selection of Heaney's work in his 1985 *Faber Book of Contemporary Irish Poetry*. In its subtle way, it does, however, register a number of reservations about the younger writer's poetics. Whereas Heaney, most famously and controversially in *North* (1975), responded to the endless bombs, beatings, and assassinations of the Troubles with a poetry that sought rituals and symbols "adequate to our predicament", as he phrased it, and which allowed him to acknowledge his own attraction to the myths underpinning Irish Nationalism, for Muldoon random death and destruction are givens to be approached in a spirit of complete detachment. Nearly all of his volumes contain scenes, images and fantasies of quite astonishing violence: his father being eaten alive by piranhas ("The Waking Father"), a girl made pregnant by the poet strangled by the belt of a whirring corn thresher ("Cuckoo Corn"), a blanket deliberately infected with smallpox "traded" during the Indian Wars ("Meeting the British"), a woman fist-fucked to death ("Blewits"), a pair of trousers worn by the Scottish scout in "MADOC" made from the skin of "at least four, maybe five, hapless Gros Ventre women", and of course everywhere dismembered and exploded bodies, like that of the local councillor in "The More a Man Has the More a Man Wants", blown up by a booby trap in a municipal car park:

> Once they collect his smithereens
> he doesn't quite add up.
> They're shy of a foot, and a calf
> which stems
> from his left shoe like a severely
> pruned-back shrub.

What is disturbing is the jocular matter-of-fact tone, the refusal to be outraged or even surprised. Muldoon is figured by Heaney as depending on these bad shootings to blow his own unexpected, small cries: the resultant poetry, Heaney seems to suggest, is startling, but uninterested in dignifying the suffering it exploits.

The Romantic model of poetry on which Heaney's own œuvre is based is one Muldoon has endlessly guyed, sidestepped, and refuted. Heaney's relationship to the reader depends, above all, on our willingness to trust the voice that explains to us how the poet evolved in relation to landscape, history, culture, and family, and to sympathize with his attempts to make sense of the experiences he describes, which we must believe actually happened. Whether or not the poet of "Quoof" in real life spent a night in a hotel room in New York with a girl who spoke hardly any English, on the other hand, is irrelevant to the impact of the poem. Muldoon tends to figure a poet simply as someone "through whom a poem [is] written", as he puts it in an Author's Note prefacing his *Collected*; the notion of a stable poetic self providing readers with exemplary "momentary stay[s] against confusion", to quote Frost's famous formulation, seems to the Postmodern Muldoon an unsustainable fiction. On the contrary, poetry should unsettle our habitual patterns of thought, lead us as through a labyrinth into the heart of confusion.

His most explicit reply to the charges levelled in "Widgeon" is "The Briefcase", dedicated to Seamus Heaney, and collected in *Madoc*:

I held the briefcase at arm's length from me;
the oxblood or liver
eel skin with which it was covered
had suddenly grown supple.

I'd been waiting in line for the cross-town
bus when an almighty cloudburst
left the sidewalk a raging torrent.

And though it contained only the first
inkling of this poem, I knew I daren't
set the briefcase down
to slap my pockets for an obol –

for fear it might slink into a culvert
and strike out along the East River
for the sea. By which I mean the "open" sea.

The poem alludes to a passage in an early Heaney poem, "Lough Neagh Sequence", in which he marvels at the eel's ability to migrate across the Atlantic, and wriggle inland into the heart of Ireland. "The Briefcase" was written shortly after Muldoon himself settled in America, and on one level might be taken as a parody of Irish diaspora culture's sentimental longing for "home". Heaney's vibrant, organic, instinctive "gland" undergoes a highly characteristic Muldoon transformation into a luxury briefcase, one to be held "at arm's length" – rather as the poem's form (again a sonnet, but this time with in / out rhymes, i.e., *abcdefgfgedcba*) seems quizzically at odds with the metaphor of "living form" the poem comically literalises. But Muldoon is not simply proclaiming here the virtues of the kind of poetic self-consciousness his work embodies; he is also satirizing the possibility of a poet's controlling the range of a poem's meanings, and the uses to which it might be put.

From the very outset of his career Muldoon has shown himself acutely aware of the need for poetry to be held "at arm's length", not only from writer and reader, but also from the political and cultural circumstances of its historical moment. This issue is a particularly pertinent one in twentieth-century Irish literature: "Did that play of mine send out / Certain men the English shot?" Yeats dramatically demanded in "The Man and the Echo" of his patriotic verse drama *Cathleen Ni Houlihan*. "When, for fuck's sake, are you going to write / Something for us?" an angry Fenian berates Heaney in "The Flight Path" in his 1996 collection *The Spirit Level*. Muldoon resists such pressures by insisting on the hypothetical space in which each poem exists – and often, as in his account of Coleridge and Southey's exploits in America, by developing ostentatiously hypothetical narratives. One of the most pervasive themes of his astonishingly precocious first book, *New Weather* (1973), published when he was 21, is the precariousness of identity, how many roads not taken diverge from and shadow the one that was. In one mini-parable a somewhat Audenesque spy-figure falls in with a woman, also on the run, who suggests she steal papers for them both, that they escape the following night by boat, and then marry. We never learn, needless to say, of his response to this alternative life suddenly presented to him, but are offered instead these cryptic afterthoughts:

> I have been wandering since, back up the streams
> That had once flowed simply one into the other,
> One taking the other's name.

This time when streams "flowed" – or seemed to – "simply one into the other" without resulting in hybrid offspring is as close as Muldoon will come to indulging in the illusions of innocence. This poem, called "Identities", is about evading the complications and consequences of sex, and the poet's nostalgic wanderings, or wonderings, are analogous to his evoking the word "quoof" in strange beds.

More often, though, Muldoon's poems explore the peculiar conjunctions and transformations attendant upon accepting – or making – proposals such as that of the woman in "Identities". In "Whim", for instance, an unnamed he picks up an unnamed her in the bar of the aptly named Europa hotel. He invites her back to his flat – not that they make it that far:

> They would saunter through the Botanic Gardens
> Where they held hands, and kissed.
> And by and by one thing led to another.
> To cut not a very long story short,
> Once he got stuck into her he got stuck
> Full stop.
>   They lay there quietly until dusk
> When an attendant found them out.
> He called an ambulance, and gently but firmly
> They were manhandled onto a stretcher
> Like the last of an endangered species.

This little misfortune (known in slang-terms as dog-knotting) is again presented as the literal enactment of a metaphor – that of making the beast with two backs. While in "Quoof" the lovers' encounter begat the image of a creature so shy it had "yet to enter the language", the more knowing couple of "Whim" metamorphose into one about to disappear from it. Particularly characteristic of Muldoon here, in fact probably the most distinctive hallmark of his entire œuvre, is his use of the conditional tense – "They would saunter ..." We can never quite be sure in Muldoon's narratives of the borders between fantasy and reality. In a poem from the same volume (*Why Brownlee Left* (1980)) we learn of a man about to join holy orders. However,

> The night before he was to be ordained
> He packed a shirt and a safety razor

And started out for the middle of nowhere,
Back to the back of beyond.

He marries a childhood sweetheart, inherits his uncle's fortune, buys land, and is found dead one morning by his favourite grand-daughter. Only the poem is called "The Bishop", and the implication is that this is his dream on the eve of ordination of the life he will never lead. Muldoon applies the same technique to a number of poems about his father, who almost emigrated from Ireland in the 1930s. In the end he didn't, but Muldoon is much drawn to pondering the implications of this unfulfilled scheme. "It's an image", he has commented,

> that's troubled me for ages, since it underlines the arbitrary nature of so many of the decisions we take, the disturbingly random quality of so many of our actions. I would speculate on my father's having led an entirely different life, in which, clearly, I would have played no part.

He sets about trailing his "father's spirit / From the mud-walled cabin behind the mountain / Where he was born and bred", to "a building-site from which he disappeared / And took passage, almost, for Argentina":

> The mountain is coming down with hazel,
> The building-site is a slum,
> While he has gone no further than Brazil.
>
> That's him on the verandah, drinking rum
> With a man who might be a Nazi,
> His children asleep under their mosquito-nets.

And none of these children is the poet – whose conception is described in another sonnet in the same volume as an equally arbitrary occurrence, as probably dating back to "a chance remark / In a room at the top of the stairs; / To an open field, as like as not, / Under the little stars." Far from clarifying his sense of self, the attempt to imagine his biological moment of origin only emphasizes his awareness of the random: whatever the circumstances, as this poem ("October 1950") punningly concludes, "it leaves me in the dark."

"In the dark", however, is exactly how many readers feel when confronted with Muldoon's longer poems – peculiar, hard-to-define, comic-epic quests such as "The More a Man Has the More a Man Wants", "MADOC – A Mystery", or "The Bangle (Slight Return)" from *Hay*. These oblique narratives exhibit a density of allusion and word-play that brings to mind late Joyce. For although a kind of chaos-theory seems to underlie Muldoon's sense of the way events happen in the world, his large-scale poetic structures embody this randomness by its opposite, a manic over-patterning that decrees that every detail in a poem must somehow connect with every other detail in it. In his later long poems in particular, the ludic deliberately shades into the ludicrous (to use a Muldoonish pun), and the formal challenges he sets himself become ever-more demanding, and bewildering: why, for instance, does he have the rhyme scheme of his long poem "Yarrow" track that of another long poem, "Incantata" (both collected in *The Annals of Chile* (1994)? Both poems, further, bristle with references to an encyclopaedic range of myths and texts and contain more than the odd scrap of Gaelic and other foreign languages; are these allusions, too, one begins to wonder, part of some elaborate hall of mirrors?

Indeed, to decode fully much of Muldoon's recent work you'd need to have read and remembered pretty much all that he himself has read and remembered – and that's a very, very great deal. In 2000 he published a set of lectures he delivered as Oxford Professor of Poetry under the title *To Ireland, I*. These consisted of alphabetically organized entries on Irish writers, from the twelfth-century bard Amergin to Zozimus, the pseudonym of a blind nineteenth-century Dublin ballad-maker. And pretty well every writer mentioned is shown some-

how to be referred to in James Joyce's "The Dead" – or, in the entries
for post-Joycean writers such as Elizabeth Bowen or C. S. Lewis, to
contain somewhere buried allusions to Joyce's wintry short story. *To
Ireland, I* is a brilliantly entertaining and informative work of criticism, but is also almost a spoof of the genre. What it does undoubtedly
demonstrate, however, is Muldoon's unique way of reading literature
like some dazzlingly versatile, perhaps almost compulsive exponent
of the art of the dot-to-dot puzzle. Certainly it sheds an intriguing
– if not wholly reassuring – light on the intricate cross-references and
recurring tics and themes that pattern Muldoon's own relentlessly
allusive longer works. Joyce once commented of *Ulysses*: "I've put in
so many enigmas and puzzles that it will keep the professors busy for
centuries arguing over what I meant, and that's the only way of insur-
ing one's immortality." The exegesis of Muldoon's œuvre has only just
begun, in monographs such as Tim Kendall's 1996 *Paul Muldoon* and
Clair Wills's 1998 *Reading Paul Muldoon*, but it promises to evolve
into an equally time-consuming project.

Muldoon has now been resident in America for around 15 years.
Moy Sand and Gravel – which was awarded this year's Pulitzer Prize
for Poetry – is his most concerted attempt yet to evolve a poetry that
fuses his overwhelmingly Irish preoccupations with his day to day life
on the East Coast (he teaches at Princeton) with his wife Jean Hanff
Korelitz, and their two children. The mixed marriage he contemplates
in this volume, most directly in the eclogue "The Grand Conversation", is his own:

> *She.* My people came from Korelitz
> where they grew yellow cucumbers
> and studied the Talmud.
> *He.* Mine pored over the mud
> of mangold- and potato-pits
> or flicked through kale plants from Comber
> as bibliomancers of old

went a-flicking through deckle-mold.

This "conversation" also dominates the book's long concluding poem, "At the Sign of the Black Horse, September 1999" (a reference to their house in New Jersey) in which Muldoon plays off his rural Catholic Irish origins against his wife's Judaism, and ponders the mix of their disparate cultures and genes in the face of the recently born Asher ("in Hebrew 'blest'"). As its numerous references to Yeats's "A Prayer for My Daughter" emphasize, this is Muldoon at his most domestic, hymning the fragile delights of family life in the face of the forces of nature (the poem is set in the aftermath of the "haystack- and roof-levelling wind, / Bred on the Atlantic", of Hurricane Floyd), and historical suffering, alluding in particular to the themes of Irish hunger and the experiences of Polish Jews during World War II. The poem presents a series of glimpses into the lives and times of Jean's extended family, but also, as is Muldoon's wont, knits together many of the images and characters featured earlier in the book to create his densely textured intertwining loops of reference and language.

Moy Sand and Gravel is unlikely to strike Muldoon aficionados as a great leap forward, but it still offers a number of poems that demonstrate why he is regarded by many as the most sophisticated, rewarding, and original poet of his generation. It contains two of his very best sestinas ("The Misfits" and "The Turn"), some wonderful translations from Horace, Montale, and Valéry, and three poems ("Unapproved Road", "John Luke: The Fox", and "The Loaf") that make brilliant use of terza rima. Its short title poem revisits the anxieties of merging that galvanize early poems such as "Identities" and "Mules", contrasting the coming together of two movie stars in a screen kiss with the two towers of a sand and gravel company across from the cinema he used to visit as a child growing up in Armagh. Here the fantasy of balanced union Muldoon strives so hard to make credible elsewhere in the collection seems to be, if not exactly rebuked, then severely qualified. In the book's opening poem Muldoon pictures himself driving around Ireland "with a toe in the water / and a nose for trouble", keeping his "wound green". "Moy Sand and Gravel" memorably shows why – no matter how hard he washes it – that wound could never be any other colour:

> To come out of the Olympic Cinema and be taken aback
> by how, in the time it took a dolly to travel
> along its little track
> to the point where two movie stars' heads
> had come together smackety-smack
> and their kiss filled the whole screen,
>
> those two great towers directly across the road
> at Moy Sand and Gravel
> had already washed, at least once, what had flowed
> or been dredged from the Blackwater's bed
> and were washing it again, load by load,
> as if washing might make it clean.

New York Review of Books, 2003: Review of Paul Muldoon's *Poems 1968–1998* (Farrar, Straus and Giroux, 2001) and *Moy Sand and Gravel* (Farrar, Straus and Giroux, 2002).

Misfortunes and Mishaps:
James Tate's *Return to the City of the White Donkeys*

The city of white donkeys evoked in the title poem of this exhilarating new collection from James Tate is an underground metropolis just beneath the earth – or so Polly, one of the book's teeming cast of more than slightly off-kilter characters would have us believe: the inhabitants of this city "are very pale," she explains,

> "but they can
> see in the dark. Of course there are no cars or anything
> like that, but a few have carts pulled by albino donkeys.
> They live on root vegetables, potatoes, carrots, radishes
> and onions. Oh yes, and grubs, they love grubs. Their houses
> are made of mud. They've never seen the sky, or light of
> any kind, never seen a sunset, so they don't miss them. They
> fall in love, much as we do. They experience joy and pain
> and sorrow much the same," she said.

Polly knows all this because she was born and grew up there, and only escaped by accident – though "escaped" is the wrong word, since she never wanted to leave, and has since missed her family terribly. Charles, her interlocutor, has known Polly a long time, and is initially profoundly disturbed by this tale of her subterranean origins. Normally they talk about politics, of which she is an astute observer. The next time they meet Polly tells him her mother is dying and she must return home, despite certain "logistical problems":

> "I have only
> the faintest memory of where I surfaced all those years ago.
> I was only a child at the time, and the shock of the light
> is all that has stayed with me," she said.

Charles urges her to try to recall her first experience on earth, and eventually she remembers seeing a church steeple at a short distance from where she emerged. So they set off to visit the seven church steeples in the area: "At each church," he relates,

> Polly got out of the car and wandered around in
> fields, and sometimes people's yards. She looked like a dream
> out there, the wind plowing through her hair and lifting her
> white dress. She looked so happy. Then, when she had finally
> given up on the seventh, she started walking back to the car
> and something happened. It was late afternoon and the sun was
> in my eyes, so I didn't actually see it happen. All I know is,
> I never saw Polly again.

The epigraph from *Return to the City of White Donkeys* comes from Nathaniel Hawthorne's notebooks: "The trees reflected in the river – they are unconscious of a spiritual world so near them. So are we." Like the trees and their reflections, Tate's unlikely anecdotes present a beguiling mixture of the reassuringly solid and the mirage-like. However implausible their narratives, the poems are always full of the most ordinary things – shoes, vegetables, banks, TVs, shops, potato chips. Most are set in small-town America, the kind of place that has a Farmer's Supply store one might dawdle around if feeling at a loose end, like the narrator of "Of Whom Am I Afraid?", who finds himself soothed by contemplating the sacks of feed and seed. While browsing one day he falls into conversation with an old, grizzled farmer about to buy a rake:

I said to him, "Have you ever read
much Emily Dickinson?" "Sure," he said, "I
reckon I've read all her poems at least a
dozen times. She's a real pistol. And I've
even gotten into several fights about them
with some of my neighbors. One guy said she
was too 'prissy' for him. And I said, 'Hell,
she's tougher than you'll ever be.' When I
finished with him, I made him sit down and read
The Complete Poems over again, all 1,775 of them.
He finally said, 'You're right, Clyde, she's
tougher than I'll ever be.' And he was crying
like a baby when he said that."

Inspired, the narrator purchases some ice tongs, "which / made me surprisingly happy, and for which I / had no earthly use."

What earthly use is poetry? This is a question that all poems, at some level, have to address. The comic exuberance of Tate's surfaces has tended to obscure the absolute and impassioned nature of his commitment to poetry as the most effective and resourceful way of alerting us to the spiritual world so near us. His sense of the spiritual is not, of course, articulated in relation to Biblical scripture or doctrinal controversy in the manner of Dickinson or Hawthorne, those last great scions of New England Puritanism. Tate was born and bred in Kansas City, Missouri, and a distinctly Mid-Western twang is integral to the voice in which his poems develop and perform their very tall stories. Nevertheless, Hawthorne's famous description in "The Custom House", his introduction to *The Scarlet Letter*, of the way moonlight "spiritualizes" the everyday, investing a child's shoe or a doll or a wicker carriage or a hobbyhorse with "a quality of strangeness and remoteness", might be seen as analogous to the way Tate's uncanny narratives set about transforming the banal: once bathed in moonlight, Hawthorne writes, "the floor of our familiar room has become a neutral territory, somewhere between the real world and fairy-land, where the Actual and the Imaginary may meet, and each imbue itself with the nature of the other. Ghosts might enter here, without affrighting us."

"Afraid?" asks the Dickinson poem from which Tate – who has in fact lived in Amherst since the late Sixties – borrows his title: "Of whom am I afraid? / Not death, for who is he? / The porter of my father's lodge / As much abasheth me." The most obvious earthly use of poetry is the potential it offers to translate what affrights us into a realm where ghosts may return and be addressed, argued with, re-confronted and reconfigured. We are conducted to this realm, in Tate's poetry, principally through the uses he makes of surprise. Indeed, surprise is so fundamental to his methods that one is tempted to say that for Tate poetry *is* surprise, wherever, however it occurs. It is his way of creating the state of what Keats called "negative capability" – "that is when a man is capable of being in uncertainties, Mysteries, doubts, without any irritable reaching after fact and reason". There is no point in reaching after fact and reason when being told by an old friend that she was born in an underground city where people eat grubs and have carts pulled by white donkeys. Such a claim puts us, as it puts Charles, in a quandary: should we dismiss her as a lunatic, and, to quote from the same Keats letter, "let go by some fine isolated verisimilitude caught from the Penetralium of mystery, from being incapable of remaining content with half knowledge"? Or should we, as Charles eventually does, suspend our scepticism and inhibitions and participate in the way events unfold, even if this means accepting an unnerving loss of control?

Tate's poetry seems to me to illustrate, with almost obsessive fervour, the importance of learning to live in uncertainty. His outlandish narratives are designed to induct us into a kind of limbo where the Actual and the Imaginary meet in the half-light of half knowledge, and where we find ourselves sliding from the mundane to the absurd in a pleasurable, all-accommodating trance. When we awake, at the poem's conclusion, we may well wonder on what level we should interpret the story, or what kinds of anxiety or inner conflict inspired it. Such wonderings, however, are precisely what the poem aims to confound, for a surprise will stop being a surprise if it can be glossed as embodying a particular set of meanings or concerns. Many critics appear to have found this aspect of Tate's poetics frustrating; for although highly esteemed, indeed prize-laden, and a significant influence on the work of many younger poets, his œuvre has not as yet generated much illuminating or sustained analysis. This may in part be because he rarely goes in for the kinds of epistemological speculation that make, say, John Ashbery or the Language writers so appealing to contemporary academic discourse. Tate's poems, in contrast, are wrapped up wholly in themselves; each devotes its energies solely to the challenge of developing out of its given premise, its "fine isolated verisimilitude", a sinuous labyrinth of the unexpected.

Surprise depends on outflanking or overturning the reader's expectations; we don't expect the narrator of "Of Whom Am I Afraid?" – even if we recognize the source of its title – to demand so peremptorily of the old farmer if he's read Emily Dickinson, and still less do we expect the farmer not only to have done so, but to have gotten into fights with his neighbours over her. On the other hand the poem, like most gathered in this book and in Tate's previous collection, *Memoir of the Hawk* (2001), is explicitly in the tradition of the poem based on an encounter: the narrator meets someone, has a peculiar, often mystifying conversation with them, and ends the poem invigorated or consoled, or somehow re-angled:

> "God," said I, "be my help and stay secure;
> I'll think of the Leech-gatherer on the lonely moor!"

exclaims Wordsworth at the conclusion of what is perhaps the archetype of all encounter poems, "Resolution and Independence", in which the poet's chance meeting with a venerable collector of leeches enables him to overcome a crisis of anxiety over his poetic vocation. While the nature of the exchanges in Tate's encounter poems tends more towards the wacky and irreverent than is the case in Wordsworth, who nearly always reports himself admonished and uplifted by conversing with his various outcasts, the structure of the resultant poem is still roughly similar. "Of Whom Am I Afraid?" for instance, follows exactly the stages of the "Resolution and Independence"-style encounter lyric: the narrator finds himself "a little at loose ends", just as Wordsworth falls prey to "blind thoughts"; he seeks solace in nature, that is the seed and feed sacks at the Farmer's Supply store, meets an old man whom he accosts with a "stranger's privilege", as Wordsworth puts it, and from whom he receives a reply that is contrary to his expectations, but which immeasurably cheers him up. In both poems the narrator's happiness is released by the way the old man's replies refute the imperatives of what Wordsworth calls "getting and spending", the utilitarian capitalist world that considers poetry "prissy"; both encounters allow the narrator-poets to recover a sense of the importance and potency of poetry, however "useless" it may seem, and more generally, create a space for the expression of sentiment – in a delightful reversal, Clyde's pugnacious neighbour cries like a baby when forced to acknowledge the "toughness" of Emily Dickinson. Tate's narrator is not, however, seduced by the farmer's unexpected validation of poetry into believing his vocation sets him above or beyond the everyday world of commerce; rather, in another neat reversal, the poem's conclusion suggests the possibilities of a poetic approach to capitalism: it is the purchase of a pair of ice tongs for which he has no "earthly use" that renders him "surprisingly happy". One might say that this particular poetic narrative has "spiritualized" ice tongs.

Many of Tate's encounters can be read as negotiations between a generic outsider and the institutions of a body politic he or she can neither escape nor endorse. Despite the bizarre turns of event that have them ricocheting like pin-balls through the arc of each poem, most of Tate's characters seem as ready as Charles to adjust to the

279

unlikely. Perhaps the one who suffers the most acute mental anguish is Leon, who one day receives a call from the White House, from the president himself, asking him a personal favour:

> I like the president, so I said, "Sure, Mr.
> President, anything you like." He said, "Just act
> like nothing's going on. Act normal. That would
> mean the world to me. Can you do that, Leon?" "Why,
> sure, Mr President, you've got it. Normal, that's
> how I'm going to act. I won't let on, even if I'm
> tortured," I said, immediately regretting that "tortured"
> bit. He thanked me several times and hung up.

But acting "normal" is not easy as soon as it becomes your "Bounden Duty" (the poem's title). Poor Leon is almost instantly seized by devastating paranoia: is he dressed in a "normal" way, or in a way that reveals he is trying too hard to look "normal"? Is that car outside his house "normal"? And the injunction to act as if nothing was going on forces him to wonder exactly what *is* going on: that farmer on TV the president shook hands with yesterday – was he a real farmer? Eventually Leon manages to leave the house to go out and buy milk; at the store he runs into Kirsten, who asks him what's going on. "Nothing's going on," he replies tersely, and explains he is just buying milk for his cat. "I didn't know / you had a cat," she returns. "You're right," he concedes, "I don't have a cat":

> "Nothing's going on, Kirsten, I promise
> you. Everything is normal. The president shook
> hands with a farmer, a real farmer. Is that such
> a big deal?" I said. "I saw that," she said, "and
> that man was definitely not a farmer." "Yeah, I
> know," I said, feeling better.

This brilliant riff on the conspiracy theory puts one in mind of Delmore Schwartz's remark that even paranoiacs have real enemies. A still more extreme example of Tate's topsy-turvy conjugations of the interface between public and private is "The Kennedy Assassination", in which the narrator is interviewed 40 years on by two law enforcement officers, Antliff and Merino, who want to know where he was on the afternoon Kennedy was shot. He embarks on an extended reminiscence about an ex-girlfriend called Rosemary Goldberg, who had fallen under the influence of a certain Carol; that afternoon he was spying on them as they played tennis in matching white outfits, but the news that the president had been assassinated makes both suddenly seem to him

> unbearably silly and irrelevant to anything
> that mattered in this world. They couldn't stop laughing, and it
> made me sick to my stomach," I said. "So that was it for you. The
> president getting shot freed you from Rosemary," he said. "I guess
> you could say that," I said, "though I never thought of it like that
> before." "Then it was a good thing for you," Antliff said. "What
> are you getting at?" I said.

In the event no charges are pressed, though it does indeed turn out he was a major beneficiary of the Kennedy assassination, which probably saved him from becoming an unsolved murder case himself: he asks the officers what happened to Rosemary:

> "Housewife, mother
> of three on Long Island. Apparently strangled her husband in his
> sleep, but nothing's been proven," Merino said. "Still quite a good-
> looking babe, if you ask me," Antliff added.

The elegant symmetries and dead-pan derangements that Tate orchestrates throughout this book often had me almost weeping with laughter. I think it his best so far. Like those collected in *Memoir of the Hawk*, its poems all consist of a single, sometimes pages-long, paragraph, and the line endings are again so arbitrary as to make them almost prose poems – indeed on their first appearance in magazines and other publications some were actually printed as blocks of prose. It seems to me they work much better with the ragged right hand margin, for it gives them that little extra bounce, and makes them feel more hybrid, impure, and unselfconscious than when presented as exhibits in the long tradition of the prose poem, with its illustrious pedigree and origins in the hallowed work of nineteenth-century French poets such as Baudelaire, Mallarmé, and Rimbaud.

The prose poem was also a crucial genre for many of the European Surrealists whose work had an important effect on the evolution of Tate's poetry in the period after he won the Yale Younger Poet's Award in 1967 for *The Lost Pilot*. I suspect that one of the reasons Surrealism appealed to him was that it offered a way of escaping the narrowness of a regionalist style of poetry, to which he seems from the outset to have been averse, without committing him to presenting himself as an all-knowing arbiter of culture, in the fashion of Eliot or Pound or Lowell. Of the modes of international Modernism inherited by America's post-war generation of poets, Surrealism had the advantage of being implicitly iconoclastic and anti-authoritarian – despite the fact it was the brain-child of a group of elite, highly educated Parisians, and the official "Surrealist Movement" was controlled by its figurehead and founder, André Breton, with a rod of iron. There has always, however, been something insistently American about Tate's uses of the absurd, as Charles Simic pointed out in a review of *Memoir of the Hawk*: "If Tate is a Surrealist," he observed, "then he belongs to that native strain to which Mark Twain, Buster Keaton, and W.C. Fields also belong."

Tate himself has suggested that American poets – and American popular culture – have made such diverse and thoroughgoing use of the innovations of Surrealism that the word has become almost meaningless. One of the measures of the success of the poems in this volume, and of those collected in the almost equally good *Memoir of the Hawk*, is how completely they develop an idiom that fuses the excitements – and seriousness – of the surrealist project with the colloquial speech-patterns and unheroic dilemmas of everyday life. Tate has stripped his language of both grandeur and extravagance; and if the characters in these poems are occasionally vouchsafed glimpses into the spiritual world so near them, it is not as mystic seekers after elemental truths, but as victims of the illogic of farce and the humiliations of the pratfall.

Tate's poetry has always sought to span the gap between the mishap and the sublime. His most direct expression of this compulsion is still the title poem of his first collection, "The Lost Pilot", an elegy for his father, whose plane was shot down over Germany in 1944, a few months after Tate was born. Lieutenant Tate's body was never, however, recovered, and the poem figures him endlessly orbiting the planet "like a tiny, African god". The terms the poem uses to account for the distance between the unreachable, deified father, and the earthbound, abandoned son cast an interesting light on Tate's subsequent development of a poetry that aims to approach the spiritual through slapstick:

> My head cocked toward the sky,
> I cannot get off the ground,
> and, you, passing over again,
>
> fast, perfect, and unwilling
> to tell me that you are doing
> well, or that it was mistake
>
> that placed you in that world,
> and me in this; or that misfortune
> placed these worlds in us.

"Mistake", "misfortune" – even after numerous readings of this poem I find the restraint of these words extraordinarily moving; they translate the helpless lurch in the line break between "doing" and "well" (what does it mean to be "doing / well" as a tiny African god orbiting the earth?) into a determination to live with what Keats called "half knowledge", to accept life's randomness and unknowability. And it is, I think, the conviction that this acceptance is somehow shared by his father that provides the frail link between the two in the poem's haunting final statement that "misfortune / placed these worlds in us."

While few of Tate's subsequent poems have emulated the solemn cadences of "The Lost Pilot", most can be seen as dramatising its search for ways of balancing the cosmic and the quotidian. One might argue that the Polly of the title poem of this new volume is the orbiting father's female antithesis; while his features are imagined growing "dark, / and hard like ebony" as he spins across the "wilds of the sky", she returns to a lightless kingdom of pallor and mud. Both, in their different ways, make use of the tradition of metamorphosis, and indeed *Return to the City of White Donkeys* is as packed as Ovid's compendium of legends with the supernatural, with strange creatures such as flesh-eating moths, feral babies, a hungry dead man, a giant turkey, a talking raven, and with transformations that occur when one's least expecting them. Margot, for instance, stops to relieve herself in the woods in the course of a Sunday drive, is bitten by something, and contracts the flying disease. Her companion glimpses her gliding above the woods and perching on trees:

> I was speechless, and in awe
> of her grace. It appeared so effortless and natural.
> "What am I supposed to do?" I said. "I think you'd
> have to put an arrow through me," she replied.
> I don't have an arrow," I said, "and besides I
> could never do that. I love you!"

Like Polly she vanishes in a blur of light. "She was being called," he decides; "By who, I don't know. / But I could feel it and it was very strong." And life, he ruefully concedes in the poem's final line, is truly made of just such mishaps: "A / Sunday drive, a pee in the woods, and now this."

New York Review of Books, 2004: Review of James Tate's *Return to the City of White Donkeys* (Ecco Press, 2004).

Love and Theft

One of the most eloquent denunciations of plagiarism is delivered by
Tristram Shandy. "Shall we forever make new books, as apothecaries
make new mixtures, by pouring only out of one vessel into another?" he
asks. "Are we forever to be twisting and untwisting the same rope?" It
was not noticed until some time after Laurence Sterne's death in 1768
that this passage was itself plagiarised from Robert Burton's attack on
literary imitators in his introduction to *The Anatomy of Melancholy*.
"As apothecaries," Burton observed, "we make new mixtures every
day, pour out of one vessel into another ... Again, we weave the same
web still, twist the same rope again and again." Sterne acknowledged
his borrowings from writers such as Cervantes and Montaigne, but
was curiously silent about his many thefts from Burton. They were
first spotted by John Ferriar, a Manchester physician, who in 1793
published a sympathetic but puzzled essay on Sterne's indebtedness to
the *Anatomy*: "I do not mean to treat him as a Plagiarist," he writes.
"I wish to illustrate" – to celebrate – "not to degrade him. If some
instances of copying be proved against him, they will detract nothing from his genius, and will only lessen that imposing appearance
he sometimes assumed, of erudition which he really wanted." Five
years later Ferriar issued an expanded discussion of the matter, *Illustrations of Sterne* (1798), in which he adopted a less lenient attitude
towards his author's habit of making "prize of all the good thoughts
that came in his way". This book promoted a lively debate in various
magazines about the ethics of Sterne's "borrowed plumes": was he "a
literary pilferer", "a servile imitator", or should one, rather, admire the

286

"ingenuity" with which he incorporated the works of other writers into the patchwork tapestry of his compendious masterpiece?

In *The Savage Mind* (1962) Lévi-Strauss distinguished between the "bricoleur" who happily assembles constructions from a heterogeneous array of materials, and the more scientifically minded "ingénieur", who is driven by the search for abstract concepts. The dividing line between bricolage and plagiarism is a fine one, and the case of Sterne – and of De Quincey and Coleridge after him – is still in many ways unresolved. Sterne aficionados tend to see the joke as being on Ferriar, especially since Sterne obliquely signalled his debt by choosing as epigraphs for Volumes V and VI of *Tristram Shandy*, in which the majority of his borrowings from Burton occur, two Latin quotations, one from Horace and one from Erasmus. Both were lifted from a passage in Burton's *Anatomy*, and the Erasmus "quotation" includes a reference added by Burton himself to Democritus, the persona he adopts in the *Anatomy*. Did Sterne intend his readers to pick up on this? The gist of the quotation is: "If anyone should complain that I am speaking in a tone that is too frivolous for a divine or too biting for a Christian" – and here Erasmus ends and Burton begins – "not I, but Democritus said it." Sterne was himself a divine who had been accused of speaking too lightly, of indulging in extravagant praise of folly, and his Burton-inspired defence is that he, Sterne, was simply adopting a persona. The hybrid allusion links him with two earlier masters of satirical comedy, with the further twist that certain passages in the volumes that follow were indeed first spoken by Democritus.

In his 1989 book on plagiarism, *Stolen Words*, Thomas Mallon excoriated the academic special pleading that elevated Sterne and Coleridge from literary shoplifters into masters of bricolage and intertextuality. Their cases are analysed along with that of the Victorian novelist Charles Reade, and the American writer Jacob Epstein, whose first novel, *Wild Oats* (1979), included a number of sentences taken straight from *The Rachel Papers* by Martin Amis. These plagiarists, he found, nearly always used the notebook defence: they'd copied out passages by authors they admired into their notebooks, but forgot to add quotation marks and attributions; this material then somehow got mixed up with their own. Mallon showed himself a staunch advocate of a no-nonsense approach to the issue, but conceded in an afterword to a new edition of the book, published in 2001, that the internet had blurred still further the demarcations between legitimate and illegitimate appropriation. Virtual information that appears on your own screen tends to seem, viscerally, less someone else's than when it's printed in a book with the author's name on the cover. The "boundless textual promiscuity" (Mallon) of the web has also decisively altered the way we think about information; the point is not so much to be good at remembering things, as to be good at finding them quickly. Already web skills are playing an important role in the evolutionary struggle for survival. Will future historians turn first to the wrist and clicking finger in assessing a corpse from our era? Will those who develop RSI be the information revolution's lepers? How soon before our relatively recently acquired skills become as obsolete as the ability to kill a mammoth with a spear or write shorthand or programme a VCR?

I found myself pondering all this while writing a poem about the demise of the passenger pigeon. The idea for the poem came from a comment in an excellent book by Tony Sharpe on Wallace Stevens, in which he speculates on the flocks of pigeons mentioned in the last lines of "Sunday Morning":

> And, in the isolation of the sky,
> At evening, casual flocks of pigeons make
> Ambiguous undulations as they sink,
> Downward to darkness, on extended wings.

Sharpe wonders whether Stevens might be referring to the passenger pigeon, once the most numerous bird in America, perhaps on the planet, but by the time of his birth in 1879 on the verge of extinction.

The possibility adds an edge of menace to Stevens's celebration of American spontaneity and independence, and complexly shadows the utopian vision of a "supple and turbulent" ring of men singing a secular hymn to the sun in the poem's previous stanza. One of the most powerful experiences of Stevens's early manhood was a seven-week camping and hunting holiday in the Canadian Rockies in the summer of 1903, in the company of his first employer, the attorney W.G. Peckham. His long journal entries from this trip (published in 1977 in *Souvenirs and Prophecies*, edited by his daughter Holly) suggest that Stevens rapidly metamorphosed into an adept backwoodsman, merrily shooting deer and living off the land like a latter-day Natty Bumppo. It's hard to square our usual image of Stevens as a doggedly conscientious master of surety and fidelity with this carefree frontiersman, though his life in the wild is surely evoked in "Sunday Morning", with its ideal of a "chant of paradise" uniting his ring of men with the land they inhabit:

> Their chant shall be a chant of paradise,
> Out of their blood, returning to the sky;
> And in their chant shall enter, voice by voice,
> The windy lake wherein their lord delights,
> The trees, like serafin, and echoing hills,
> That choir among themselves long afterward.
> They shall know well the heavenly fellowship
> Of men that perish and of summer morn.

It may seem "far-fetched", Sharpe acknowledges, to connect the "casual flocks of pigeons" that close the poem with the demise of a particular species, but he points out that "Sunday Morning" was composed not long after the death of the last passenger pigeon, named Martha, in Cincinnati zoo on 1 September 1914. The world's attention was fixed, of course, on other events, and the intensity of Stevens's vision may reflect not only the masculine camaraderie he so enjoyed on his trip with Peckham, but his mixed feelings about not participating in the even fiercer male bonding rites of military service: the "heavenly fellowship" is of "men that perish". Perhaps the doomed casual flocks of pigeons look back not only to the extinction of the *ectopistes migratorius*, but across the Atlantic to the mounting casualties of Flanders.

Unlike most of his Modernist contemporaries, Stevens tended to avoid references to facts or information in his poems; he would have agreed with Wittgenstein's admonition in *Zettel*: "Do not forget that a poem, even though it is composed in the language of information, is not used in the language-game of giving information." Nevertheless, my experience of swooping down and roosting on various websites in search of facts about the passenger pigeon brought to mind another Stevens poem, "A Postcard from the Volcano", which is also concerned with extinction:

> Children picking up our bones
> Will never know that these were once
> As quick as foxes on the hill;
>
> And that in autumn, when the grapes
> Made sharp air sharper by their smell
> These had a being, breathing frost;
>
> And least will guess that with our bones
> We left much more, left what still is
> The look of things, left what we felt
>
> At what we saw.

The children blithely picking up the bones of their ancestors, unaware of and indifferent to the sensual fullness of being they once enjoyed, seemed to me to act in a way analogous to my behaviour in cyberspace, hopping from site to site, converting whatever I picked up to a flickering simulacrum of itself, to what Stevens, in the same poem, calls "a tatter of shadows":

> The spring clouds blow
> Above the shuttered mansion-house,
> Beyond our gate and the windy sky
>
> Cries out a literate despair.
> We knew for long the mansion's look
> And what we said of it became
>
> A part of what it is . . . Children,
> Still weaving budded aureoles,
> Will speak our speech and never know,
>
> Will say of the mansion that it seems
> As if he that lived there left behind
> A spirit storming in blank walls,
>
> A dirty house in a gutted world,
> A tatter of shadows peaked to white,
> Smeared with the gold of the opulent sun.

My passenger pigeon poem acknowledges that the information it contains has been gleaned from the internet, but it also deploys the Sterne/Burton defence by taking in some allusions, including the "opulent sun":

> The bird's sad demise is chronicled on many websites. Children
> Visit these for homework, and learn how far and fast the pas-
>   senger pigeon
> Flew, and that its breast was red, and head and rump slate blue.

As the opulent sun set, raccoon-hatted hunters would gather
   with pots
Of sulphur, and clubs and poles and ladders; in a trice
   they'd transform the dung-
Heaped forest floor into a two-foot carpet of smouldering pigeon.

Like too many of my poems, this one ends up being about empires, their rise and fall; for undoubtedly the seething activity of cyberspace will one day disappear as conclusively as the vast clouds of passenger pigeons that once darkened the skies of America; one can only hope some institution of the future will be able to preserve a relic or two in honour of it, as the Smithsonian now preserves the stuffed remains of Martha.

Should the Sterne defence seem unconvincing, however, the modern poet can always fall back on the notion of the "found" poem.

How nice to read a new book by Wittgenstein!
But how much nicer to read "A new book by Wittgenstein
will naturally be felt to illuminate
whatever topic or subject it treats of.
Not that the present offering is exactly
a new book by Wittgenstein at all.
'The first thing to be said about this book
is that nothing contained herein
was written by Wittgenstein himself.'"
Oh, reading about Wittgenstein,
even when it is not exactly about Wittgenstein,
is so much better than reading Wittgenstein himself.

This is one of my favourite found, or nearly-all-found poems, Edwin Morgan's "A New Book by Wittgenstein" (1966). The found poem brings into question notions of authenticity and individuality more

directly than any other poetic genre: it is poetry's version of Duchamp's urinal (signed R. Mutt). Morgan's found poems include pieces
derived from the letters of Cowper and Keats, and a sequence collaged
from A.S. Alexander's *Tramps across Watersheds* (1925). Other British
exponents of the genre include avant-gardists such as Tom Raworth,
cris cheek and Bob Cobbing. Cobbing, who late in life even took
to cutting up his own cut-ups, was also a master of concrete poems,
sound poems, and what he called "word-nets", in which the poem is
figured as a net catching whatever acoustically related words or verbal
fragments come its way.

Implicit in such experiments in minimalism is a challenge to what
we think constitutes the poetic. At the other end of the scale – by
far the longest work ever published to be based on the principle of
the found poem – is Charles Reznikoff's *Testimony: The United States
(1885–1915): Recitative*, which consists of hundreds of stories taken
from law reports and organised according to region, date and category;
for example, "Social Life", "Machine Age", "Property", "Negroes",
"Children", "Railroads". Reznikoff trained as a lawyer, and worked
for several years for the legal encyclopedia *Corpus Juris*. He became
fascinated by the literary potential of witness statements, and in 1934
published the first version of *Testimony*, a prose anthology or collage
based on summaries of court reports. The "recitative" version, however, issued in two volumes in 1965 and 1968 and running to more
than five hundred pages, presents its narratives taken from legal briefs
in loose, free-flowing verse. Here is "Episode in the Life of a Schoolteacher" from "The South (1901–10)":

> The Negro schoolmistress gave birth to a child –
> her parents did not know and she did not want them to –
> gave birth in the school's water-closet
> and left the child under the water-closet on the ground.
> Three Negro girls who went to the school
> at recess saw the baby under a hole in the seat.

One of the girls had jumped up and said,
"Oh, there is a baby!"
It was raising its hands and kicking its feet
but its eyes were shut
and its mouth full of sand.

Although Reznikoff avoids revealing the legal outcomes of the cases
he includes, we are always aware while reading *Testimony* of the legal
conventions governing the way each story is told. The versification
is rarely intrusive; but in a subtle, almost subliminal way, it dignifies
and deepens the events that triggered the intervention of the law: the
railroad accidents, the cold-blooded murders, the gross examples of
corporate negligence, the thefts, the suicides, the labour disputes, the
mining disasters, the racial conflicts, the *crimes passionnels*. The poem
also might be said to cast a quizzical, even sceptical light on the titanic
efforts of an American Modernist poet such as Hart Crane to impose
on American history an overarching, all-comprehending myth or narrative: the sheer multiplicity of its characters and their stories defeats
all impulses and attempts to generalise. Reznikoff was active in left-
wing circles, and clearly thought of his project as an instrument for
social justice; but like the organisers of Mass Observation in Britain in
the 1930s, he wisely decided to let the evidence speak for itself.

It was the work of two poets with a very different political agenda
that most conclusively established the notion that one might use the
words of others in one's own poem. Eliot and Pound weren't great fans
of democracy or equality: indeed their allusions often serve to exclude
or ridicule the ignorant masses ("Ta ta. Goonight. Goonight. / Good
night, ladies, good night, sweet ladies, good night, good night"), as
well as to furnish any reader who is ready to be initiated into the
mysteries of the high-cultural elite with a comprehensive reading list.
Borrowings from an array of texts are interspersed throughout *The
Waste Land*, some acknowledged in Eliot's notes to the poem and others not. To read *The Waste Land* properly, one has to understand how

its various allusions fit together, and the interpretation of cultural and literary history they develop. Eliot and Pound were both bricoleurs, but they were purposeful: the great chunks of Jefferson and Adams and Confucius that find their way into *The Cantos* illustrate Pound's version of history, and are intended to show how the chaos of the present might be redeemed if we could only be led to make sense – *his* sense, that is – of the past.

But not all Modernist poets used source material in such a coercive way. Marianne Moore, for instance, was as dependent as Pound or Eliot on the use of other texts, but her quotations are often taken from recondite works, helpfully signalled in her extensive author's notes, such as *Report on the Introduction of Domestic Reindeer into Alaska, Antiques in and about London, Animals of New Zealand,* and a Bell Telephone leaflet called *The World's Most Accurate Clocks.* Moore's borrowings are scrupulously signalled by quotation marks in the poem itself, and often contain plenty of information: "'In Buckinghamshire hedgerows,'" one begins, quoting, so a note informs us, E. McKnight Kauffer,

> "the birds nesting in the merged green density
> weave little bits of string and moths and feathers and thistle-
> down, in parabolic concentric curves" and
> working for concavity, leave spherical feats of rare efficiency.

Moore seems to me Modernism's purest bricoleur, weaving her poems from shreds and patches. Her poems also foreground the ordinary act of reading: she delights in a newspaper article on the Brooklyn Dodgers or the report of a conversation between a couple of horse-trainers – and this gives her assemblages an air of being scavenged from the everyday, as if anything at all could be grist to her poetic mill.

There was a strong documentary element in much late Modernist American writing, and epics such as William Carlos Williams's *Paterson* or Charles Olson's *Maximus Poems* (set in Gloucester, Mas-

sachusetts) are in essence enormous collages that attempt to capture
the spirit of a place by combining memoirs, histories, town records,
overheard scraps of speech, newspaper clippings, and lyric descriptions of landscape, riverscape, townscape, and seascape. In *Paterson*,
Williams included extracts from letters from Edward Dahlberg, Allen
Ginsberg, and from a woman called Marcia Nardi, who had turned
up in his surgery in Rutherford in the spring of 1942 with a sick son
and a sheaf of poems. Williams liked these a great deal, and wrote
to say so. He also tried to persuade his publisher, James Laughlin
at New Directions, to take her on, though to no avail. In reply he
received from Nardi a long series of bitter missives that castigate him
for smugness and selfishness, and reveal her own despair: "Your whole
relationship with me," she tells him, "amounted to pretty much the
same thing as your trying to come to the aid of a patient suffering
from pneumonia by handing her a box of aspirin or Grove's cold pills
and a glass of hot lemonade." These letters play a vital role in the
dialogue between the genders that *Paterson* attempts to orchestrate,
and are among the most gripping pages of the poem. He used them
without her permission, for she had disappeared, but was able to salve
his conscience somewhat when she resurfaced in 1949; he gave her
small amounts of money, obtained for her a grant of $250, and even
managed to get some of her new work into print.

The dilemma over a poet's right to incorporate another's words into
his or her work came back with a vengeance when Robert Lowell
decided to include in his 1973 collection, *The Dolphin*, a number of
sonnets based on letters from his ex-wife, Elizabeth Hardwick. Lowell
had left her, and their daughter, Harriet, for England and Caroline
Blackwood; *The Dolphin* tells, as he put it in a letter to Christopher
Ricks, "the story of changing marriages, not a malice or sensation, far
from it, but necessarily, according to my peculiar talent, very personal.
Lizzie is naturally very much against it. I am considering publication
in about a year; it needn't be published, but I feel clogged by the possibility of not." It's not hard to see why Lizzie was against it. Lowell

called the work "half-fiction", and one can't confidently tell what is verbatim transcript of her letters, and what has been doctored. The sonnets in her voice are disturbingly private:

> "I love you, Darling, there's a black black void,
> as black as night without you. I long to see
> your face and hear your voice, and take your hand ..."
>
> ("In the Mail")

Friends such as Stanley Kunitz and Elizabeth Bishop (who a few years earlier had been dismayed to find one of her own distressed letters to Lowell recycled as a sonnet) begged him not to publish: "*Art just isn't worth that much*," she insisted, asking if he "wasn't violating a trust" and declaring it "cruel" to "use personal, tragic, anguished letters that way".

Pound defined the epic as a poem including history, and Lowell eventually decided the hundreds of sonnets he composed in the late 1960s and early 1970s should be arranged chronologically and presented as an epic collage, which he called *History*, and which takes us from Genesis to the death of John Berryman. The Modernist impulse to introduce historical documents and sources into poems evolved partly as a reaction against Victorian notions of the ideal poem as a pure, lyric expression of the poet's genius, a view brilliantly popularised by Palgrave – with a little help from Tennyson – in his best-selling anthology. Incorporating material from other sources and people is bound to make poetry impure, messy, diverse, inconclusive. The historical collage-epic is still going strong: Tom Paulin's *The Invasion Handbook* (2002), a mix of letters, translations, newspaper reports and poetic portraits arranged to illuminate the origins of the Second World War, is a recent example.

Found or collage poems underline the truism that all writing depends on other writing: a poem may aspire to stand alone, but any piece of writing presented as a poem inevitably triggers the read-

297

er's assumptions about what kinds of thing a poem should be or do, which it confirms or modifies or challenges or refutes. And no poet can be for long unaware that however new a "mixture" may at first seem, to return to Sterne borrowing from Burton, it is also a pouring "out of one vessel into another", the result of love and theft, to quote the title of a book by Eric Lott on the origins of blackface minstrelsy in 1820s and 1830s America, a title itself stolen – as he acknowledges by the use of quotation marks – by Bob Dylan for his latest album, *"Love and Theft"*. At a 1965 press conference in San Francisco, Dylan was surprised to find himself asked not if he was still a folk singer or a protest singer or the voice of his generation, but if he thought he might ever be hung as a thief. The questioner was Allen Ginsberg, and Dylan, whose loving thefts from a vast and eclectic array of musical and literary sources have kept armies of Dylan researchers busy, could only reply, giggling: "You weren't supposed to say that."

London Review of Books, 2004

A Note on the Author

Mark Ford was born in Nairobi, Kenya in 1962, and attended schools in Lagos, Chicago, Colombo, and London. He has a B.A. and a D. Phil. from Oxford University, where he specialized in American poetry. From 1991-93 he was Visiting Lecturer at Kyoto University in Japan. He now teaches in the English Department at University College London, where he is a Professor. He has written widely on nineteenth- and twentieth-century British and American literature. His first collection of poetry, *Landlocked*, was published by Chatto & Windus in 1992, and his second, *Soft Sift*, by Faber & Faber in 2001 and by Harcourt Brace in 2003. He has also written a critical biography of the French poet, playwright and novelist, Raymond Roussel (*Raymond Roussel and the Republic of Dreams*), published by Faber & Faber in 2000, by Cornell University Press in 2001, and by Ediciones Siruela in a Spanish translation in 2004. He is a regular contributor to the *New York Review of Books,* the *Times Literary Supplement,* and the *London Review of Books.* Recent publications include an edition of the poetry of Frank O'Hara (*Why I Am Not a Painter and other poems* (Carcanet, 2003), two anthologies of the work of poets associated with the New York School (*The New York Poets* and *The New York Poets II,* Carcanet, 2004, 2005), and a book-length interview with John Ashbery, published by Between the Lines in 2003.